Donated
By B.A. Buttz

This book is an unedited version and contains some typographical errors. If you find an error of any kind, <u>read on</u>. The content is more important than the mechanics.

As a novice writer, and in my haste to get out the word, I moved too quickly to get the book printed. The edited version is on-line at Amazon.com

Health, happiness and inner-peace. You're worth it.

Born to be Damned

Tapestry of a Gay Man

B.A. Buttz

authorHOUSE®

AuthorHouse™
1663 Liberty Drive
Bloomington, IN 47403
www.authorhouse.com
Phone: 1-800-839-8640

First published by AuthorHouse   11/8/2010

ISBN: 978-1-4520-9468-7 (e)
ISBN: 978-1-4520-9467-0 (sc)
ISBN: 978-1-4520-9466-3 (hc)

Library of Congress Control Number: 2010916430

Printed in the United States of America

This book is printed on acid-free paper.

Certain stock imagery © Thinkstock.

A tapestry made for a gay man manifested itself in genetics,
religion and environment. I am that man.
"A Self-Analysis"
One of God's Children

Contents

Dedication

I dedicate my heart and my writing to my children, Jennifer and Jason, as well as my partner of 25 years, William F. Cogan.

In addition, I devote the purpose and intent of this book to the memory of all gay and lesbian men and women who were victims of hate crimes such as Matthew Shepard and/or who, in desperation, as did Tyler Clementi, took their lives because they were not able to tolerate or live their birthrights as gay human beings.

In times when sexual orientation is still so misunderstood, the burden of responsibility and education falls to senior members of gay society. If one life or one soul can be saved, it's worth the sacrifice to "come out". I am one of those senior members.

You can't run from your birthright.

"The hardest battle you're ever going to fight is the battle to be just you."L. Buscaglia 1

Special Dedication to the family of Tyler Clementi, Rutger's University student, and the memory of Matthew

Shepard, University of Wyoming student murdered in 1998. Never again!

Acknowledgements: Editing, Mr. Lynn Pansch and Mr. Clifford Warwick

Introduction

"Where good and love are, God is there.
Christ's love has gathered us into one.
Let us rejoice and be pleased in Him Let us
hear, and let us love the living God.
And may we love each other with a sincere
heart."

Song "Ubi Caritas"
Composer Maurice Durufle' 2

If only it were so!

If only we loved one another with a sincere heart instead of religiously and emotionally judging the 8.8 million gay and lesbians residing in the United States. If only the shame of living one's birthright didn't resound in a 1/3 teen suicide rate among gay teens. If only gay men and women were viewed as human beings with different genetic birthrights. If only! (Internet: Wordiq.com)

Our gay population is neither understood nor accepted within the norm of our society. Bullying, hatred, and even death are not foreign to the one-in-ten gay population. (Internet: Wordiq.com)

Would one really choose to be a member of this socially rejected group of people? This book was written for the purposes of awareness, education and assistance for all who read it.

I share my feelings, emotions and experiences as someone who lives the life and not as one who studied, researched or theorized about the life. My writing credentials are personal life's experiences. Only if you live it, do you know it and feel it. Your birthright dictates the destiny of your soul.

If one gay, lesbian or straight person finds their inner-being and some aspect of inner peace from reading this book, then my primary objective has been accomplished. Maybe someone will find their story in my story and be able to come to grips with a sense of authentic self and personal well-being regardless of sexual orientation.

We need a vaccine to inoculate prejudice in order to earn respect, acceptance, compassion, tolerance and understanding as to what it means to be gay in a world filled with prejudice, hatred and ultra-conservative norms. Hopefully, increased education will be that vaccine.

In reality, gays are viewed as second class citizens.

Prelude

Webster defines a tapestry as "a heavy woven cloth with designs and pictures to be used as a wall hanging." (Webster's NEW WORLD DICTIONARY, July, 1983)

Personifying that concept, the fabric of my being is a composite of genetics, religion and environment. Each aspect of the tapestry is a critical component to my evolution as a gay man. I share that evolution with you, the reader.

As a mid-western born child, I grew up in a world of loneliness, frustration and confusion regarding my sexuality. I felt isolated and often thought I was insane.

I had no one to converse with or ask questions about how I felt. In the 1940's - 1960's, no books were generated chronicling gay life. Personal computers and the Internet didn't exist. Homosexuality was a taboo topic and was never discussed publicly.

I remember such endearing terms as "fag", "homo", "queer", "weirdo" and "pervert" resounding through the social conversations in the straight world. In particular, high school and college were depositories for derogatory innuendos about gay men. Comments about lesbians were seldom heard. "Fag" always referenced a man.

As a child, I never knew gay descriptors would apply to me, but I knew their connotation was something unacceptable in our society.

As a young man, I lived in a world of torment in and among societal expectations, morally acceptable behaviors and structured religion.

America has become so culturally diverse, it's hard to comprehend lack of tolerance or acceptance of/for gays. However, within the context of religious interpretation, being gay is a damnable choice. Hence, the stigma is perpetuated.

How can we, as gay men and women, expect to be understood or accepted within a society which can't eliminate domestic, child or animal abuse? How can a misunderstood, taboo topic be evoke acceptance or even tolerance?

Homosexuality is a religious, moral and social issue, but many reasons exist as to why is it so difficult to address any social issue in the 21st Century? A synopsis...

First, within the social classes and various socio-economic groups, what is accepted in one class, is not in another.

What is right for some individuals, is wrong for others.

What is normal in some families is foreign or abnormal to others.

What is taken for granted in one social class, isn't even known or experienced in another.

What is believed in one family, isn't a part of faith in another.

Finally, what is routine in some lives, constitutes survival for others.

It is within these differences that philosophical dogma surrounds sexuality. Being gay appears to be a conscious act that arouses ire in each of the social classes, cultures and socio-economic environments.

As a former elementary school principal, I know cultural and family differences create obstacles for education.

To illustrate, when the school year begins, and new students enter a teacher's classroom, they bring with them 25 diverse family cultures each functioning with its own set of values, norms and traditions. In the past, all students were educated equally and in the same manner. One prescription fit all, but not anymore. Assimilation into our culture was a goal. Today, cultures and religious beliefs are maintained within the label "American citizen" and individual educational prescriptions are expected and are the norm. Every child learns differently.

Religious dogma, cultural and social mores, (folkways), personal beliefs, and political correctness become challenges or impediments to instruction. Teaching within parameters is doable, but difficult.

However, step out of the norm and add a gay child to the class, and social stigma barriers arise instantly. We make concessions for cultural and religious differences but avoid others indiscriminately, especially sexual orientation.

Each day we arise and begin a day filled with personal choices and decisions. Some choices are easy; others are more difficult. Simple choices constitute such things as showering, brushing teeth, clothing,, food, etc.

More difficult choices come later and include such things as dating, drinking, smoking, drugs, college, matrimony, housing, transportation, etc. Our society is the product of conscious choices.

However, have you ever thought about the choices we don't have as newborn children?

We don't choose our parents, race, names, size, weight, hair color or even gender, nor do we choose our socio-economic status, where we will live, or our genetics. Even though we have no say in these choices, as we mature, we must assume responsibility for the choices we didn't have or make at birth, including being gay.

Philosophically, choices are always emphasized as decisions we consider and make in life. We are always responsible for our choices. Yet, no one ever mentions the choices we don't have which are critical components to our direction and journey in life.

Will society ever understand how or why being gay is so misunderstood and/or feared? Personally, I think not.

I was born to Missouri Synod Lutheran parents of German and Polish backgrounds. I didn't pick my religion or my genetics.

As a teenager, due to early religious training and social stigma, I surmised I was born to be damned.

"The whole purpose of education is to turn mirrors into windows."Sydney Harris 3

My parents in 1940. Helen Galamback, (Polish) and Ralph E. Buttz Jr., (German).

CHAPTER ONE

A Prayer For Bobby

Inspiration:

I needed inspiration or an event to move me off center to share my life. I have led a fulfilling life even though people have suspected I might be different. Life is easy just rolling along living within cultural and societal expectations, but stepping out of the box or expressing ideas that are contrary to public belief, can have ramifications. Indeed, sharing one's sexual orientation does have consequences. However, when facing mortality, one must ask, what have I contributed? What have I done with my life or better yet, what do I still need to do?

My entire life has been a search for purpose. What does God want me to do with my life? Why am I here?

Am I just a statistic waiting to be tallied on some medical chart?

Often, events can, and do, inspire or motivate us to do or act in a manner not of the norm in our lives. My personal event came with a Lifetime, made-for-television movie entitled "A Prayer For Bobby".

I didn't really want to watch the movie, as I knew it was about a gay teenager. I had lived "that" life and it wasn't fun. However, my partner and I decided to share the experience. I wasn't excited about seeing someone suffer as I had, but I was curious as to how the title of the movie applied to Bobby's life.

The story-line occurred as follows: A young teenage boy comes to grips with being gay. His mother does all she can to try to change him. She does not accept his gayness and seeks any form of rehabilitation for her son. She prays to God and asks Him to change Bobby and make him well. She believes prayer will cure Bobby or change his thinking and choices about his sexuality.

As Bobby experiences the disappointment and shame his mother is feeling, he is tormented and heart-broken. He doesn't understand why he was born gay and he certainly doesn't understand his mother's reactions. I didn't know why I was born gay either.

As the story progresses, Bobby realizes he can't change. He must learn to live with his affliction and/or do something about it. He searches for answers but is filled with anguish. He can't change.

After continued pressure from his mother, Bobby's torment leads him to a desperate act. The scene is so emotionally moving I found myself sitting, then standing, then yelling, "No", then crying.

Bobby is on a bridge which spans an interstate highway. He flashbacks to encounters with his mother and is sobbing. Slowly he mounts the rail of the bridge and stands starring down the busy interstate.

He continues to have flashbacks until the shame of being gay overwhelms him. He sees a semi-truck speeding towards the bridge and almost without conscious thought, turns his back to the highway.

Bobby stops crying and the sadness in his face is riveting. I had felt the same sense of worthlessness and disappointment in myself.

As the semi nears the bridge, Bobby releases his grip, holds both arms out as if to fly and soars backwards to the interstate below. As he hits the semi, the scene flashes away. Bobby is gone and the movie is only half over. What next?

I looked at Bill, my partner. We were both weeping. Why? What a waste of a valuable life. Why did Bobby have to live as he did? Why do so many young gay people want to end it all? Why is our society so unforgiving; so quick to judge?

The next scene flashes to Bobby's funeral. What sadness permeated the room. The ache in his family's heart could not be soothed with words of comfort.

As the movie continues, Bobby's mother commits to a mission, a mission of inner-peace and understanding. She begins to talk to gay people, the clergy and people who knew Bobby. She tries to comprehend why her son chose to be gay and what forced him to commit suicide.

The most powerful moment in the movie occurs at the end. His mother is verbally addressing a mixed group of gay and straight people. Bobby's mom relates how she misses him and loved him. She did not understand what he was experiencing.

She states the issue of Bobby's gayness was more about her, than it was Bobby. More about what people would think, or say, than it was about Bobby's well-being. She had believed Bobby could change if he really wanted to.

In the finale, Bobby's mom tells the group she prayed for God to help Bobby. She prayed long and hard. She asked God to make Bobby well, but God didn't listen.

Then, she realized her assumption, that God did not listen, was wrong. Indeed, he had listened.

After all her prayers, the reason God didn't change Bobby or make Bobby well was because nothing was wrong with Bobby. NOTHING WAS WRONG WITH BOBBY! God created Bobby as he was, and God does not make mistakes.

The Creator didn't change Bobby because he didn't need to be changed. He wasn't mentally ill or sick. He was perfect just as he was. I sobbed as I knew the story could have been mine.

This movie changed my life and my need to find continued purpose in life.

As a teenager, I lived Bobby's life and meandered through it with little confidence and no pride. The prayer for Bobby could have been a prayer for me.

I, too, prayed to God to change me, he didn't. I didn't need to be changed, but I thought I did. I fought my birthright intellectually, emotionally and religiously, but I couldn't change it.

If my story can help one Bobby to choose life as opposed to a desperate end, then God did give my life purpose. If so, then all I have believed to be wrong about my life, is right. All my suffering and mental anguish will be worth it.

I was moved to stand up and be counted as a senior member of the gay community. Someone to open his arms and offer assistance to others who may be contemplating a life ending decision. In a word, "Don't !".

My tapestry is in the formative stages.

"Stars are not seen by sunshine."
John Wodroephe 4

Decatur, Illinois, 1930
Industrial center and middle class utopia

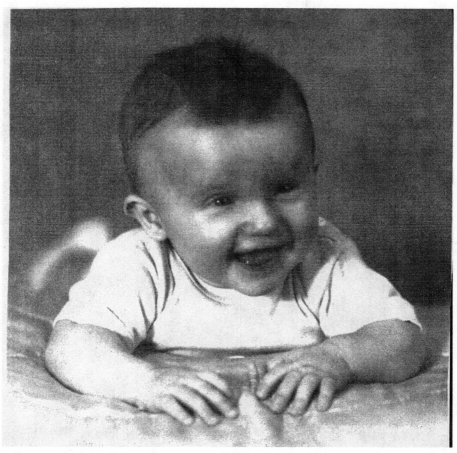

Barry Allan Buttz ; So innocent, yet already gay.

"If God had wanted me other wise, He would have
created me otherwise."Goethe 5

CHAPTER TWO

The Formative Years and My Mother

Birth In Bean Town:

Growing up in the 1940's, '50's and 60's, life was easy, the future predictable and America, as I knew it, would endure forever. It was an age of innocence.

The setting is Decatur, Illinois, a town of 94,000 people located three and one half hours south of Chicago. Decatur is an agri-center housing Archer Daniels Midland, (ADM), and Tate and Lyle, formerly Staleys. As soybean processing companies, they give Decatur the title "Soy Bean Capital of the World."

At the time, a growing Decatur had 44 schools and

a student population of approximately 23,000. Stephen Decatur High School had 5000 students in grades 10-12, and families were involved in their children's education. Dads worked and Moms ran the household.

Most of the working masses were blue collar and worked in such plants as General Electric, Firestone, Caterpillar, Signal Depot and Mueller Company.

In addition to these well-known companies, Decatur was the hub for the Wabash Railroad. Enterprise was thriving and it was a good time to be alive. It was safe to say, America's birthrights were alive and well in the industrial city of Decatur, Illinois.

I was born on a bone chilling night, November 20, 1944, at Decatur Memorial Hospital. Ralph and Helen Buttz were the proud parents of a 7lb, 10 oz. baby boy.

Ralph was of strict German descent hailing from the Blankenburg and Frahlman families. Helen was of Polish descent having the sur names of Golomback, (Galamback), and Kashefska, (Kashefski). What proud traditions each of these European cultures had.

A child's name is one of the greatest gifts parents can give to their children, but selecting an appropriate name can be challenging. A name is so personal that research should be done before a child has a permanent label, one of the non choices in life. Hence, Barry Buttz was born.

I hear you laughing and know you are thinking, "How could any parent do that to a child?" I felt the same way. I think my parents' research was limited.

Supposedly, my parents named me after a movie star named Don Red Berry, but I can't remember him in any movies other than Class B westerns.

After five days in the hospital, I was taken to my first home on 23 St. Our home was a four room, one bedroom bungalow in a very modest neighborhood. My paternal grandparents, Ralph Sr. and Minna, lived only one block away on 22nd Place. I remember nothing of my life in this house.

We lived one year on 23rd St. because Mom and Dad decided to move across the street from Dad's parents on 22nd Place. Socio-economically, we hadn't moved up in the world as our new home had the same number of rooms and only one bathroom, accessible only through my parents' bedroom. The house sold for $1,400.00.

The neighborhood was stable and filled with other relatives. Aunts, uncles and cousins surrounded our home and presented a secure environment.

It was the 1940's and life in the Midwest was slow paced and recovering from World War II. Due to the war, employment was still plentiful. As the government had commandeered railroads and all of my father's family were railroaders, they were exempt from military service.

Life appeared to be predictable and living day-to-day was normal.

In 1948, my only brother was born and the Buttz family signified all that America was supposed to be, "USA, Chevrolets, Apple Pie and the Fourth of July".

Thus, began my life as a middle class boy being raised in a family of four within the American Dream.

Postscript:

Decatur's population reached upwards of 96,000 people in the 1960's, but as industry died, so did the city. Today, the city's population is below 80,000, only 18 schools are left, and the student population is barely 8,900. A town that once needed five high schools, now has two and talk exists of consolidation. The Pride of the Prairie needs an economic over-haul.

~

Impact: My Mother

An old Jewish Proverb reads, "God could not be everywhere, therefore, he made mothers." Rudyard Kipling, 6

As I sat in church this Mother's Day, 2010, I tried to digest that proverb and find some truth in it for me. Mothers are always hailed as heroines of the family.

As research has shown and publications have stated, opposite sex parents establish a foundation for sexual identity and introduce their children into manhood or womanhood. Fathers lead daughters into sexual identity and meaningful relationships with boys and mothers demonstrate to sons how to relate to women and become a man.

As a responsible, loving role model for daughters, a father provides a sense of security and sets the tone for adult interaction with males. Mothers are supposed to do the same for their sons.

Unfortunately for me, I found no truth in the proverb as my sense of sexual identify was stripped from me by my mother early into my formative years.

My first recollection and memory in life was at age four. One night I went to kiss my dad good night and my mother said, "Barry, you can't kiss daddy any more. Go on to bed."

I replied, "Why?" She responded, "Well, boys don't kiss boys."

"But Mommy,", I replied, " I want to go kiss Daddy good night."

"No", you can't", she said, "You can't kiss Daddy He doesn't want to kiss you because boys don't kiss boys."

Thus, began my introduction to the gay world. Boys don't kiss boys.

I didn't understand. I had always kissed Dad good night. The issue wasn't boys kissing boys, it was me wanting to kiss daddy good night. I was only four years old and had no comprehension as to what Mom meant. I wanted Dad to know he was special. I needed his love and the security his presence gave me.

I went to bed feeling I had done something quite wrong and Dad didn't love me any more. What had I done? I was a good boy. I never gave Mom or Dad any trouble. I cried under the covers. It was the longest, loneliest night of my early life.

I held my blankey tightly and repeatedly said, "Daddy doesn't love me anymore. Daddy doesn't love me anymore. I was a bad boy."

I woke up the next morning feeling distant and unwanted. I didn't know if I was supposed to say "good morning" to my dad or just slip away into a corner. Silently and crushed, I sat in the corner on a warm coal-driven heat register. Life was never to be the same.

Dad left for work and I sat quietly in the corner until Mom told me my peanut butter toast was ready. I have never recovered from this incident and it initiated an ill-fated attempt at a life of perfection.

In my four year old mind, I was imperfect. I didn't please my father. Something must be wrong with me.

Maybe if I were perfect, Dad would love me. I had to try to earn his love. I had to.

Someone had just taken a thread out of my young tapestry.

~

Emotional Holes In The Heart:

Other psychologically damaging incidents occurred repeatedly during my formative years. Mom constantly reminded me Dad had wanted a girl and not a boy. In my attempt to be perfect, did that mean I had to be a girl or pretend to be one? I wasn't sure, but I was very impressionable, sensitive and had my feelings hurt easily.

If I were upset or needed emotional comfort, Mom often called me sissy, pantywaist, big baby, and cry baby. Coming from Mom, those names must be accurate. I internalized the comments. I was a sissy.

As any child would do, when I would get my feelings hurt or would physically incurr an injury, I would cry.

Often Mom would say, "Are you a big baby? Do you have lace on your panties?" or "Come to Momma and get some ninny, (breast milk). Come to Momma.", clutching her breasts. I was never a breast fed baby.

Once I said I was running away. Mom opened the

door for me and said, "Good-bye". I got to the corner and stopped at the street sign. I was crying and looked back at the house. Mom was standing in the doorway and motioned me back. Her comment was, "Come on, big baby, come to Momma for some ninny." I hated those comments. The "ninny" comments embarrassed me and carried sexual overtones.

I thought Mom's breasts were for babies or sissies and immediately became "turned off" to the thought of seeing or touching women's breasts. I learned to abhor women's breasts. They repulsed me.

The verbal harassment I took was constant from ages 4 through 10. When in need of emotional comforting, I was made to feel like a weakling and a baby. Interpretations became distorted and I couldn't process intent. To me, what was said was true. I was nothing.

~

St. Louis Zoo:

At age four, I remember going to the St. Louis Zoo and was totally excited about the trip. I had never been to a zoo. As we approached the zoo entrance, Dad was holding my baby brother and I was walking with my Mom. She said she was hot and took off her blouse. Underneath, she had on a "tube top". It was yellow with white ruffles on the top and bottom. Mom's breasts hung freely. All I saw were ninny breasts. I was so embarrassed I quickly dropped back and would not walk with her.

She said to me, "Get up here. What's the matter with you?"

I commented, "What is that thing?"

She said, "What thing?"

I pointed and said, "That thing, you're naked."

She pointed to her breasts and said, "Come up here and Momma will give you some ninny."

Yes, that's how it was. I wanted to die. It might have been sexy to Dad, but to me, it represented a source of irritation and disgust.

I soon learned all women had ninny breasts. Sick! I couldn't look at them because I associated degrading comments when I saw them. In some ways, I became afraid of women. They were mean.

One piece of my tapestry was lost but another took its place.

~

Compensatory Creativity and Imagination:

I felt physically and emotionally abandoned. Lost was my feminine guide to the world of manhood.

As a result of Dad's perceived rejection, and Mom's ridicule, I began to look for a new daddy. I remember playing Author's, (card game), and telling everyone Nathaniel Hawthorne, (Author), was my daddy. He was handsome and someone I wanted to hold me. I always sought the approval of older men. I constantly searched for "my daddy" and wanted a daddy to love me as mine didn't.

I pretended other children's dads were mine and I belonged in their families. I languished for some man to care for me. Pretend families were fun, but my role always seemed to be that of a girl. I didn't know how to be a little boy. Anyway, didn't dad's always want little girls?

I created Mr. Weathers, my imaginary Dad, and called upon him at bed time to soothe me to sleep. I could see his face; feel arms around me. He gave me security. All was well in this soft place to fall, Mr. Weathers. I was compensating for the emotional loss of a father.

My pain was deep and justified. I was supposed to be held, loved and told what a good boy I was. Instead, I was cast aside, left alone and never built up emotionally. I had no self-esteem and didn't even know what it was. I just didn't have and inner-self.

~

The Spider and The Tonsils:

Added to the feelings of isolation and loneliness, when I was four I had to have my tonsils taken out. In 1948, it was not uncommon to have one's tonsils removed in the doctor's office. Shortly thereafter, it became illegal. We were on our way to Dr. Brown's office.

I remember Mom walking me into the doctor's office. It was a cold, dark, damp atmosphere. The walls were concrete and discolored. I looked down the long hallway and wondered what would happen to me. I remember tile floors that looked like diamonds. I didn't want to have my tonsils out, but I couldn't breathe. My tonsils were closing.

Someone took me by the hand and walked me down the hallway. The hand was cold and thin. I looked up, but it wasn't Mom. A lady dressed in white was walking with me. She had on a white hat too. Mom was nowhere to be seen. I didn't know what it meant to die, but I thought I was about to experience the sensation.

The room the nurse took me to was all white. Everything was white. The white bed was steel and had bars on the back of it. The air in the room smelled funny and it was freezing.

I remember the ether mask being placed over my face and the awful smell. As I drifted off to sleep, my dreams began. I was caught in a large spider web and couldn't escape.

I was screaming and kicking and couldn't get free. Then, I noticed the eyes, those terrible big, black eyes looking at me. The spider! It slowly moved my direction. I kicked harder and harder, but only became more entangled. I could feel the giant, black arachnid closing in on me. I was its prey. I wanted to scream but couldn't as I no longer had a voice. I couldn't yell for help. This was death; it had to be.

The spider taunted me and played with me before the final attack. As the huge black creature came closer, I gave one final thrust to escape. I think it had me. BAM! I heard my name being called, "Barry, Barry, wake up." I awakened to find one nurse standing over me. My tonsils were out. I looked around the room. Where was the spider?

I had to lie perfectly still for one hour and during that time I looked for the spider. Then, a treat came forth as I was offered ice cream. I had remembered someone saying if ice cream were eaten, one would vomit. I refused, but vomited blood anyway. For sure, I was dying. Blood filled the bed and turned the white sheets apple red. Where were my parents? I had no idea. I wanted to go home. More blood. I screamed and screamed but the nurse told me the more I cried the more I would bleed. I had to stop.

I was cleaned up and the bed was changed. It seemed like days, not hours, that I was alone in that white room. Finally, my Mom and the doctor appeared in the doorway.

He looked in my throat and said it looked good. Quietly, he left. Mom stood near the bed.

Within an hour we were on our way home. I had heard the nurse reference bleeding and death. I thought Mom and Dad would let me sleep with them, but I was wrong. Alone, I lay awake all night in the back room watching shadows dance on the ceiling and praying the huge spider would not find me.

I knew the spider was behind the curtains or under the covers. I couldn't sleep. At long last, hidden under the covers, I drifted off to sleep. No spider, no.

I wasn't sure why I was not being monitored as the nurse's words were very clear in my head, "Bleeding, death". I waited for the shadow of death but it never came, nor did the spider.

~

Brownie:

Another major mind-altering incident occurred when I was five. I had wanted a puppy to care for and love. Dad had been told the neighbor's dog had a new litter of puppies. When the puppies were six weeks old, we walked down the street and selected our first pet, a little mutt we named Brownie.

I loved Brownie and had finally found someone to love me as much as I loved him. I had a responsibility.

About two months after we got Brownie, he and I were outside playing. Brownie began to run around the house yelping and screaming uncontrollably. I was terrified. I cried for Dad who came out, picked me up and rushed me into the house. I begged to know what was wrong with Brownie. Mom wouldn't let me go back outside. I couldn't hear Brownie any more. Where was he? Dad was outside with Brownie for more than two hours.

When Dad returned, he told me Brownie was fine and was resting in the garage. The next morning I bounded out of bed and went to the garage to see my pet. He wasn't there. Frantically, I ran into the house and called for Mom and Dad. Brownie was gone. We all went outside and Dad said Brownie had gotten out under the garage door and had run away.

"NO!", I screamed. It couldn't be. How could Brownie leave me? Brownie didn't love me enough to stay home. Why? Brownie! No one loved me! No one!

Mom and Dad made no attempts to look for Brownie. Therefore, each day I arose and got on my small bicycle, (with training wheels), and rode the neighborhood looking for my dog. I rode and rode yelling his name, "Brownie, Brownie, come home. Please Brownie!"

Tears poured from my eyes and I couldn't see. I begged Brownie to come back. My legs ached and I couldn't eat or sleep. I knew I would find him. I knew it. I just had to search harder. Brownie must be looking for me; he must be. I needed him to come back, please!

I spent over a month searching and praying he would come home for me to love. He never appeared.

I learned Brownie didn't run away. He had rabies and Dad had taken him to be put down. I needed my pet. Dad lied. I was 15 when I figured it out.

The issue? Why hadn't they simply told me the truth? Why did they let me spend one month scouring the neighborhood crying, pleading and searching for Brownie? To make matters worse, my little bicycle didn't even coast. The wheels turned all of the time and I had no respite from constant peddling.

Older children laughed at me and went faster than I could peddle. They, too, left me as I searched for Brownie. I trailed behind. I was always behind. Truly, I didn't belong anywhere.

To me, my parent's decision was an abomination. As it was, Brownie was lost to me either way. Had he died, I would have learned an early life's lesson, death.

However, in running away, he was lost to me in a different way but I perceived his absence as a lack of love for me. It was one of many mistakes they made trying to raise a very sensitive boy who already felt he had no one to love and was loved by no one.

Their decision not to tell me the truth was another lie which helped to increase my need for love and perpetuate my search for someone to love me. Trust was a word that eluded my vocabulary. To this day, I have problems trusting people. I have had to depend on myself for so long, it is also difficult for me to accept help from other people, as I don't trust them. I'd rather do what needs to be done myself.

In addition, the perceived emotional loss of my father and now the tangible loss of Brownie, created in me a life-long fear of loss. Within this loss was the emotional need for male love and approval. I craved them.

During the formative years, my mind was tattooed with indelible ink and I would never recover from the scars of the needle. A needle generated by persons who gave me life and ones I was supposed to trust unconditionally, my parents.

The emotional losses I experienced would manifest themselves in an introduction to homosexual life when I was 38 years old. This introduction will be explained in Chapter 10.

Vulnerability, depression, and genetics would prove to be too much for a man to comprehend.

Time was ticking and a gay tapestry was in the making.

1948, Age Four
Degraded, alone, I had the fear of loss instilled at the tender age
of four.

Maternal Grandfather   Father and Son

~

Starting Formal Education:

In the late '40's, children could start school in September at age four if they were five by December 1st. My November 20th birthday qualified me for early entry. Throughout my school years, I was always socially immature because I started school at age four.

I was not happy about starting school and wanted to stay home with Mom. I was to enroll in Kindergarten at Roach Elementary School, which was 15 blocks from home. Mom walked me to school that first day.

She said, "Remember how we are going. You will have to walk yourself to school and you don't want to get lost, do you?"

When we finally arrived, I didn't want to stay. I met my teacher, Miss Davis, and she showed us around the classroom. Other kids were there but I didn't want to talk to them.

After a while, Mom left and so did I. I hid in the "cloak room", waited until the bell rang, went out the back door and started walking home. In our industrial town, safety in the '40's was not an issue. I didn't know anything about safety, and just wanted to go home.

I plotted my route as best I could remember and started walking. Streets were familiar but houses were like chess pieces. Everything looked the same, but if I could find Vilmure's Market, I knew I would be near home. I watched for cars and crossed two busy streets. I wasn't sure if I would ever see my Mom or Dad again. Maybe I had made a mistake leaving school. I thought about going back, but I had come to far.

Finally, after many turns and twists, I saw the intersection I knew at the corner of Wood St. and 22nd St.. Vilmure's Market was in sight.

It took me 45 minutes to get home. I walked upon the front porch, peered into the window and saw Mom.

I said, "Hi".

She screamed, "What are you doing home? How did you get here?" I didn't have time to answer either question. She threw me in the back seat of the car and back to school we went. "Car seats" didn't exist. Mom was livid and I felt I had done something terribly wrong.

Once apologies were offered to the teacher, Mom promised she would stay in the back of the classroom. I was sobbing. However, when Mom said she would stay, I was pleased and secure. After about 10 minutes of rug time, I looked to the back of the room and Mom was gone. Mom lied. I panicked. "Where is Mom? Where!," I screamed.

Classmates looked at me in horror. My teacher moved me up by her chair and quickly reminded me only babies cried. Yes, babies cried, but I was only four and had just been lied to by my mother. I was alone and it was my second lesson in not being able to trust family.

Postscript:

Can one imagine allowing a four year old to walk to school unattended? Times were different, but four years old is too young to be on any street alone. I seemed to be more of a nuisance to my mom than anything. I think the walking home experience impacted my fear of never getting home and never wanting to leave home. In my adult life, I dream of my childhood home nightly. It may be hard for you to believe I dream of the home nightly, but it's true. I don't know why unless something happened to me I have repressed or the house was a substitute for human security. Readers, any ideas?

~

A Life-long Cancer:

In my formative years, school became my biggest source of anxiety. I had my first experience with my wonderful christening, Barry.

Children can be cruel, and even in the '40's, one could find bullying and discrimination. My name became a plague. Barry soon became bare-butt, bare-ass, big butt, big ass or the worst of all, hairy butt. No one else had a name with a curse word in it, BUTT. Words can't describe the self-loathing and self-hatred I felt being Bare-Butt. I was humiliated to the point of wanting to be invisible.

The name calling was relentless and daily. As a very sensitive child, I ran home, crying all the way. Why were kids making fun of my name? I hadn't hurt any of them? When I got home, I told Mom what happened.

True to form, I got, "Don't be a big baby. If you cry, they will tease you more." That didn't help me understand why I had to be "bare-butt".

I hated school, hated my name and hated my mom. I was branded for life. This cancer became a life-long struggle. No cure existed.

Postscript:

As I wrote the paragraphs above, I found my words did not adequately portray the discrimination and hurt my name caused me. In times when children didn't curse, my name in itself was "bad". The brand my parents put on me would have life-long consequences. I will die hating my name, which should have been a source of pride.

To illustrate my humiliation as an adult, my name has been bastardized both verbally and inprint. Some of the mail I have received over the years has been addressed to B.a. Butty, Beldy Euttz, Ba Butty, Barry Boots, Betty Bartz, Betty Batty, A Butt, and my favorite, Barney Tuttz.

Funny, to the casual observer, yes, but to me, a horrific mistake by my parents. I have lived in fear of hearing my name announced at events, being introduced as a guest and even as an award recipient. It has been a life-long cancer eating away at my sense of value as a human being. Some day, the cancer will consume me.

~

Second Grade:

Every year of elementary school was filled with name calling and teasing. I never adjusted to being called "sissy" or "Bare-butt". Mom called me sissy and it cut to the core of my tapestry.

I had no interest in sports as my Dad didn't share any time with me or any of his love for sports. I didn't like to get dirty, (still don't) and I wasn't one to play in the mud or make mud pies. All efforts to expose me to macho activities failed for lack of reason and/or logic to me.

I remember in second grade, my teacher had to show me how to hold a bat. Her comment was, "Haven't you ever held a bat before?" The answer was, "No". I hated softball.

Being accepted was so important to me, I learned to lie to seek approval. Mom and Dad lied, so why couldn't I?

In the second grade reader, we were reading a story about pets. After the story, everyone was asked to share what kind of pet each had. Of course, I had none and would have loved to share the story about a three year old doggie named Brownie, which I didn't have.

When my turn to share came, I told the class I had a German Shepard named Rascal. I described him in every detail and told the class how he slept with me to protect me.

However, Rascal wasn't mine. He was my aunt and uncle's dog. The class was so impressed. I had the best and biggest dog in the class.

I moped around all day thinking about the lie. In Sunday School and church, the Commandment said, "Thou shall not lie". I felt dirty inside and as though my Sunday school teacher would be mad at me. Miss G. was my Sunday school teacher.

I was smart enough to make the right decision. I told Miss G. Rascal was not mine. After school, we talked for a long time and she asked me why I lied. I was too young to know.

Rascal and I
I pretended he was my dog

~

Fifth Grade:

Third and fourth grades were full of adventure and typical school events, but the name calling continued. I was bullied and physically shoved around. I did not want to go outside at recess or lunch and often stood beside the playground supervisor for security. I marked time until I arrived in fifth grade.

I loved my fifth grade teacher and had a crush on her. Mrs. Baker was kind and insightful. She knew I needed special handling and she gave it to me. I was assigned many classroom tasks in order to bolster my self-confidence and self-esteem. I loved her.

During the course of elementary school, my parents

and teachers tried many strategies to stop the name calling. Nothing worked. Now in fifth grade, Mom insisted my middle name, Allan, be used. I was to be called Barry Allan. At least a consonant "n" was in front of Buttz and not a long e.

However, too much time had passed and the students already had history with "Bare Butt". It was too hard for them to forget the name which hurt me so much. I became emotional every time I heard it. The name change didn't work and I still hated to go to school.

Bare-Allan-Butt lived on.

Image Boost:

As a part of a fifth grade reading project, I was chosen to be on the local radio station reading the part of Paul Revere in "One If By Land", a play. Another boy and I shared the reading. At school we practiced and practiced and finally, taped it for broadcasting.

On the night it was to be aired, my family sat eagerly waiting in the living room. The announcer came on the air and gave the format and rationale for the activity. Then, he related, "As a part of our celebration, we have two students from Mrs. Nanna Baker's fifth grade class at Roach School narrating the play. We have Steve Hatch reading as------, and Barry Buttz playing Paul Revere."

I dove under the couch. To hear my name on the radio was more than I could take.

The story began. Steve read first and sounded great. Then, Paul Revere entered the scene. How could a girl be reading such a significant part? Well, it wasn't a girl, it was me.

A family member said, "He sounds like a girl." I already knew it. I had ears. What was to have been a proud moment, turned into a personal tragedy.

My parents laughed at me and I could only imagine what my classmates would say the next day at school. I got sick, (not really), but Mom made me go to school.

The students' reaction was as I expected, but Mrs. Baker praised me. Oh, how I loved that woman.

Security Gone:

In November of the school year, Mrs. Baker became ill and was out for over a month. We had a substitute teacher named Mrs. England. I gave her pure hell. It was so unlike my character, but Mrs. England had replaced the one person in my life who made me feel secure. I couldn't believe my own behaviors. One day Mrs. England asked me why I was being so rude to her. I explained my feelings and included how Mrs. Baker made me feel. She seemed to understand. She asked if we could be friends and I said yes. She was nice. I hadn't given her a chance.

After our discussion, I liked Mrs. England because she

also seemed to care about me. I opened my heart as well as my arms. I loved fifth grade.

~

Walk In The Rain:

As I grew older, I did little to displease my parents on purpose, but one incident hurt my psyche and entrenched a major scar on my heart.

My brother and I had received shiny, yellow rain slickers for Christmas. In those days the yellow slickers came complete with rain headgear that snapped under the chin. One Monday morning, as it was raining, Mom sent my brother and me to school wearing the slickers and high rubber boots that snapped up the front.

Although, it was raining, she never volunteered to take us to school in the car. The last thing she said was, "Now stay dry and don't walk in the puddles."

The rain was steady and coming straight down. Mick and I made it to school and were dry. Once we arrived at school, off came the boots and the slickers. School was routine but it rained all day.

After school, as we walked home, the water level was higher on the sidewalks than it had been in the morning. We came to an alley and it was covered with water. Knowing we were equipped for the weather, Mick and I waded into the alley.

Whoops! The water poured over our boots and soaked our pants. I began crying before we got home. I knew what to expect.

Once in the doorway, Mom looked at us and said, "I thought I told you to stay dry!" Get those clothes off and get in your room. You are both going to get a spanking." I tried to explain but she told me not to "smart mouth" her and to get moving. She did not listen.

I was naked, wet and scared. When Mom got to our room she was carrying a leather belt. I begged for mercy, but to no avail. She looked at Mick and told him to get out of the room. Supposedly, he was too little to make decisions and I was to blame.

I remember that belt hitting me across the buttocks at least three times before I screamed so loudly the neighborhood could have heard me. Mom made me feel like I had done something terribly wrong. I honestly thought accidentally getting wet was a being a bad boy or even a "sin". My butt had red marks on it.

It wasn't the punishment that really bothered me, it was the anger in Mom's eyes and her voice tone that scared me. I never understood why she always wanted to hit me rather than talk to me or listen to an explanation. Mom's best discipline method was "guilt" and when that didn't work, she immediately reached for a discipline tool, the belt or a bolo-paddle.

Mom was always angry at me when I was a little

boy. More than once I heard, "Stop crying or I'll give you something to cry about". Those words resonated in my head to the point I made myself immune to tears. I knew she would give me something to cry about because she had done it before.

I'm not sure why Mom expected me to be perfect, but she did. I tried my best to be a good kid, but little things like the puddles and boots were always a deterrent to my road to perfection.

~

Sixth Grade:

The following year, sixth grade, I had a male teacher and as a role model, Mr. M. was "laid back" and not too dynamic. He was easily offended if you told him you didn't understand a concept he had taught. He did nothing to meet my emotional needs. He didn't do much for my self-esteem either. Once, Mr. M. told me I needed to grow up and stop being a baby.

Would it never end? I had trouble with basic math concepts such as fractions. He told me I didn't' understand fractions because I didn't want to understand them. Right! Explain to a 10 year old why he needs common denominators to add fractions. I never digested the concept of adding fractions utilizing common denominators.

Shortly after the start of the year, I was named patrol boy. I had to wear one of those yellow slickers when it rained and I had a patrol boy strap I wore around my waist and over my shoulder. My station was four blocks from school and was on one of the busiest streets at the time. I tried hard to fulfill my responsibilities to please Mr. M. I was fine until the bullies told me Bare-Butt was not going to tell them what to do and they stepped out in front of traffic. I got in trouble.

I tried to please Mr. M., as I needed his approval too. He did motivate me enough to perpetuate my straight A report card.

For me, in my family, the male role model went to work, came home, gave Mom his undivided attention, and went to bed. Children were to be seen and not heard, but in my case, I was not to be seen nor heard. Males were fickle figures to me, even though I needed one so badly. I loved them and hated them.

Postscript:

The year after I left Roach school, Mr. M. was named principal. He served in that capacity until the mid 1980's. In 1984, I was named principal of Washington Elementary School and we became professional contemporaries. He loved to tell people I was his student. Later in our lives, I was promoted to the school district's central office and became his boss. That is irony. The baby had grown up.

~

The Fan Club:

As a sixth grader I continued to find male substitutes for my father. Two girls and I started a movie star fan club. We met weekly at one of the young lady's homes.

Our center of attention was Clark Gable. I was elected the president and we sent away for pictures. When the pictures came, I kept a picture of Mr. Gable and put it above my bed.

Later, we added other female movie stars to our club, but I focused on Clark Gable. My imagination and creativity were unlimited. Living in my imagination was more satisfying than reality for me. I created so many men to love me I was often overwhelmed. Of course, I was just pretending.

Our club lasted for six months; then we were bored and moved on, but I didn't take down my picture of Clark Gable. He was such a handsome "daddy".

~

Cub Scouts:

Also, in sixth grade, my parents tried Cub Scouts as a resource for masculinity and male role models. What a disaster. Bare-Butt lived in Troop 19 too, as no one had forgotten my school name and all of the Den members were school classmates.

Cub Scouts were a threat to me because the activities were supposed to be macho in nature. I couldn't build anything, didn't want to be physically fit and hated sports.

I couldn't even get the basketball up to the net, yet alone into the rim. What fun I had. Plus, camping out meant bugs and going to the bathroom in some little house with holes in the floor. I looked into the holes only once. No explanation needed.

The worst experience I encountered was being forced to paint my face black with over-emphasized white lips in order to sing and dance to Al Jolsen's "Mammy". The act was supposed to be funny, but I wasn't laughing.

Two of us were chosen for this performance. The other boy and I were embarrassed and humiliated. I'm sure in today's society, the activity would have been considered racist. In reality, it was.

Who cares about badges and patches on their Cub Scout uniform? I failed at every project I had to do in order to earn those darn badges. The Pack meetings were worse than the Den meetings because after much pageantry, the macho boys received badges I could never earn. Besides, each of the macho boys had fathers who did things with them. I didn't have that advantage.

For me, Cub Scouts was a pathetic excuse to make boys do stupid things that never came out like the picture in the book. It did not teach me how to be a good citizen or even a better boy, but it did teach me how to experience failure. I hated Cub Scouts.

I dropped out of Cub Scouts after one year. I just wanted someone to make it all go away. How does a child rid himself of his name, his genetics, or even his opinion of himself?

The look on my face tells it all.
I am in the back row, upper right.

Public Display of Decency:

One additional anxiety grew quickly in public school education. I wouldn't use the restrooms at school because I preferred privacy. Why were no doors placed on the boy's restroom stalls? My kidneys would ache until I got home, but even through high school, I never used the bathroom.

I often wonder what my parents instilled in me to make me ashamed of my body or be afraid of this natural body process. I think it stemmed from their reactions to personal nudity and the use of the restroom at home. I was never allowed to see either of my parents nude and the use of the restroom was off limits if a parent was in the room. The problem was, we only had one restroom and it was located just off my parent's bedroom.

I remember Mom telling me I was going to start swimming classes at the Y.M.C.A. I was excited until I learned boys swam nude. I screamed, kicked and threw a fit until the idea was dropped. I wasn't about to swim nude with people I didn't know. I learned to swim in the lake with my swimming suit on.

I was equally terrified in high school when "gang" showers were required after physical education class. I never understood why it was an accepted practice for a group of guys to stand nude in a shower while girls took private showers behind individually curtained shower stalls. Why could girls bathe in private but not boys? Society's expectations made no sense to me and they were in conflict with what I experienced at home.

To this day, it is difficult for me to use public restroom facilities. I will almost always choose a restroom stall than stand at a urinal. For me, this choice eliminates the "bashful kidney" syndrome. It's shocking what "home training" can do to an immature mind as it attempts to function in an adult world full of personal differences. The carry over is life-long. Some memories are indelible and last forever.

On the way to Roach School
Meadow Gold Milk Horse, 1952
I am the boy on the left.

~

Annual School Events, Winner Take All:

At recess, I often played games that were simple and not competitive. I didn't like to lose and it was difficult to win if one had no experience with street games. I was fond of circle ball, hop-scotch, dodge ball and rope jumping. I was interested in the all-school marble tournament, but had never played marbles. I tried, but couldn't do it. The boys all seemed like experts and had tons of beautiful marbles. I had none.

In the spring of the year, an annual sixth grade marble tournament was held for boys and a jump rope tournament for girls.

Instead of entering the marble tournament for the boys, I joined the jump rope tournament for girls. I was the only boy in the competition. After two grueling hours of jumping double-dutch finals. I won. After the tournament, I had the strangest feelings. I was torn between being a winner and being a winning loser. Why? The boys rejected me because I didn't play marbles and I lost the friendship of the girl I had beaten in the jump rope contest. I won, but I lost too.

When I got home, I told my parents. Neither of them seemed to know how to react. I could tell by the expression on my Dad's face he was disappointed in me and Mom actually put her feelings into words, "You big sissy".

Not only did I lose friendship in winning the jump rope contest, I lost self-esteem. I had never won anything previously and I thought the feeling would be much different. Mom put it accurately, I was a sissy.

I was happy that sixth grade was nearly over and I could move on to junior high school. I knew most of my classmates were going to the same junior high as I, but maybe they would forget the tournament and I could start over in my quest to be a boy.

Postscript:

Life in the '50's should have been so simple, but it wasn't. I should have been just another little boy in elementary school who was learning how to function in an educational and social setting. However, I didn't have the proper emotional perspectives nor did I have the appropriate recreational and social skills. As I look back, I'm not sure which was the greatest detriment, my age, my name or my (forced) gender identification. I was confused, but I wasn't stupid.

Follow-Up:

Roach School closed in the late 70's. Today it stands in the ghetto burned out, gutted and boarded up. It does not deserve this disrespect for it served the educational community for nearly 65 years. I often drive by just to restore memories of my past.

Actual photo of Roach School marbles tournament (1940)
I jumped rope with the girls.

~

The End of the Formative/Early Adolescent Years:

As the formative years and early adolescence came to a close, I had learned my dad wanted a girl, I couldn't kiss boys, Mom thought I was a sissy, women's breasts were unappealing, I was a panty-waist, and bare-butt was my life-time plague.

I could not trust family members because Mom and Dad had openly lied to me which led to greater suspicion, rejection and a sense of worthlessness. Brownie had run away and never came home. Not even a puppy loved me.

The central figure in my sexual identity, Mom, had left me with scars no one could repair. How could the person who gave me life, be so cruel?

I wasn't a girl, but felt I should have been one. I absorbed the emotion, but not the intent of Mom's behaviors.

These events during my early childhood impacted my sense of well-being, or lack thereof. I had to constantly compensate for being Barry Buttz and sexuality was yet to impact my foundation as an adolescent.

Dad was a railroader and was often gone for three or four days at a time. I would stand at the screen door for hours waiting for him to come home, only to be discarded when he rushed to my mother's arms. He never saw me, nor did he speak to me. I was so unimportant and so lost. Sometimes, I felt invisible.

To get attention, I used to watch Mom feign illness when Dad came home. She was fine all day, but the minute Dad's car drove in the driveway, she developed a headache or didn't feel good. My brother and I always knew if Dad was coming home, as Mom headed for the couch. Dad would always accommodate and fix dinner or do the dishes after dinner. I learned early on what it was to be phony.

Mom and Dad loved each other so much that children were competitive for their time, attention and love. In reality, they probably would have been happier had they not had children. Mom was a true study in co-dependency. When my dad was away, she had fears that did not resonate when he was home. He was her rock, her security.

Unfortunately, I absorbed Mom's fears. Nothing seemed right until Dad got home from work. Mom was fearful of everything. She didn't like male dogs, worried excessively when traveling, hated big cities and expressed bigoted statements about other cultures. I digested most of the fears but was able to discern the strength of cultural differences for myself. I am overly fearful, worry when I travel and don't like big cities.

However, I was an excellent student, but I was not what my parents had wanted in a son. I was a personal disappointment to them as I was born the wrong gender.

It was too much for a child to comprehend knowing he was born a boy but should have been a girl.

Indelible perceptions led me to believe I was the unwanted male child and I did nothing to please my father. As a result, my adolescent life had been one big search for an older man to care about me. The stage was set. Environment can influence and direct the predisposition to be gay and establish permanent mindsets in young children. It did for me.

At this point, I would plead with all parents-to-be to research their children's names and make sure the chosen name is powerful and meaningful and not a source of ridicule or ego destruction. A name should resonate pride. Choose carefully.

In my case, no name with an ending vowel sound before Buttz could have been used. I needed a first name that ended in a consonant, such as Thomas, William or even John to avoid being teased. I asked my mom what my name was going to be had I been a girl. She said, "Sherry". I rest my case.

My sexuality evolved very slowly. During pre-school years, my psyche had been violated but I was too young to know how or understand the ramifications that would follow. No threads of love were creating my tapestry at this time.

As an adolescent, all I wanted was to belong----to be loved. I never found emotional security. I was a parent's dream as I was respectful, polite, well-mannered and never got into trouble at school. Trouble, for me, was always subject to my mother's definition and interpretation. I was 10 years old in sixth grade but I felt like I was 20. School and academic life were so easy, but nothing in my social and emotional existence was ever "normal" or easy. Truly the age of innocence had been lost, forever.

CHAPTER THREE

Adolescence and the Church

Structured Religion:

As a part of my growth as an adolescent, structured religion became a focal point. My parents made me attend Sunday School and church every Sunday. Church started at 8:00 a.m. and Sunday School began at 9:00 a.m. A later service was held at 10:30 a.m., but Mom thought good Lutherans had to sacrifice sleep and attend the eight o'clock service.

I walked to Sunday School which was before church and often walked home. Church was five blocks away and Mom felt it was good for me to walk. Of course, she rode in the car.

As a devote youthful academian, I wanted to learn

all I could and be a dedicated servant of God. I listened and comprehended all I could about God and Jesus. It was said God the Father is full of love and gives it to his sheep. Well, as Dad was a father, and I did well in church and Sunday School, he would love me as one of his sheep. I could win Dad's acceptance and earn his love by attending church. How could he not accepted me as a dedicated Christian boy. Christians were good.

However, all of my Sunday School teachers were "old maids" and sisters from one large Lutheran family. Within this family, six children existed but only one had married. Needless to say, the slants expressed on sex were biased and not based on personal experiences.

Interestingly enough, one of the Sunday School teachers was my second grade teacher at Roach School.

The teachings in Sunday School were about God, Jesus and living a good life. As side-bar issues, such things as respect for women, not fondling girls, no pre-marital sex and not doing "evil" things with women were taught. I digested every word and vowed to obey.

In many ways, the Church's teachings only confirmed my beliefs that breasts were bad. Boys weren't supposed to touch breasts or do bad things with girls. Mom had thrust nasty "ninny" breasts at me and I hated them. I wasn't going to touch those things. No problem here!

Confirmation:

In fifth grade, I had to begin Lutheran Confirmation classes. About 16 of my school-mates began the long four year trial with confirmation classes meeting every Saturday from 8:00 a.m. until 12:00 p.m. during the school year. Confirmation started in fifth grade and continued until the end of eighth grade. When confirmed, I would be a communicant member of the church.

My life on the weekends was filled with rote religion. I had little free time as Saturday and Sunday mornings were dedicated to my religious instruction. In addition, I had to attend VBS, (Vacation Bible School), in the summers.

Never was I allowed to miss one class. Rigidity was Mom's middle name, but maybe she just wanted me out of the house so she could have Dad for herself. Needless to say, complaining all the way, I went.

As confirmation paved my way for admittance to the church, I continued to learn girls were evil. As was the case in Sunday School classes, women were labeled "Jezebels", "Salomes" and ungodly adulterers. As per my youthful analysis and formed opinion, women made men do corrupt, horrific things in the eyes of God.

After all, look what Eve did to Adam, or so it was said.

Hollywood movies seemed to confirm what the church preached.

I wasn't sure what confirmation meant, but my knowledge about evil women was being confirmed. Even Biblical movies such as THE TEN COMMANDENTS, showed Moses being tempted by an evil woman. No wonder Mom acted like she did. Mom was the temptress and possessed those evil breasts which seemed to seduce men to do evil things.

Hence, my feelings for girls were suppressed, as I didn't want to do anything to anger God or disappoint my parents or the church. In my immature mind, girls were nice to have as friends, but serious relationships could lead to sin. What did I know, I was nine years old.

No Safety or Sanctity In Church:

As was the case in public school, the name calling never ceased. I was tormented by being "Bare-Butt" at church and in confirmation classes. In addition, I was at least a year younger than most of the other kids. I was defenseless.

Two of the older boys were merciless. They were brutal to me and called me "F.... Nuts", "Dip S...", "A... H...", and other endearing names. Mostly, I was called "hairy ass". The worst threat was trying to pull my pants down to see for themselves. It wasn't true, I wasn't hairy ass; I was only nine.

I avoided the boys as much as I could but knew if they caught me, they would de-pants me in front of the girls.

My fears of nudity and even using the restroom were compounded.

Many times at recess they chased me but I ran faster than they could. Anticipating the embarrassment was as bad as if they had actually caught me. Church was no safe-haven for Bare-Butt.

Bullying seemed to be my albatross wherever I went. Now, I was scared to go to confirmation classes. More anxiety developed and I didn't want to leave the house. At church, I stayed within the safety of the girls' circle during activity time. I made sure the pastor wasn't too far away either.

Cheerleader:

One Saturday the pastor told us the church was going to have a basketball team. Our church had never had a basketball team. The team would play one game, and it was out of town. Tryouts weren't necessary as we had only enough boys to make a team. I couldn't get the ball to the basket, so I told the pastor I would be a cheerleader.

True to form, we did travel out of town on a school bus and I was a cheerleader. Truthfully, I didn't have a clue what I was doing other than making a fool of myself. I think the pastor was as disappointed in me as my dad was. However, what no one knew was, I was disappointed in myself. I really wanted to be on the court with the boys playing basketball, but I didn't know how nor did I have the physical strength or skills.

Our team lost the one-time game, but the biggest loser was I. I boarded the bus after the game and no one was pleased with me or my performance as a cheerleader. I sat by myself, shunned. The boys laughed and taunted me and the girls sat in evil-eyed wonderment. More than anything, I seemed to establish a reputation for myself that would brand me a "faggot" even though, at the time, I had no sexuality. I was not like other boys.

Induction Into The Church:

I literally missed four years of Saturday morning cartoons because I had to get up and go to confirmation classes. Mom was relentless.

After four long years, I was confirmed in May of 1958. My parents made a major production of my confirmation and held a huge party at the Staley Club House located on Lake Decatur. As Grandpa Galamback worked at Staley's, we had access to this beautiful stone building which sat high above the lake. The building had an elegance, that, for the times, was almost like a small chateau. We danced, ate and sang for hours and I almost thought my Saturday sacrifices were worth it.

I knew I had been confirmed, but intellectually, I did not grasp the over-all concept of body and blood for the forgiveness of sins. The best part of confirmation was the $100.00 cash I received as gifts. I was 13 years old at the time.

I was now a communicant member of the Missouri Synod Lutheran Church and religious rhetoric cluttered my mind.

My confirmation verse read, "If ye continue in my word, then ye are my disciple indeed and you shall know the truth and the truth shall set you free." (HOLY BIBLE). Looking back, I believe truth meant freeing my inner-self, the real me. As with God's Word, once found, you are free. I was anything but emotionally free.

However, with that verse came a guilt trip. If I strayed from God, I would surely be damned to Hell. It was up to me to remain within the moral confines of the church. I could never let myself, my parents or my God down. I set a goal for myself that no human being could possibly keep, never "mess up". The point had been made and I took it seriously. I had no concept what it meant to be human.

Postscript:

As a 65 year old man, I am in church on Sunday mornings.

~

Junior High School:

In 1956, I entered junior high school. Of particular importance was my age; I was 11. The student age range was staggering and frightening for me as I was 11 and some of the 9th graders were 16. Many of the older boys looked like men. It was the first time I encountered movement from class to class as all elementary classes were isolated in self-contained classrooms via grade. I was not eligible to ride a bus to school as I lived two blocks short of the distance regulation. Thus, I had to walk, ride my bicycle or ride a city bus the mile and a quarter to school.

Johns Hill was a three story, 1925 vintage brick building seated atop a large hill over-looking Pygott Football Field where all of our high schools played football. The school housed approximately 800, seventh, eighth and ninth grade students. In 1957, the 9th graders left mid-year as Eisenhower High School opened as our high schools became four year schools. Prior to 1957, our only high school, Stephen Decatur High School housed tenth through twelfth graders.

The change to two year junior highs was very significant because previously, all junior highs had sports teams much the same as a high school. All schools were "feeders" for Stephen Decatur. We had four large junior high schools, Roosevelt, Woodrow Wilson, Centennial, and Johns Hill. Junior high sports had bitter inter-city rivalries. As many people attended the junior sports as they did high school.

The grade changes brought an end to competitive junior high sports and the establishment of high school freshman sports teams. No girls sports existed at this time. My dad was a star player for Johns Hill's football team and left me a legacy I could not fill.

Decatur was flourishing as five high schools existed amid economic wealth. MacArthur, Lakeview, St. Teresa, Eisenhower and Stephen Decatur housed over 5.000 students. Employment was plentiful and Decatur's future was very promising.

I was now in junior high and many events played an important role in my physical, intellectual, emotional and sexual growth and development.

Physical Education/Gym Class:

For the first time I had physical education, P.E.. I did not look forward to those classes. Why? Well, in the 1950's gym class was a precursor for military service.

We had a regiment of calisthenics and military drills which found us lining up to commands of "Attention", "Dress right", "Dress". As the Korean Conflict had just ended, the expectation was that all boys would serve their country in the armed forces and students were being prepared physically. Physical fitness was more the purpose of P.E. than was an introduction to sports or sport's activities.

As a World War II baby, I had seen too many movies depicting death and slaughter of American boys. Post war movies were never complimentary to the Japanese or Germans. I didn't want to learn about being a soldier nor did I want to be a soldier. I didn't want to be killed. I hated gym class, "Hup, two, three, four..."!

In addition to military service preparation, students had to wear gym uniforms. White T-shirts, blue shorts, canvas tennis shoes and a "jock" strap.

While dressing for class one day, Coach Garver came by and said, "Boy, what are you doing?". I was dressing for class.

I replied, "Putting on my jock, sir."

He commented, "Well, why in the hell are you putting it on backwards?"

I said, "I'm not, the pouch goes in the back, doesn't it? My mom says football knocks the poop out of you and I want to catch the poop in the pouch when I get hit so it doesn't fall on the ground."

The coach pounded his head and walked away.

In truth, I didn't know front from back. Neither Mom nor Dad had pre-empted the wearing of a jock. It was simply a required article of clothing. To me, it was like wearing jockey shorts with no back. I was ten years old.

~

Another gym class incident didn't help my standing with the boys. While playing supervised basketball, I had no idea what to do. During team play, we were moving down the court and Steve Hatch threw me the ball. I took off running. The coach blew the whistle and stopped play.

He said, "Buttz, don't you know how to play basketball? You have to dribble."

Dribble? Vocabulary, that was my problem, vocabulary. I didn't know the sport's "lingo". I thought dribbling was what my dad did on the toilet seat. Mom always said Dad dribbled on the seat because he didn't pick it up to pee. God how I loved gym class. Total humiliation.

~

In seventh grade, the final gym class fiasco was the rope climb. We had to climb a thick rope to the top of the gym, touch the rafter and come down. Right ! The rafter was approximately 30 feet up. I had never had any weight training and couldn't pull myself up one notch. I tried and the coach told me to go sit down. I was a total failure. I wasn't functioning in a man's world.

Then came the showers. Those dark, dank, stinky shower where everyone ran around nude and played "grab-ass". Not me, I stalled until everyone was dressed and then I got dressed and left. I never took a shower at Johns Hill and no one knew the difference. The male world made no sense.

For sure, Dad would never like me. I began to believe I was a sissy. I was smart enough to compare my abilities with the other males in the gym class, and I knew I didn't measure up.

Something in me was lacking. Why couldn't I be like the other boys? I felt like a girl in a boy's class. A good grade in gym class didn't appear to be on the horizon. I was doomed. "Sissy Bare-Butt."

~

Hall Guard:

In eighth grade, I had yet another junior high school "ego bust". I was an excellent student and was chosen to be a "hall guard". Hall guards were honor students who got to leave classes early, wear an "HG" arm band and stand in stair wells to make sure students were orderly and didn't skip steps. They were trusted, respected and honored. I was in a position of power and authority. Surely, acceptance would be assured.

Things didn't go as I planned. About two months after I had been a hall guard, I caught an African-American young man skipping a step. As per regulations, he had to walk the steps again. When he got back to the top of the stairs, he said, "I'm kickin' yo a-- after school." Terror filled my veins. I worried all day and couldn't eat my lunch.

After school, I carefully checked the playground and went out the back door. I sprinted to my aunt's house about five blocks away. I remember running down the large hill, past the football field, across Jasper Street and down Decatur Street. Finally, my aunt's house was in sight and I was safe. My aunt telephoned my parents who came and picked me up.

Verbal intimidation? No one had a name for verbal intimidation in those days. To me, it was an overt threat and I believed my butt was going to be kicked. Conversation was sparse on the way home.

I didn't want to go back to school the next day but I had to. Hey, being a hall guard wasn't all it was cracked up to be. Maybe power and authority weren't for me. When I saw the young man again, he simply smiled at me. Intimidation?

The next day, after hall guard duty, I had gone to my locker to get books for my next class. A fellow hall guard stopped by his locker next to mine. I told him what had happened the day before and he looked at me and laughed.

Then, he made a big ole' "hocker" and spit it on me. It splashed off the collar of my shirt and hit my face. I was angry, hurt, crushed.

"Why did you do that?", I asked.

"You're a punk and your name is an embarrassment to me", he replied, "You're a sissy pants. Bare-Butt!. No one is named Barry Buttz."

He laughed, pushed me and went to class. This

incident was the most humiliating experience I had ever faced. To make matters worse, I didn't defend myself because I didn't want to get in trouble, be kicked off hall guards and the church said not to fight. It wouldn't have mattered, I was too little to defend myself anyway.

At that moment I knew no matter what I did, nothing would change the fact I was Barry Buttz. I didn't report the incident to anyone as that's what a punk would do, but I never forgot who spit on me.

Ironically, when I was teaching junior high school, I had both of the man's daughters. I loved the girls, but remembered their father's treatment of me some 12 years before. I never shared the story with the girls. I wonder if the man even remembers what he did?

I can't explain how much this incident affected my self-esteem. I was trash.

~

The Female Species:

The most perplexing aspect of junior high school was relationships with girls. I liked them, but remembered what my Sunday School teachers had said. Every girl was a potential Jezebel.

Many of the boys told me what they had done on dates with girls and I knew they were headed for Hell. I didn't want to go to Hell. Touch boobies, no way!

Junior High was to be a time of exploration and happiness, but girls complicated my inner being and produced contradictory emotions. How could I like them, but be afraid of them? The church said if I fornicated, I would be damned.

I dated three girls in junior high school but thankfully, dating meant dancing, eating popcorn and going to movies. In those times, especially in the Midwest, sexual encounters were rare at the junior high school level. Holding hands was about the limit of sexual contact.

Sexually, I didn't even know how babies were made! At 13, I hadn't even kissed a girl. Fornication? Who knew what that meant?

~

An Adoptive Family:

At times, adolescence was a happy time for me. I was safe in a repetitive world of school, holiday vacations and summer vacations. I was secure because I knew what would happen each month of the calendar year, a similar schedule of events.

We never went on family vacations because my aunt and uncle owned cottages at Lake Decatur. Our summers were spent swimming, boating, fishing and water skiing at "the cabin".

One such happy time started in the summer of 1957.

I was asleep at the cabin and we had the back door open for air to pass through. About midnight, a large group of people came to the cottage next door. Cars full of people laughing and having a good time. I couldn't imagine who they might be.

When I awakened the next morning and went outside, I met the Stembel family from Gibson City, Illinois, a small town about an hour north of Decatur. Doc, Fat and Kay were Dad, Mom and daughter.

Kay was a 13 year old, blond, blue-eyed beauty who was entering high school like I. I hit it off with Kay right away and Doc was a true father figure. He was tall, gray-haired, dignified and handsome. Fat, was a motherly gal who had never had a son. Her real name, Eva May, was a funny name like mine and that's why she adopted the nickname, Fat. I identified with her because we each had silly names.

I soon filled my sense of family void and became an integral member of the Stembel family. They were class act people. Doc was a sophisticated male role-model, Fat adored me and Kay was a sister I never had.

Kay loved my dad. Mom always said she was the daughter my dad would have wanted. Mom's comment was the norm and confirmed my belief, I should have been a girl. I didn't hold Mom's comments against Kay. We were best friends.

For the next eight years, our families met for holidays

and summers at the lake. I felt special. The Stembels had one of the biggest boats on the lake and tied it up at the major marina. I often pretended the boat was mine as people would watch me tie it up for the night. I enjoyed being perceived as rich.

Fat had a red and white 1957 Ford convertible. I was super special when people saw me in that car with the top down. I had found a family and parents to love me and care for me. However, I knew it was all just pretend, but it was better than being worthless in your own family. Fantasy was more soothing than truth.

Kay and I were like brother and sister. At 13, we slept in the same bed, hung out together and soared down the lake in the big boat. We built a tree house in the empty lot across the street and had secret yells to announce our arrival. We were so innocent. Sexuality? No one thought about sex. We were kids enjoying one another's company. This was the norm in that era. These years were the best in my life.

In the summer of 1962, I was asked to work at the Stembel family farm in Gibson City and I jumped at the chance. I was treated with love and respect. I was their son; the son they never had. Oh, I didn't know much about farming and stepped in cow poop the first day, but we all laughed together. Fat just patted me on the head. The pat meant, it's alright, you don't have to be perfect here.

Doc let me drive their new 1958 Chevrolet before he

did Kay. He trusted me. Doc is the man taught me how to drive on the highway, not my father. It was my first experience with a father-son relationship and was very special for me. I felt like a respectable, trusted young man for the first time in my life. I earned my keep and worked hard on the farm. Doc wanted the barn painted as well as the fence that enclosed the house and out buildings. With pride, I accepted the challenge.

Even though I felt a happiness in the Stembel household, I never went on vacation with them. Each year they spent time at the beach in Biloxi, Mississippi. They asked me to go every year, and once I almost accepted, but I had my mother's fears and refused. Looking back, I truly missed cultural and environmental experiences by being so fearful. I wish I had gone.

These times were my happy times in adolescence and I loved my adopted family, but all was about to change as real life crept into the fantasy.

Her senior year in high school Kay became pregnant by a classmate of hers and our innocent lives seemed to change rapidly. She seemed distant and frustrated. As an only child, I know she felt as though she had let her family down and teenage pregnancy in those days was truly a social stigma. Her parents had had so many dreams for her. College, taking over the business, running the farm; the dreams were shattered.

Our childhood innocence was over and only I was left

to face the trials of youth. Kay had moved on into an adult world.

Postscript:

Fat died of a brain hemorrhage in 1962, my freshman year at ISU. Kay married the boy and together, they had one daughter. Later they divorced and Kay moved to St. Louis. She fell down a series of steps, broke her neck and died at age 34. She died instantly. Doc lived to be an senior citizen, passing away in 1996 while in his 90's. It all seemed surreal.

My adopted family was gone and I felt a void. I had memories no one could take from me. For the first time, I had belonged to a family, no strings attached.

~

The Visit:

The Stembel family was one of two which had a major impact on me and my life. As the Buttz family owned two cottages at the lake, a family from Illiopolis, Illinois, rented one of them. The Smith family, (name changed), was much like my own. Ron, (Dad), Victoria, (Mom), and two boys, (Dave and Don).

Ron was a dark complexioned, handsome, hairy older man who was kind and considerate. Victoria was a school teacher and the boys were a year or two younger than my brother and I.

In August of 1958, the Smith's asked my brother and me to stay all night at their home. Illiopolis is about 20 minutes west of Decatur. Excitedly, we accepted and headed out of town in their red, 1958 Ford convertible. It was one of the first "hard-top" convertibles made. What a car.

We shared dinner, played catch and time passed quickly. Bedtime came and I assisted my little brother with the rigors of teeth brushing, etc. All four boys slept in one room in separate beds.

Ron came into the room and it filled with masculinity and security. His smell was all male. He went to both of his boys, kissed them and told them good night. Then, he stopped by my brother's bed and bid him pleasant dreams. I knew from my own home life, I would be skipped. Neither Mom nor Dad tucked us in or came to our bed sides to tell us good night. We never got a good night kiss.

As Ron turned, he came to my bed, put his hand on my head, and said, "Good night, Barry. We are glad you and Mick are here."

I said, "Good night, Ron. Thanks, we are glad to be here."

Ron left the room and I began to cry. The tenderness melted my heart and I envied Dave and Don so much. How lucky they were to have a dad like Ron. What a man he was. What a role model for his boys. I felt warm and wanted. I was validated as a son someone might want.

The visit to their home has never been forgotten. I learned how our family could function, but never knew why it didn't.

Postscript:

The following year, Ron was on his way home from the Illinois State Fair in Springfield, Illinois. He was traveling east on old Route 36. It was dark and he missed a curve. The top was down on the 1958 convertible and it rolled over and over, crushing Ron. He died instantly. My parents reacted as any friend would have, but I reacted as though I had lost someone who cared about me personally. I had lost one of my pretend dads.

~

Movie Magazines, Sex and Religion:

The impact of the church during adolescence was tremendous. I had to be a good boy or I wouldn't get to Heaven. Girls complicated issues and boys seemed not to relate to me at all. Sexuality was elusive.

However, I couldn't explain the urges and surges I had when it came to movie magazines. Our family was at my aunt's house playing cards one night and I was on the couch reading LOOK magazine.

In the middle of the book was a full page picture of

Clint Walker without his shirt. I experienced a rush I had never felt. What was this feeling? I began to stir in my loins and felt embarrassed. The man was so handsome and manly.

I was drawn to the massive amounts of hair on his chest. I wanted to look like that. What a man! His chest looked like my dad's. What's this, an erection?

I quickly turned the page and a picture of Rod Taylor appeared. He, too, was bare-chested. His chest was also loaded with hair and I was in heaven. I had no idea why I felt as I did. I was experiencing my first sensations of sexuality.

Why did I feel like I was doing something bad, being a sinner?

Looking through the women's lingerie section of the catalog didn't make me feel funny inside but, I wasn't supposed to look at naked women anyway, as per the church and Mom.

It didn't matter, the pictures of the bare-chested men were alluring and I spent all evening with my face in the book. Nothing had ever made me feel like I did inside. I was "turned on" and didn't know the feeling.

~

Bare-Chested Males:

We lived three blocks from Nelson Park golf course and I would often find myself riding my bicycle around the perimeter roads to see if any men were playing bare-chested. I wasn't sure what the feeling was, but I needed to see if they had hair on their chests. Something was so stimulating seeing bare backed males and hairy chests.

In addition, my world history teacher lived down the street from us and her husband was a "dream boat". He would often wash his orange 1957 Buick convertible and wear only short plaid swimming trunks. He was such a handsome man. His chest rippled and his legs were so strong. I wanted him to hold me and make me feel safe. I created wonderful, safe places and it always seemed to be in the arms of a man, (my dad).

I must have ridden by the hunk twenty times every time he was outside washing that car. I wanted to ask him if he needed any help, but I couldn't make myself do it.

In the evenings, he and his wife would drive by our house and he always wore dress clothes and a white straw hat. He was testosterone personified. The couple had no children.

~

Twisted:

As time passed, I became more and more confused. According to the church, I wasn't supposed to fall prey to evil girls, but at the same time, I wasn't supposed to like boys. I didn't like boys but I did like older men. No one in church said I couldn't like older men, but it felt strange as all of my buddies were talking about female body parts.

Remembering that my mom had explicitly told me about boys kissing boys in reference to my father, I thought, "If girls are bad and boys don't kiss boys, then what is sex?" I fought my sexual feelings and the decrees of the church. My emotions were like a whirlpool and I was being pulled down, drowning.

Adolescence didn't end frustration, it created a new chapter of ignorance. At age 13, I had never masturbated or even known what it meant to wake up in the morning with my underwear wet. I was as innocent as a newborn.

Physically, my body was talking to me, but I didn't know what it was saying. In 1957, sex education was to be done in the home, and my parents never spoke of the topic. The word, S-E-X, was always spelled out and whispered by my mother. It had to be a bad word.

The first time I woke up after a "wet dream", I thought I had urinated in my underwear. Urinating my pants was stigma enough to buy my silence. My mind and body were not working together.

At age 4, Mom had used guilt to stop me from wetting the bed. I did it one time and she told me "big boys" don't wet the bed. I never did it again. I not only live with guilt, I lived in it too.

Analyzing Adolescence:

Adolescence was to have been an innocent time of growth and maturation. For me, it was a time of processing and analyzing all of my experiences. What a series of contradictions!

For example, Dad wanted a girl; I was a boy. Dad liked sports; I didn't know what a jock was. Dad was hairy-chested; I was drawn to hairy-chested men. Dad loved Mom; Dad had no room in his heart for me. School was important; School was a place of torment and social rejection. Girls were evil; boys didn't interest me. Nothing made sense.

My world was filled with contradictions and I wasn't mature enough to analyze them or infer meaning.

I didn't recognize it, but my life was simple and protected. I had little worldly knowledge and limited intellectual resources to dissect the normal progression of life's events. My thoughts were predicated upon good and evil. I was not able to recognize learning experiences or identify them as opportunities for growth.

My religious background seemed to ingrain predestined journeys for me and I believed I was living a patterned life. Life was a series of steps, one, two, three..... Each step was like a puzzle piece. When the steps were completed, my puzzle would be complete and I would be a an educated, well-adjusted, mature man.

As a child, I had no inner self to rely on and no parental guidance to assist me in decision making. Religion was my rock and my guide, but its applications didn't seem to fit into what I was experiencing emotionally and physically.

The one place I could go for answers, the church, only confused me more. Religion was to have been a guide for life's direction, yet everything I heard and learned in church indicated I would be damned if I were not perfect. I was not perfect and received no biblical answers that applied to my life on earth.

I believed if I were a good boy, did what I was supposed to do, go to church, obey my parents, do well in school, not cause trouble, etc., my life's puzzle would take form and all would be well. How wrong I was.

In reality, I simply became a pawn. People moved me around the chess board one step at a time.

I learned pawns don't have the authority of a king, but it was the queen who had the real power. As a pawn, I didn't have the strength to change much and certainly had no knowledge what it meant to be "check mated". I was in check-mate position and didn't know it. I was a pawn but destined to be a "queen".

My tapestry was a kaleidoscope.

Some lessons aren't taught in a classroom.

CHAPTER FOUR

High School Years

A New Start:

Registration:

In the fall of 1957, I started high school at the ripe old age of 13. Dwight D. Eisenhower High School was newly constructed and I would be in the first four year graduating class, the Class of 1962. Eisenhower was beautiful and housed approximately 1,900 students. Gray brick, tons of glass windows, 45 degree angle auditorium, new gymnasium, huge parking lot, science labs; everything was new. The edifice was an educator's dream. I couldn't wait for orientation and registration day.

However, excitement was quickly over-shadowed

during registration day. I sat in the back of the auditorium with my buddies and each new student's name was called and assigned to a home room. I dreaded hearing Barry Buttz called before all of those incoming freshman. I didn't. Instead, I heard the name, "Betty Butes" called.

I got up and the gang yelled, "Sit down Buttz, that's a girl's name."

I looked back at them, and in silence, ambled slowly down the steep stairway to the bottom of the auditorium. As a group, we exited via the lower east door and went to Homeroom 62 somewhere in the dungeon basement.

In homeroom, the teacher read the role. When he called Betty Butes, I said, "Here".

He laughed and said, "Are you sure."

I said, "Try Barry Buttz".

He looked longingly at the roster and then replied, "Oh, yeah, I guess that is Barry Buttz".

By this time, obscurity was gone and I was now fair game. Homeroom was in a state of hysteria, at my expense.

Pecking Order:

I was hoping to find a fresh start in high school, but found myself in the same state of affairs I had been in all my school life. Compared to other freshman, I was young, 13, but some of the 19 and 20 year old seniors were grown men. It was difficult finding my place and my social status.

During freshman year, I took the brunt of the "name" jokes. "Bare-Butt" lived on but it got worse. One day I was going to class and a classmate said, "Hey, Dingle". I had no idea what a "dingle" (berry) was. At first I thought is was probably a cool nickname. Maybe I was "in" with the social elite.

When I asked a buddy and found out it's true meaning, I ached inside. I never forgot who called me that insidious name. I had been equated with fecal material. "Bare-Butt" had taken me to the depths of metaphoric hell.

In addition to Dingle, I was referred to as "Fairy", simply because of the similarity to Barry. Many of the "dudes" would come down the hallway and say, "Hey, Fairy.". I cringed.

In the '50 and 60's, another interesting spin developed with names. It was trendy to call other male students by their mother's middle name. My mother's middle name was Bertha. I lost again as Bertha was referenced in a rock and roll song by the Trogladites, "....Bertha Buttz...". As it would be, "Fairy" or "Bertha" was a loser. The taunting never stopped and humiliation became a fact of life. I carried and hid it well.

Compared to Bare-Butt, Dingle Berry was far worse.

Names seemed to drive the engine of despair for me as I rolled along the tracks of depression. I was probably clinically depressed in high school, but didn't know it. I was just sad and empty.

~

Another high school sexual issue was the connotation of being gay referenced by the gestures of passing one's penis off to someone in the hallway. The wording was "root" with a hand gesture from the groin. I hated the game and was a victim more than once.

Teenage males would verbalize the words, "sib-a-chob" and pass the root. None of this made sense to a young man who was already in a state of questioned sexual identity.

I smiled, played along, and appeared to be in control. I passed the root too. My saving grace was that the root was being passed to everyone and not just me. What a break!

At this point, I had no self-image and my grades, honor roll and class status were my personal salvation. I was smart, but I wasn't socially acceptable due to my name. Over-coming the name became a life-long pursuit, as I had to earn respect in some social, academic or athletic arena for the name to be respected. I didn't respect my name and could hardly expect others to. I was at the bottom of the pecking order. Pass the root.

New Image:

Finally, I had had enough. I had a decision to make regarding my persona and I made it. It was up to me to change my image. I told myself I was tired of being the brunt of sissy jokes, and decided to change my image. The first thing I wanted to do was be an athlete. So, I took an interest in sports. Besides, maybe Dad would be able to share some conversation with me and we could have common interests.

I loved basketball and learned how to play quickly. My buddies and I played in all weather conditions. Lions Park was close by our homes and in the winter, we shoveled ice and snow in order to play. We went to all high school games and supported the Eisenhower Panthers. Although I loved the sport, I was never good enough to make a high school team. Not being a participant did not deter my interest in the sport.

My interest peaked and I began following the University of Illinois Fighting Illini as well as the Decatur High Running Reds, another Decatur high school which eventually won the state basketball tournament in 1962. The St. Louis Cardinals was my baseball team of choice and in football season, the Chicago Bears were my favorite.

Most fans outside of Illinois do not know the Chicago Bears started in Decatur, Illinois as the Staley Bears. George Halas, (Hall of Fame), coached the Staley team and later moved the team to Chicago. It is a proud heritage for our community. I sincerely loved sports. My metamorphosis was quick and the transition from sissy to athlete was in progress. I was determined and for my own salvation, had to make my dreams come true. Now, I was the master of my own destiny, not the name callers.

~

A Run For New Life:

I made honor roll regularly my freshman and sophomore years and in the spring of my sophomore year, I decided to go out for track and field.

The first organizational meeting took place in the school's auditorium. I remember thinking to myself, "What am I doing?" I had told no friend or my parents I was trying out for the team.

A huge football player acknowledged my presence with, "Hey punk, what are you doing here? This is a sport for men?" I wasn't even shaving.

I wanted to turn and run, but instead, I stayed. I had a right to try and I was not going to be dissuaded by someone who didn't even know me. The handsome coach, Mr. Innis, welcomed me and asked me what track or field events I wanted to concentrate on. I didn't know. He told me to report for practice. Excitedly, I did.

Practice was long, hard and enduring. I challenged myself to limits I didn't know I could experience. I wanted to be successful and contribute to the team. I had never pushed myself to do anything, but the coach encouraged me to work hard and I responded.

With my personality, I was the kind of athlete who grew with praise and assistance. Yelling, screaming and "cursing me out" were not tools of motivation for me. I needed confirmation, not more rejection.

As practice continued, weak links were weeded out. Many young men quit the team because practice was too hard and they didn't want to devote the time and energy it took to make it or they simply didn't have the talent.

It was time to chose events and find our spots on the team. Practicing different events, I found I had speed. I was running the 50 yd. dash in 5.4 seconds. We converted those practice times into reality events and I ended up running the 100 yd. dash, the 220 yd. dash and was a member of the 880 yd. relay team. Today, all of these distances are measured in meters.

My first meet was sensational. We traveled to Taylorville, Illinois and ran against a strong Taylorville Tornado squad. I was second in the 100 yd. dash, second in the 220 yd. dash and our relay team came in first. I remember riding the bus home from Taylorville and felt on top of the world. I felt like one of the boys.

My sophomore year I earned my athletic numeral. An athletic numeral was a 6 " round embroidered appliqué that had your sport and graduation year on it. It was to be placed on a school athletic jacket.

I vividly remember the awards assembly in the spring of 1960. When my name was called, my favorite history teacher, Miss Casserotti, stood and cheered.

Coach Innis said, "We expect great things from this man next year as he has contributed to our team on and off the field. We are proud of him." Are you kidding? Someone expected great things from me! Someone was proud of me! It couldn't be, but it was. I'll never forget that day.

I asked my parents to buy me a black and white Eisenhower letter jacket for Christmas. I wanted to display my work efforts and identify with other athletes. I was proud to wear my school jacket and carried myself proudly when I wore it. I had found something athletic I could do, represent my school and improve my image.

The athletes who initially ridiculed me, now wanted to walk home with me. "Hey Buttz, wait up. I'll walk home with you.", I often heard. It was a far cry from the old Bare-Butt image. Acceptance? I was skeptical but I relished it.

My new image was enhanced by African-American track team members. A. Taylor and I became good friends and ran together as buddies. Patterson, Harvey, Polk , and the Livingston brothers encouraged me to beat all challengers, even other African-Americans for my spot in the relay. I had found a new avenue of acceptance and I identified with the athletes. The multi-cultural experience would prove to be invaluable later in my professional career as an elementary school principal.

In my senior year, I earned 21 points, enough for my school letter and I was thrilled with myself. Points were earned by placing first, second or third in events. First place was worth five points, three for second and one for third. If a relay team won first place, the team split the points.

Sadly, track and field is a spring sport and my letter jacket was to heavy to wear in the spring and summer. I had my grandmother sew my letter on it anyway and wore it to the drug store. It was 90 degrees out. I was proud.

Postscript:

I proudly wore my letter jacket to Illinois State Normal Univsersity as a freshman and was told that high school letters were not worn and only college letters and letter jackets were allowed. One could wear his high school letter jacket without the letter. I took my block "E" off my jacket and put it on the bulletin board in my dorm room.

That "E" was all the image I had. Today, it's in a box under the bed.

~

Student Athlete: Attitude and Academics

As an athlete, a major change occurred in my attitude toward physical education. In high school I looked forward to gym class. I was fast and everyone wanted to run the required physical fitness 50 yd. dash with me so their time would be better. I ran 10 or 11 times in gym class to assist other guys with their times. No one ever beat me.

That darn rope climb was accomplished in 11.9 seconds and no one laughed at me this time. I was a leader and had earned respect.

Nothing stopped me from being accepted. "Buttz" was an acceptable athletic label and I wasn't chosen last for teams any more as had been the case in junior high school. The name calling diminished and for the first time in my life, I walked the hallways as an equal to other male students.

Senior year, Mr. Diller, one of the coaches, called me aside and complimented me for being a student athlete. I was being inducted into the National Honor Society that evening and he took the time to tell me how much he appreciated my representing the school as an academic athlete.

I had done what I set out to do. My exterior image was in tact, but inside, I was still struggling with my identity. I felt like I was living my life just to be socially accepted but the real me lay somewhere inside the outer veneer.

I knew I would always have to prove myself to over-come Barry Buttz. Life offered me nothing; I had to earn it.

~

Assistant Track Coach:

For a while, all thoughts of feeling weird were gone. I had a new girlfriend and was rock solid in my role as boyfriend and jock.

I was functioning as a normal teenager until one day our assistant track coach stepped out of the hallowed P.E. office and to my surprise, he had no shirt on. His muscles rippled and that chest was full of hair. I nearly choked. I shivered. God he was a hunk of man.

I found an excuse to head downstairs to the office area hoping that he would emerge shirtless again. He didn't. He was gorgeous. What was it about men who looked like this? Why did I react to hairy-chested men? I was momentarily ashamed, and quickly left the area to go home. His image permeated my vision all the way home.

My girlfriend never gave me that kind of a feeling. She was great, but the feeling I just had never emerged in her presence. Was I a freak? What was going on in my mind?

I wasn't aroused when all of the guys were taking a shower after practice. I was never turned on by other boys. If girls didn't turn me on and other boys didn't turn me on, then what was this stimulation by older men? Older hairy men.

My attractions for men were always for older, hairy-chested men. Not boys, not people my age, but older hairy-chested men. Even then, if an older man was not hairy chested, I had no interest in him. My orientation appeared to be filled with a fettish derived from my hairy-chested dad.

Indeed, I was still seeking my "father figure". I simply was not able to separate love as being other than physical. To me, emotional love evoked physical love, no matter what one's gender. I had confused the need for love and the expression of love within the confines of male approval. Love equated to approval, which meant, in a physical sense.

~

The Preacher's Son:

While in high school, one circumstance added to my emotional, moral and sexual frustration. One of the girls in my church confirmation class was dating the preacher's son from another church. That church was also Missouri Synod Lutheran and the boy was a "friend". He would regularly brag about "banging" his girlfriend.

What? The preacher's son having sex with the angelic girl in confirmation class? It can't be! He bragged so much and told us where he went in his car to "do it". As dudes would be, we went to the site and found all of the used condoms thrown from the car window. He wasn't lying.

I never thought a good Lutheran girl would have pre-marital sex and certainly, a preacher's son, should be the pillar of society and a role model for other youth to follow. My image of morality went up in flames. I had done all I could do to inspire my Christian spirit and live a good life, and these two were living a life of sin. Well, sin as defined by my Sunday School teachers.

How could the world be so contradicting? Church, sex, natural inclinations, morality...none of it made sense.

~

Student-Faculty Game:

The preacher's son was instrumental in an ego damaging incident my senior year. Tryouts were held for the student-faculty basketball game. The preacher's son was the students' coach. He chose all of the very popular guys but included me and a buddy. The stipulation was, we would be on the team, but not get to play. It was an ego-image thing and being on the team was personal to me and meant validation for my expanded athleticism.

At game time, all of the teachers were introduced as well as the students. When my name was called, a huge cheer was heard. I hadn't had such a reception ever. The gym was packed and tension was fever pitch. This was the year the students were supposed to beat the faculty, which had never been beaten. It wasn't to be.

The faculty was pounding the students and with 15 seconds left to go in the game, the faculty called a time out to put teachers who hadn't played into the game. I asked our youthful coach if my friend and I could go in. The preacher's son screamed, "No".

He looked at me and laughed. Without saying a word, he let me know I was not worthy of 15 seconds. As an ego-maniac, he never knew how important 15 seconds were to me. He was a three year letter man and was cocky and self-indulged. His message to me was, I wasn't good enough to be one of the "boys". It was a blow to my newly formed male ego. He was a jerk.

Postscript:

The preacher's son and his girlfriend broke up shortly after graduation. He graduated from the seminary and became a pastor. He has his own church in St. Louis, Missouri. He did not attend our last class reunion. His former girlfriend did, and all I could think of was her tarnished image, at least in my eyes. He is still a jerk. In the name of the Lord.

As far as the student-faculty game, no one remembers the score or the fact that I didn't play. (I remember.)

~

High School Honors:

I graduated from high school in the Class of '62. I had earned high honor roll status, a place in Honor Society and lettered in track and field. My class rank was 7th in a class of 236 and my grade point was 4.75 out of 5.0. I was a 16 year old senior and had just received my driver's license.

In addition, I was voted "Best Mannered" and "Best Dressed" in the senior class . However, a senior class officer approached me and asked me to give up "Best Dressed" . I had received two awards and the runner-up in the "Best Dressed" category, hadn't received any. Unless I gave him one of mine, he would have none.

He was the star pitcher on Eisenhower's 1962 state championship baseball team. It hurt, but I gave up the award. I had earned two, but only received one. I truly needed the self-image confirmation. He didn't. Three cheers for the gay guy, right! To this day, the star pitcher does not know the circumstances of this incident.

~

Graduation:

As graduation night approached, I was asked to sit on the stage as one of the recipients of the Gold Delta award for academic excellence. The delta was a small, 10K gold triangle with Latin inscribed on it which signified academic achievement. Only 12 of us in the senior class received them. I felt a sense of academic pride for the first time in high school. Ironically, I had to enjoy the moment, for it was the last night I would ever be in that building.

My parents did attend the graduation ceremony, but half way through, I noticed my dad's chair was empty. Mom said he became ill and had to leave.

As I drove away from graduation night, I looked back at Eisenhower High School. In some ways, I felt a sense of academic and athletic accomplishment. I knew I would never again drive down 16th Street and pull into the parking lot as a big senior. My public school education was over. I hated to see it end.

However, anxiety abounded as nothing had changed within me. I was still unsure of my emotions while dating girls, and had some kind of an emotional void the size of a grapefruit in my abdomen. Was life always going to be this frustrating? I was totally unsettled and was not living in the moment.

In addition, I recalled my high school counselor, Miss Hedrick, telling me I was an over-achiever and would never make it through college. She tried to discourage me from going for a college degree. I asked her why she thought I was an over-achiever, and she gave me some counseling "jibberish" which made no sense. What a message coming from someone who was to assist students.

I was 7th in my class and wouldn't make it? What she said to me left its mark on an impressionable young mind. Did she know something about me that I didn't know? Literally, I went to college believing I would not graduate.

What lay ahead was unknown and I was terrified. I had been accepted at Illinois State Normal University in Normal, Illinois, and intended to purse a career in teaching. My sexuality was undefined at this time, but little did I know the sexual saga was just beginning

~

Processing Life:

Through high school and the early teenage years, I never came to grips with my authentic self. In fact, I didn't know I had an authentic self. I lived for others and tried to please. I was a "crowd pleaser".

I never felt any sense of personal accomplishment. Whatever I tried, I expected to make it work. What ever I did, it was expected of me. If I were successful, I was supposed to be successful. Achievement was never enough. I think perfectionists find this scenario to be the norm. As one hurdle is completed, another takes its place. The mind is never settled and a sense of urgency prevails to meet the next challenge.

I appeared normal, but I certainly didn't feel normal, whatever that meant. Something inside was missing.

Something was wrong. For me, life was mechanical. I was going through the motions. I was being what everyone wanted me to be, a robot.

As I look back, inspite of it all, I truly enjoyed my high school years. It's contradictory, but while home created anxiety for me, the physical structure was my safe-haven. I felt secure and safe from the world. Even though I felt emotionally abandoned, Dad's presence gave me security. Everything was alright when Dad was home. It was a false sense of security, but I felt it anyway. Mom and I were both less afraid when Dad was home.

As mentioned before, to this day, all of my dreams surround my home on 22nd Place. The child in me seems to still be looking for what I never had in that house. Dad, I think.

When I was five, I dreamed Dad had died in the grade-line, (small inside porch to the basement). My brother and I had found him dead and were playing in his blood. This dream occurred shortly after Mom told me I couldn't kiss him good night anymore. I think the psychological implications of the dream were that emotionally, I no longer felt I had a dad and in essence, he was dead to me.

As a child, the dream was just a nightmare and I didn't analyze it. Years later, as an adult, I discerned its meaning. The house is always in my dreams. Sometimes Dad is in the dreams. It's a safe place to be and I look for him there.

I had literally gone though four years of high school and felt I had learned nothing about myself. I was a jock. I was intelligent. I was a good kid.

However, I was not authentic, and I knew it. Who was I? I didn't know.

An stain existed on my tapestry.

Senior Picture: An ironic inscription under my yearbook senior picture read,

"Not too serious, not too gay. An alright guy in every way."

Even though gay meant something different "back in the day", I couldn't win!

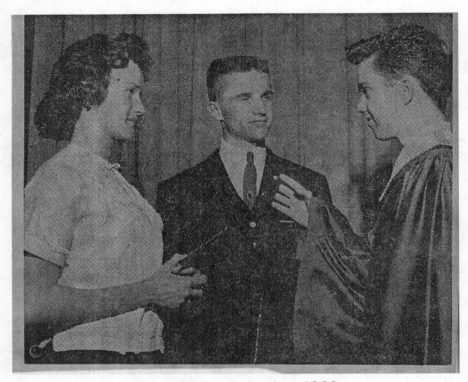

Honor Society Induction, 1962

"It takes courage to grow up and become who you really are." Cummings 7

I had no courage and I didn't know who I was.

CHAPTER FIVE

College and the Early Twenties

"And gladly would he learn and gladly teach."
Motto/Illinois State Normal University, 1857

Entering College:

In the fall of 1962, Mom and Dad drove me to Illinois State Normal University in Normal, Illinois. A teacher education scholarship worth $36.50 paid for books and tuition. Having been a big senior in high school, it was difficult being a freshman again. I was starting over and wondered if Bare-Butt would invade college too.

I was assigned to Room 148 at Walker Hall, a men's dorm which had previously been a women's residence hall. I looked forward to having half a room to myself. After unloading my clothes and setting up the room, it was time for Mom and Dad to leave. Mom gave me a hug and Dad echoed some utterance that I did not distinguish.

I stood and watched from the dorm porch as they drove away, but quickly turned to enter a new world of free-thinking, independence, choices and decision-making. It was a foreign world.

My roommate was an Eisenhower High School graduate who played football and was also a member of the 1962 state championship baseball team. His dad was a minister and we were friends in high school, but not close.

Over the course of our freshman year, we became great roommates. About 21 students from the E.H.S. Class of '62 were all going to I.S.N.U. and we felt secure having old and immediate friends. My high school girlfriend was one of those students.

Freshman year would be trying and challenging, but I had vowed I would not go home until at least Thanksgiving. Some of the kids from Decatur were going home the first weekend. To me, that made no sense. I was ready for my new life.

Believe it or not, Bare-Butt appeared to be gone.

As the school year began, events occurred that would guide and direct my sexuality. I'll share those experiences.

Panty Raid:

As a freshman, I tried hard to fit in with the guys at ISNU. In August, our campus staged a major "panty-raid". It was insane. Male students were chaotically running from dorm to dorm screaming and yelling while the girls were throwing under-wear from the windows.

It was a feeding frenzy. Males were grabbing panties, bras or anything being thrown. I was completely overwhelmed. To appear interested, I dashed about as though I was a member of the frenzy.

Someone yelled, "Hey the senior girls are on the roof taking them off on the spot. Boobies." The place went nuts and everyone headed for Fell Hall, the senior girls' dorm. What a display!

Breasts were being exhibited, bounced and stroked. Some of the guys were emotionally "dying" out there. One guy yelled, "Hey, this damn thing is still hot."

I could hear voices in my head telling me what I was doing was wrong. The pastor, my Sunday School teachers, and the church were all talking to me at the same time. In reality, it was my conscience.

This wasn't supposed to be happening and it wasn't what I went to college to do. I had my first opportunity for a major choice. I was embarrassed and decided to go back to my room in Walker Hall. Was this really higher education? I was disappointed in other students' choices and behaviors. I couldn't continue the sham. I was disappointed in myself.

After three hours, the campus police finally quelled the "riot". It made newspaper headlines and was featured on radio and television. School administrators forbid students to repeat the event or face expulsion.

That evening, back in the dorm rooms, guys were saying and doing really bizarre things with the underwear. Some of the idiots had panties on their heads and one guy was rubbing his penis with a bra. Another idiot said to me, "Here Buttz, smell these." I left the room and vomited.

Truly, these behaviors did not express my character nor did they excite me in any way. I was pretending to be one of the crowd, but I knew the other males were not acting.

The panty raid displayed no respect for women and was not indicative of what college men or women should do. In some odd way, I didn't blame the girls, just the guys. Personally, I thought they had no class or dignity.

~

The Hairy Greek God:

As a 17 year old freshman, my class schedule was miserable. The dream of "sleeping in" was a joke. I had four 8:00 a.m. classes. One of the classes was swimming on Monday, Wednesday and Friday. An eight o'clock swimming class during the winter semester didn't make much sense to me, but it was required.

Fortunately, Walker Hall was across the street from the Fairchild Hall pool and I was able to wait until the last minute to get to class on time. In the good ole' days, students were required to use university issued swimming suits and in order to get a grade, you had to take a shower before and after class. Conformity was critical and following the rules essential.

About a week into class, I went to the pool a little early one morning and discovered this 6'3" totally sexy older male standing nude in the shower. He was the first nude, mature male I had ever seen. He was striking! Hairy, muscular, well-built and mature. I was totally enamored with him. He would stand so his back was to the shower head and all body parts were visible. A hairy Greek god. I was awed. He had it all.

Being totally conscious of my boyhood, I was embarrassed to stand facing him. Compared to him, I was a little boy. I stood facing the shower head and he viewed me from the rear. Little did I know at the time, that's what he wanted.

In class, he was introduced as the assistant swim coach. Wow, I thought about going out for swimming immediately. It was a weak moment.

Thereafter, each morning I would arrive early to see

if the coach was showering. He was. His hairy body was wet and matted. Totally sexy. I quickly included him in my nighttime sexual fantasies to lull myself to sleep.

As a naïve kid, I had no suspicions about the reasons for his daily presence, as we were all required to shower. I did find it strange he would be in the shower at 7:30 a.m. and not come out dressed for class until 8:00 a.m.. He stayed in the shower until all boys were finished and in their swimming suits for class.

One morning after class, one of the guys said to a classmate, "Hey, was he watching you today?"

"Who?", I wondered.

The classmate responded, "Yeah, he really gets his jollies on, doesn't he? Be careful, man, I think he likes you. Ha Ha Ha! Don't let him see your a---".

Who were they talking about? I didn't have a clue. Was someone secretly watching us? One of my Eisenhower classmates was in the class and I asked him if he knew what was being discussed.

He looked at me and wrinkled his face, "Sure.", he said.

I said, "Well?".

His reply, "The coach. He approached me last week.

Wanted me to come to his office after class. I rejected his offer." What? I couldn't believe my ears.

"What did he want to you to do?", I asked?" My friend just looked at me and rolled his eyes.

I was enthralled with the idea of being asked to the coach's office, but I was scared he would and I might accept. What a man he was.

He never asked me. I guess that's what I get for being a kid. At 17, maybe I was "jail bait".

In truth, I couldn't believe a coach would sexually approach a student. I had a lot to learn.

This totally handsome hunk of macho man was believed by students to be gay. Sadly, he was a pedophile.

All of the guys equated being gay with being a pedophile. It became a campus joke. No one dared tell authorities because of his status with the university. In kind, he was never accused of any sexual indiscretion. Besides, in those days, who would believe a kid?

Postscript:

I never saw my father nude, nor had I ever seen any other mature male nude before this incident. I was curious and captivated.

During my senior year I learned a number of my female

student friends not only had affairs with professors, some of them actually moved in with them.

Life was more complicated than I ever imagined. I longed for the intellectual safety of my past; little or no decision-making on my part. Just amble through life without detours or roadblocks. I honestly thought that's what life would be.

Follow Up:

Some years later the coach's son coached basketball at one of your local high schools. He was a very good looking man like his father. However, he had a problem. He was released from duty due to in appropriate behaviors in his office. Students told stories of him inviting male basketball players into his office and he would be standing nude with a full-blown erection. Sounded familiar to me. I had to wonder, had he been the his father's first victim? He was repeating history and I was empathetic. Poor kid never had a chance.

~

Meeting And Not Meeting Expectations:

As the semester progressed, my girlfriend and I shared time together as much as we could, but it didn't take long before I spotted another young lady who I wanted to date.

In October of 1962, it was homecoming time and everyone expected me to ask my high school girlfriend to the game and dance. I didn't. I asked the other young lady and friendships began to shatter. My new interest lived next door to my high school girlfriend. I truly cared about this new young woman and we dated for two years.

In the end, neither young lady became mine. My high school girlfriend dropped out of college after first semester, and my new interest lost her father. He was killed in a farming accident. She withdrew from everyone. She was an only child and never recovered from her dad's loss. She dated, but never seriously. We remained speaking acquaintances throughout college.

As the first semester came to a close, I made average grades. I made three B's and three C's but realized if I continued at that grade point level, I could and would graduate. Take that, Miss Hedrick. I had proven that "old maid" wrong. However, I was no longer the straight "A" student and found myself in academic purgatory.

~

Friendship and Sexuality:

Big Brother:

With grades established, second semester brought about my first sexual warning signs. My next door neighbors were two I.S.N.U. football players from rural Bloomington and a Chicago suburb. Both were sophomores. I became friends with Sean, (name changed), and we hit it off. He was tall, (6'3"), dark complexion, and hairy. I finally had someone to play basketball with, go swimming with and socialize with in an acceptable manner. A role model. An older brother.

His roommate, Joe, (name changed), was stocky, muscular and rough edged. He was more the buddy type for me. The boys gave me an acceptable nickname, "Shotgun". I was in! I was runnin' with the big dogs.

Almost immediately I found myself trying to decipher the difference between loving someone as a friend and loving someone in a physical sense.

Sean was straight and had a girlfriend. I was jealous of her and the time he spent with her. She was confiscating time he could be spending with me. I often displayed anger at Sean and he didn't understand why, nor did I. He got angry with me because I was often moody around him and he sensed I didn't know what I wanted from our friendship. We were both frustrated.

One night he said to me, "What is it with you? Do you want to s---k my d--k? If you do, here, I'll give it to you right now."

I replied "No", but I think I really meant "Yes".

Just the thought of being gay was repulsive to me and I was afraid to act upon my impulses. We never spoke of that night again. We spent a lot of time together and enjoyed one another's company. We went to church and once hitch-hiked to his home in Dolton. I was grateful for the experience.

The next year Sean moved into an off-campus apartment. I saw little of him but we stayed in touch.

I lost the sense of sexual stimulation and the need to be accepted, and I was relieved. The strange sexual feelings were gone. However, I missed the camaraderie. I didn't understand why I was not able to separate friendship love and physical love. I loved Sean but seemed to need a physical relationship, even though I never acted upon those impulses.

Sean and I remained friends throughout college and are still friends today.

~

The Giant:

My next sexual encounter came during sophomore year. My Decatur roommate had decided to move into an off-campus apartment. A random roommate was assigned. He was from northern Illinois and we didn't get along.

One morning I was heading to the bathroom and I angled around the corner and bumped into the biggest man I had ever seen. He was 6' 4" tall, had one hairy chest, the biggest arms I had ever seen and was totally handsome. He said hello and I replied accordingly.

I had never seem him in the dorm before and didn't know if he was visiting campus or an I.S.N.U. student.

I learned he was my neighbor on the other side of my dorm room and he, too, was unhappy in his living arrangements. Casually, we became friends and shared our concerns about our living arrangements.

At semester, we moved in together and became inseparable friends. He wasn't the best student and I did all I could to help him improve his academic status, as he was on academic probation.

I bought him clothes, tutored him and let him drive my '57 Chevy. We were called "Buds". I was functioning as the big brother and rather enjoyed the roll.

Everyone knew we were "tight" and did everything together. Jim, (name changed), and I played intramural basketball, football, softball and coed-softball. Our popularity grew and we were both sought after by the girls. Oddly enough, I didn't want the girls. I just wanted to be with Jim.

One of the craziest things we did was to play coed-softball. One of the girls named our team, The Masterbatters. Soon, we were feared as a team and eventually won the all school championship trophy. The Masterbatters reigned supreme.

I stopped dating girls and rumors abounded all over

campus. As per campus opinions, I was gay. I didn't feel gay, I felt normal, but campus suspicion existed.

One weekend Jim and I drove to Decatur to visit my parents. My brother, a friend of his, Jim and myself decided to stay at the lake cottage. That evening the boys slept on the porch and Jim and I slept in the master bedroom. At bedtime, he took off his shirt and pants and stood before me in his jockey shorts. I did the same and we crawled into bed on our respective sides. My heart was pounding.

Once he was asleep, I lay awake and stared at him. I wanted to touch him so badly. My fingers crawled across the sheets like an insect until they were close enough to touch the bulge in his shorts. I hesitated and then went for it. I touched his manhood. He never awakened. The erection I had was insurmountable. Without touching myself, I blew up. What exhilaration.

Yet, once my orgasm was over, I felt ashamed. I had never slept with or near a girl and I wondered if I would have had the same results.

The incident was my secret but I harbored guilt which escalated with each memory of that night .

Jim was a true ladies man and didn't concentrate enough on his studies. It was up to me to see to it he made it to his junior year. He didn't. I couldn't take his final exams for him and he didn't pass them. He flunked out.

I was very emotional the day he left campus. I was back to square one regarding friendship and sexuality. As with Sean, the sexual feeling subsided as soon as Jim left campus. Again, I felt relief, but I missed our friendship. My mind was in intellectual and emotional turmoil.

About a month after he flunked out, I called him at home and he told me his mother said our relationship was not normal. He asked me not to call him again. We have never spoken since. Wow!

What I felt for Jim was unusual, and the rush was exhilarating. When he left campus, I was so confused. I missed him but I didn't. Suicide? Lutherans feel only God has the right to end life. I remembered my religious training and made the right choice. I was relieved.

~

Summer Job:

In the summer of 1963, I had my first job. Prior to this time, I cut grass for neighbors and earned 50 cents per yard, but this was my first paying job. I was to start working for the Illinois State Highway Department.

My dad was a democratic prescient committeeman and all state highway jobs were patronage positions. The garage, as it was phrased, was located on North 22nd St. and was a series of buildings housing state trucks, grass cutting machines and salt for winter snow and ice storms. Starting day was a Monday morning and I arrived at 8:00 a.m. Dressed in a T-shirt, jeans and tennis shoes, I was nervous, but ready. I asked to speak to Mr. Kirby, the man in charge and my dad's friend.

Mr. Kirby's son, Kent, and I were assigned to a truck that worked from Decatur to Clinton, IL. Three men were already on that route and had been working together for years. Frank, 67, was the lead man and he drove the truck most of the time. George, 66, was the "spot man" and worked with torches and hot blacktop. Ted, 35, was the youngest of the three and he was the "jack-of-all-trades" person. Ted was dark headed, handsome and a "player".

Our summer responsibilities included painting bridges, grass mowing, burning off erupted blacktop, checking on motorists and any other repairs needed. Once in a while we had to pick up "road kill". I was fine until we had to pick up a dead Collie dog. I let Ted do the dirty work. My heart sank every time we found a dead animal.

The summer was hot and the work even hotter. We "road the route" and often stopped for drink breaks at local pubs along the route. As a non drinker, I got soda, but so did the other men, as they were on duty.

As we rode the route, one of the fun things for the men to do was ride along side a car and look to see if the women had their skirts pulled up. Ted and Kent went "ape" if a gal were showing legs, panties or more. Some of the women accommodated and pulled their skirts up for the men to see. Sometimes, one didn't need an imagination. I was in social and culture shock as I had no idea women were so bold. I played along and acted interested.

One afternoon, it was so hot we all took off our shirts. When Ted pulled off his shirt, I nearly came unglued. What a chest full of hair. I couldn't look at anything else.

As we rode by women in cars, I looked at Ted. I wanted to run my hands through the hair on this chest and see what it was like to touch a man. Ted was all man.

Finally, it came my turn to learn how to use the torch to burn spots. I was a rookie and needed help. Ted got behind me and showed me how to move the torch to complement the shovels being used by the other men. When he did, the hair on his chest touched my back. I had to stay composed on the exterior, but inside, I was near emotional overload.

I failed to mention that Kent also had his shirt off. By now, the story is predictable, and of course, Kent was of no interest to me. First, he was my age and secondly, he had no hair on his chest. My sexual arousal pattern was permanent. Hairy older men!

I earned enough money to buy my first car, a light blue over dark blue 1957 Chevrolet. I paid $700 for the car and utilized every cent I had earned in the summer. My summer job was fantastic as I was earning money and I got to be with a hairy chested man every day. At the time, arousal was enough. I was satisfied. I never saw Ted again.

I read his obituary ten years later. Life was short.

A Year Of Emotional Peace:

My junior year was unremarkable sexually, but I had the best roommate ever. John, (name changed), was short, stocky and terribly funny. He was from the Peoria area and had two brothers. We truly were compatriots.

He and I played sports all the time and I had no attraction to him physically. What a great year. Often, I would go home with him for holidays and weekends and I felt accepted in his family. I always wished my family would interact as his did. I think part of the success of the year was attributed to the fact I had no sexual interest in John. I was free and didn't have to worry about acting on feelings I didn't understand. Now, I was just a "dude" having fun with another "dude".

~

Spring Break 1964:

In the spring of 1964, four of us decided to go to Daytona Beach, Florida, for spring break. We planned the event early in the fall and began to take cereal from the cafeteria so that we would have breakfast food during our week in Daytona. Our intentions were to camp out in order to save money. Our mode of transportation was to be my '57 Chevy.

Finally, spring rolled around and the "dudes" were ready to go. We wrote, "Spring Break, Daytona Or Bust" on the side of the Chev and headed out. We had all of our camping equipment and little or no room for clothing. I had $35.00 total for the entire week's trip.

The reason we wrote "Spring Break, Daytona Or Bust" on the side of the car was more informational than it was social. The times were violent and the Civil Rights Movement was in full progress. President Kennedy had been assassinated in 1963 and no one felt safe.

Three students had been killed in Mississippi because of their involvement in the "Rights" movement and we wanted to identify ourselves as "Spring Breakers", and nothing more. We were fine, but cities all across our nation were burning and riots were common.

The worst memory I have of the times was the mass slaying of students at Kent State University. How could students be gunned down on a college campus by national guard troops? It happened.

Therefore, our decision was to drive straight through to Daytona and not stop except for gas. We were going to take turns driving, but once underway, I nixed that idea. I had earned the money for my car and didn't want anyone else to drive it.

Twenty-five hours later, we rolled into Daytona. We located the camp grounds we had seen in a brochure and it looked like Gator Haven. Screw that idea.

We drove up and down the strip looking for a cheap hotel. Most hotels had "No Vacancy" signs posted. Finally, we saw one old, green hotel with a vacancy sign. I went to the reception area and an old woman told me she would rent us a room for $10.00 for the whole week if we didn't drink, party and tear things up. I promised.

As we settled in, we bought bread, bologna, milk and beer. I didn't drink but the guys wanted beer. We utilized all of the cereal we had taken from the cafeteria and saved more money.

Off to the beach. The first day we tried to walk the beach. No one told us it was 23 miles long. The guys were going nuts looking at the girls and we simply ambled along until the sun was setting. I pointed out that however far we had come, we had to go back that same distance. We had walked for six hours.

I hardly noticed any of the girls but the older men in their Speedos on the beach drove me nuts. I pretended to notice the girls, but they were not the subject of my excitement.

Once we returned to the hotel, our white northern bodies were lobster red. I awakened the next morning with blisters all over my head, shoulders and chest. I should have gone to the hospital, but I didn't. I spent the next four days indoors. What a spring break.

The last night in the room, the boys wanted to drink and have a party. I told them I had promised not to drink or party. I became angry and got in my car and drove to a movie. The movie was "Cheyenne Autumn", which I have now see 30 times. When I got back to the hotel, I slept in the car, thus keeping my promise.

The next morning I heard a tapping at the window. It was the old lady from the hotel. She said, "Did they kick you out?".

I responded, "No, they wanted to drink and I promised you I wouldn't."

She looked at me and said, "You're a good kid, thanks for keeping your word."

I told her I would inspect the room and make sure it was cleaned up. The fellas hadn't done any damage and the night was never discussed.

We left for home and I returned to campus with $12.50. What a trip. The visions of those older men in Speedos drove me nuts. The beach was a great place. Spring Break 1964 was over and I knew I was different.

~

Student Teaching:

However, an incident occurred my senior year that cast shadows on my orientation and released the reality of my sexuality.

I was student teaching at Illinois School For the Deaf in Jacksonville, IL, and my roommate was from Decatur. Illinois School For The Deaf is an institutional setting which is well-over one hundred years old. At the time, the high school was located in one of the older buildings that reminded me of a haunted house. The third story had bars on the windows. I really didn't want to know why. The entire setting was filled with institutionalisms. By that, I mean regimented events, rules, controlled lunchroom settings, study hours, etc.. In a way, it was eerie.

My roommate and I had gone to high school together and he was very active in our senior class. I knew him well and we enjoyed one another's company. Wayne was the president of the senior class and I remember during the election campaign, someone had written on his poster, "Knob polisher". I had no idea of content meaning and it certainly had no sexual connotation. Why would waxing a knob be funny?

Wayne was very handsome and the desire of all women on campus. During student teaching, we lived above the infirmary at I.S.D., (Illinois School For The Deaf). Yes, we lived in and among all of the germs being spread throughout campus. I felt as though our rooms were no more than large hospital rooms. The ceilings were 20 ft. high and sound echoed off the walls and ceilings. Wayne and I shared a bathroom and made sure we were both not using it at the same time as a courtesy to one another.

One evening Wayne came to my side of the apartment and asked me to give him a back rub. I thought his request was strange, but he said his back really was tight and it hurt. I said yes and I went over to his bedroom. It was dark. We perched on his bed.

I began rubbing his back and he seemed pleased. We were both shirtless but had on long pants. I massaged his back thoroughly. He said my efforts were helping the stiffness. Finally, he turned over and my hands were full of thick, black hair on his chest. I was so stimulated and shocked I exploded.

Immediately, I got down from the bed and went to my side of the room. He came over and apologized and said not to blame myself. Wayne was gay. I blamed myself. I was humiliated and ashamed. I had disappointed myself, let my parents down, and disobeyed my church. I didn't speak to Wayne for the remainder student teaching.

I tried all forms of self-punishment and went through a period of self-loathing for years. Was I just reacting to any sort of sexual experience? Near the end of student teaching, I wrecked my beautiful '57 Chevy. Subconsciously, I think I did it on purpose to punish myself further. I loved that car. Now, it was junk.

At the age of 21, I had never had an interactive sexual encounter other than the backrub with Wayne. Prior to age 18, I hadn't even masturbated. Hard to believe, but it's true. I would pay a severe price for this encounter.

~

Physical Pain, Emotional Scars:

An event occurred prior to my senior year that I feel set the stage for my sexual vulnerability in Jacksonville.

During my junior year at I.S.U., (name changed as the university went multi-purpose), I injured my right knee during a physical education class and had to drop out of summer school. I knew I would graduate late.

At the time of the injury, I was making straight A's in the three classes I was taking. As we were studying track and field in Elementary Physical Education class, I was asked to demonstrate the broad jump, (long jump), in class. I agreed.

I was not in shape and had done no conditioning before the demonstration. It had been four years since I had long jumped in high school. I proceeded with the demonstration.

I jumped and landed to the right of the sand pit. My right leg hit the grass, hard. I heard the sound of a thousand twigs breaking. The twigs snapped and cracked and seemed to break in unison. I stood up and collapsed immediately. I could see the bottom of my right foot on my right shoulder. I couldn't move. The pain was so intense, I didn't feel it. I was in a state of shock.

Two large boys in the class made a chair with their arms and carried me to the infirmary across the street from the old track and football field. No emergency attention was given at the scene and no ambulance was called. My leg dangled all the way to the infirmary. Today, a lawsuit would have been immediate.

All of the ligaments and tendons in my right leg were torn and it was hanging only by the skin. The anterior cruciate ligament was destroyed as well as the medial collateral ligament. All meniscus cartilage was ripped apart.

The ISU Infirmary called my parents and said I had hurt my leg and needed to be in a hospital. The university offered no assistance. Mom and Dad picked me up in our 1957 Mercury and I rode home in the back seat in a semi-conscious condition. My leg was supported on a pillow taken from the infirmary.

Upon return to Decatur, I was admitted to St. Mary's Hospital and Dr. A. Sweet was assigned to my case. He said my injury was 100 times more severe than Joe Namath's, the famous New York Jets' football quarterback. We waited three days for the swelling to go down before surgery, but Dr. S. said, due to the pressure, blood shot to the ceiling when he made his first incision.

I was hospitalized for three weeks and was in intense pain. The pain shots helped but weakened my over-all condition. I reacted to them and had to spend more time in the hospital. Finally, I was sent home with a plaster cast from toes to hip. I wore the plaster cast for nearly three months. My leg shrunk many inches and my short-lived sporting career was over.

I walked with a limp for nearly five years and my knee would often "fall out" on me. Once I slipped and fell down the stairs at Schroeder Hall and my books and papers fell three stories to the floor. I added more humiliation to my life. I was not hurt physically.

The incident with my knee was important in a two-fold manner both of which will be explained in upcoming chapters.

August, 1965
Cast removed, recovering at home.

Postscript:

My final grades in the three summer classes were two B's and one D. I had never gotten a D in any academic class at any time in my educational life.

However, it was January of my senior year and I had one class to finish and one month to make up the work or an F would be recorded. The class was Literature for the Elementary and the exams included identification of stories, authors and characters of various children's literature stories. I had four exams to take.

The Literature professor told me if I passed one of the four exams, he would pass me with a D. At the time, I needed hours/credits and the grade was irrelevant if above an F. I passed one of the exams by one point. Fate was my ally.

~

Army Physical:

Indeed, I did get drafted and rode the train to St. Louis for the army physical. I had my train ticket in one hand and carried under my other arm a one inch thick folder explaining my knee injury.

Once at the army recruiting center, we were told to strip our clothing to begin the physical process. We were treated less than human. No one who spoke to us had a college education, yet, they were demanding and threatening. All dialogue was in the form of a command.

I hated the experience and knew I would not survive in the army.

At one station, we were all told to stand, turn around, bend over and "spread our cheeks". The scene was gross and I was sure the army personnel were laughing.

I stood firm and did not bend over.

I was shaking as the doctors approached. "Son, did you hear my order?", one bellowed.

I said, "Yes, sir, but I can't."

"What do you mean, you can't?", he asked. I handed him the file.

He read it, held his hand to his mouth, looked pensive and said, "Son, get dressed and go to the end of the line." I didn't hesitate.

As I positioned myself at the last station before receiving a 4F, physical deferment, a gruff looking sergeant took my medical papers and said, "Do you want to serve your country?"

I thought, "What? I think I just flunked the physical, How can I serve my country? I can't run through rice paddies dodging bullets. I can't run, or even bend my knee."

Verbally, I answered, "I am under a teaching contract

at Illinois School for the Deaf, and don't want to break that contract, so?"

He replied, "Hell, you're just like a G. damned Benedict Arnold, aren't you? You don't know what you want. Get the hell out of here.", and stamped my papers 4F. My head was swimming in this sea of contradiction.

Irony:

After my papers were stamped 4F, I was told to go upstairs where I met a very kind, caring man from Civil Service in St. Louis. I was offered a civil service job working with the hearing impaired in St. Louis County for twice the salary I was making.

I had been Benedict Arnold one minute and a sought after commodity the next. I wanted to accept but I was fearful and dedicated to I.S.D. I declined the job. Life continued to be full of contradictions and frustrations.

Only two of the 600 young men failed the physical that day. The rest, headed for Nam. I can only wonder how many of the young men on that train never returned from Vietnam. My body was altered, but I was lucky.

I never understood war and especially, the Vietnam War. What a waste of lives and money.

As time passed, I ached for the veterans and the horrors they lived through. My conscience would not have let me go to Vietnam if drafted. My educational skills and teaching the hearing impaired, were more valuable to children and society than my carrying a gun. God took care of my concerns. A knee injury was a small price to pay for not walking the "booby-trapped" rice paddies in Nam.

I contributed to society.

~

Senior Year Summer School:

As a result of my injury during my junior year, I had to attend summer school again during my senior year. Immediately, my character was on trial as was my religious upbringing.

I had a young professor for my Deaf Education Practicum class. He was in his 30's handsome, slender and well dressed. However, he appeared to be overly interested in me. I knew he was gay because Wayne used to get mail from him when we were student teaching in Jacksonville.

It was the first Wednesday of class and around 3:00 p.m. and a tornado warning had been issued for central Illinois. The professor suggested I spend the night at his house because of the storm threat. He reminded me of my need for the class to graduate. No pressure here.

I was commuting from Decatur and returning home nightly. I told him it was my brother's birthday, (lie), refused his offer and drove home in a severe rain storm.

I was upset emotionally and recovering physically from the knee injury.

The ride home was emotional and physically threatening. The storm was vicious but I saw no tornado.

Something deep in side of me wanted to stay, but after my experience in Jacksonville, one more guilt trip wasn't needed. I never saw the professor again. He never returned to observe me teaching.

Two weeks into summer session, I contracted a medically undiagnosed illness. My body jaundiced and I carried a high fever. I missed three weeks of summer school as I had done the year before with the knee injury.

After three weeks of antibiotics and without a diagnosis, I returned to class the last day possible for full credit. Due to the knee injury in 1965 and the illness in the summer of 1966, I graduated in August. The majority of my class had received their diplomas in May, but around 200 of us graduated together in August.

Although I earned my degree, I was disappointed I couldn't enjoy the camaraderie of my classmates in May. I was disappointed and felt I had failed because my goal was to graduate in May of 1966. I was not aware the three month delay was a blessing in disguise.

~

Analysis:

I had thought my life to be no more than the fulfillment of a series of goals which would carry me safely to the next level of maturity and success. The journey was to be easy and predestined. How wrong I was.

My college education was more than academics and I struggled to find the answers to questions that were not contained in a textbook. Life's questions proved to be more difficult than any essay or multiple choice exam I was exposed to in the classroom.

Questions without definitive answers were always difficult for me and certainly, life has no guarantees or canned answers. For me, life was like a series of "True/False" questions. Answers were either black or white, true or false. The church dictated right and wrong. Shades of gray did not exist.

Because of my expectations for "smooth sailing" through life, I fought all of the detours and roadblocks. My maturation level failed to allow me to view each roadblock as a learning experience and an opportunity for growth.

I had always looked at 21 as this mythical age when one knows and has all the answers. What a joke that was. In fact, my twenties were the worst years of my life because I felt I should know and have all of the answers to life, but didn't.

Maturity is difficult to define because at any moment of any day, one can react maturely to a situation and five minutes later, be totally immature in another situation. Chronological age is irrelevant. I never realized most of us just move forward doing the best we can.

Certainly I thought I was prepared to meet the world after graduation from college, but within two months, I learned I was a total novice at the game of life.

My story continues.

My pride and joy, 1957 Chevy

Postscript:

It was a Sunday night in November, 1967, and I was heading back to Jacksonville from Decatur. I had gone home for the weekend and had not wanted to return to "hell".

It was dusk and I was in Springfield, IL, half way back. In those days the drive was two-lane and one had to go through the back areas of Springfield to reach Rt. 36 on to Loami. In the heart of the back roads, a railroad crossing existed with an "S" curve in the middle of six railroad tracks.

I couldn't see clearly and was nearing the "S" in the tracks. I looked out the side passenger window and saw a train light approaching. I gave the car gas and plunged off the wooden crossing onto the tracks.

I got out of the car and noticed I had sheered off the two front wheels. I ran down the tracks to try to stop the train. Half way down the tracks a man grabbed me and told me not to endanger myself.

The engineer had seen me drive off the road and stopped the train 10 yards short of my car. The man who grabbed me was an off-duty police officer who happened to be the father of our neighbor in Decatur. He took me to his home across the street and called my parents.

Mom and Dad drove me back to Jacksonville and my Chevy was taken away on "the hook". I had no idea where it was going or if I would ever see it again. I did, but it wasn't the same. In street terms it was called a "side-winder", as the frame was so badly bent.

I had worked all summer to earn the money for my car and now it was junk. We got $50.00 for it at the junkyard.

The physical side of my emotional punishment was losing my car, but the emotional side was one of pure hatred, for myself. Even at this point, I didn't feel I had been punished enough for being the person I was born to be. I was truly a tormented soul.

My tapestry shed tears.

CHAPTER SIX

Panic Attacks

Definition:

This chapter is as important to me as the over-all educational purpose of this book. Understanding panic attacks is as critical for coping in life as is awareness, education and acceptance of sexual orientation.

A "Panic Attack" can be defined as the body's physical, chemical and emotional reaction to unreasonable and unfounded fears based upon a sensitized state of the mind and body. This definition is mine and I don't have to quote it from any source. I lived it.

Most of the time these unfounded fears are thought, dismissed and the individual moves on with daily life. Normal chemical reactions occur in the body but the mind does not react to them. However, if any one incident triggers unfounded fears over an extended period of time, the thoughts can be paralyzing, physical symptoms emerge and a panic attack follows.

Each individual reacts differently to panic attacks and the attacks themselves have degrees of veracity. The best way to unmask the unfounded fear is to educate one's self as to what happens to our bodies/minds during a panic attack.

No matter what the "trigger", the body will respond the same, but in degrees. My trigger was the severe injury to my knee in the summer of '65. My body had been badly shaken and my central nervous system was recovering from the severe injury and corrective surgery. In addition, add to the stress my sexual orientation concerns and a second trigger exists. Triggers vary per individual.

As a result of unfounded fears, the body reacts with anxiety, nausea, diarrhea, cramps, listlessness, depression, and even loss of consciousness. These are but some of the symptoms. However, the symptom is not the cause, it is the reaction.

When the mind is sensitized to a reactive point, any normal thought can be blown out of proportion and one usually becomes incapacitated for a few hours, days or even weeks. In my case, it was years. I had no idea what a panic attack was and thought I was slowly going mad. A cycle develops.

What is this cycle? The cycle is fear-adrenalin-fear. The

greater the fear, the more adrenaline secreted. Thus, the body is so sensitized, it reacts to every thought. This fear-adrenaline-fear cycle has to be understood, accepted and broken, to conquer the attacks.

As panic attacks result from a sensitized body which is triggered by irrational thoughts, the demons are perceived; yet, totally real to the person perceiving them. The trick is to sit in peace, think the thought, no matter how horrific, and pass through the sensitization or the panic. Once accomplished, one is on his way to recovery.

As one recovers, he/she has to "unmask" the fear and recognize it for what it is, a thought. No one thought should be more important than another. Once "unmasked", the cycle is broken.

For example, at any one time many of us have thought, "I feel like I'm going to pass out", but we don't. Sensitized people may think the same thought, create an over-load of adrenalin, and sensitize to the point they do pass out. They gave too much importance to one, simple thought in their day.

Recovery doesn't mean you will never have sensitized thoughts or another panic attack. Recovery means if you have irrational thoughts or a panic attack, you continue to function, and are not debilitated to the point of mental/physical paralysis or inability to function.

Some of the best advice I received during the pinnacle

of my panic attacks, was, sit quietly and see what happens. Live through the panic. I took the advice and sat through one of the most irrational thought patterns I had ever had. I waited, but nothing happened. I was the same person in the same place when the thoughts were over. I had unmasked the fear. My body and mind couldn't fool me any more.

In the 1960's no name existed for panic attacks. One was usually told he had a good "case of the nerves". Tranquillizers were prescribed by doctors and one was sent home to live in a world of dazed eyes and functionless, mindless worlds of sleep. Doctors treated the symptoms and not the cause.

At one time I was taking five different tranquillizers from five different doctors and washing those down with Nyquil. I often wondered how I got out of bed in the morning. Tranquillizers weren't good band-aids, and were incapacitating. I needed reasons and answers, not a "knock-out" punch. I lived in a vacuum of sleep.

Today, many drugs are available and individuals don't have to suffer as I did. To some, it is a stigma to admit they take Paxil, Effexor, Zoloft, etc., but they are wonderful drugs which "take the edge off" so one can continue to function and live his/her daily life. To this day, I take a low dose of Effexor daily and am glad I have it to take.

With this background, I will share how panic attacks affected my life.

Introduction To Terror:

It was fall semester, 1965, and I was to begin student teaching in January, 1966. I had convalesced through the summer and early August with my knee injury and had returned to campus humbled and off-schedule. I was still living in Walker Hall, Room 148, and had resided in that location for four years. Because of the knee injury and the upcoming student teaching experience, I felt like I was starting over as a freshman even though I was 20 years old and a senior.

It was difficult going up stairs as my knee didn't bend. I was allowed early exit to get to my next class but my travel time was doubled and I was very, very slow. I was often embarrassed as my knee would "fall out" of place and I would tumble to the ground. I was physically impaired.

Once I dropped all of my books down a three story stairwell and had to have help picking all of my materials up. Gone were the days of "open gym", intra-mural basketball, football and softball, and even those Friday night dances. Physically, my body had been altered.

Academically, I managed to cope for the first three months because the routine was familiar and non-threatening. In December, I began meeting with my supervisors and culminated the paper work for student teaching. The process was long and unlike other college academic work.

My first student teaching assignment was at Metcalf Laboratory School, in on-campus elementary school. I was to work with Miss Mary Rosan in the sixth grade. I had met with her a couple of times and she seemed to have high expectations for me. I wish I had had the same expectations for myself. The knee injury had destroyed my confidence and I dreaded being introduced as Mr. Buttz, the student teacher. I could hear the snickers and see the facial expressions as the sixth grade minds tried to cope with "Bare-Butt".

In late December, I returned to campus nervous and anxious after Christmas break. Finally, it arrived, day one of student teaching. I awakened early and started to get out of bed. Something snapped in the back of my neck and everything went black. I fell back into bed. I tried two more times to get up, but couldn't.

I asked my roommate to contact Miss Rosan and tell her I was ill. He did and she said to take care of myself and start the next day. That didn't happen. I was allowed to miss three days of student teaching but if I missed a fourth, I would not receive credit for the experience.

I missed all three of the allotted days. On the morning of the fourth day, I tried to get up once more and had the same reaction. I knew I had to go and forced myself to the restroom to get showered and shaved. I was very weak and could hardly stand.

I got back to the room, dressed and slowly walked across campus to Metcalf. I felt a little better with each step I took but had no idea why I felt as I did. I met Miss Rosan and we talked about my first day and what she expected of me. I was to observe the first week and prepare to take over one subject during the second week. I was assigned to teach science, my weakest subject matter area.

I was relieved I didn't have to do anything during the first week except learn the culture of the classroom and students' names. However, all of my anxieties proved to be accurate when I was introduced.

"Class, we have a new student teacher with us for the next six weeks,", Miss Rosan announced. "I would like for you to meet Mr. Buttz".

The students tried to stifle their amusement, but to no avail. I stood and told them it was alright to laugh, as I knew I had a funny name. Knowing the students were mostly professors children, it took but a second for them to process the seriousness of their laughter as an introduction to my student teaching.

One young man apologized to me later for laughing. He was a young Jewish boy who had a culturally recognizable last name and had been made sport of himself. I appreciated his grace and his maturity.

I managed to stumble my way through the next week's science lessons and learned from the students as I went along. Most of them seemed appreciative in having a male student teacher, as most males at the time worked at the secondary level.

I completed student teaching in Miss Rosan's room and received an A for the six week session. I had two additional six week student teaching assignments ahead of me but never had any reoccurrence of the strange feeling I had prior to my student teaching with Miss Rosan.

I had had my introduction to panic attacks but didn't know it.

~

Guilt:

I hadn't recognized my introductory episode as a panic attack. I thought I was ill and eventually over-came whatever it was that had afflicted me.

My first powerful set of panic attacks came after my incident with Wayne while student teaching second semester in Jacksonville, IL. The guilt I felt for having a homosexual encounter, broke open a series of unfounded fears that led to years of suffering.

At age 24, I sought counseling and medical attention, but was only given tranquillizers to calm my nerves.

The psychological counselor I saw said I was having "homosexual panic" attacks. He never explained the reasons why or the physical reactions my body would have when the attacks occurred.

He really did little to ease my mind and give me

peace. Basically, he only confirmed my suspicion, I was gay. I didn't want to be gay. Explanations! That's what I needed, explanations. If I were gay, Why? Why me? What had I done to deserve this societal curse? Why did older men arouse me? What did gay men do? I received no answers.

Damn the world! This life was a far cry from the molded, predestined life I had expected. How did I function well all of those years but now seemed cursed. I envied people who seemed to have no cares in the world and nothing seemed to affect them.

I hated my twenties as it was the most tormented time in my life. What is for most young people, the best years of their lives, I missed.

My emotional state was now causing physical reactions. My body and mind were reacting to full blown "homosexual panics". It was the first year of what would become the norm for the next 20 years. Life was a more than a bad dream. It wasn't a nightmare; it was living hell.

I was in my mid 40's before the panic attacks stopped. I never told my family what I had. In my twenties, I was ashamed and my parents offered no assistance or suggestions for addressing the physical symptoms of my illness. In lay terms, I thought I was "nuts".

I tried every punishment I could think of to rid myself

of this plague. It didn't work. Guilt, anger, anxiety, physical illness, I had it all. I hated myself.

~

Living The Unfounded Life:

As I progressed through my twenties, anxiety dominated my life and I became agoraphobic, fear of leaving the house. When I went out, I had severe panic attacks and had to go home. I can't put into words how this kind of fear makes one feel, but in my mind, I was physically ill.

I couldn't drive, go to movies, sporting events, or even church. No one had programmed me for living an unfounded life.

Each time I left one of these events, I felt as though I failed and the downward spiral escalated. For example, I was playing softball with a team and seemed to be in a daze most of the time. I couldn't hit, field or really even participate. I was in a "zone". Depression hit and all I could do was sleep. I lived on tranquillizers.

To illustrate, as I sat in church one Sunday morning, I felt like everyone was looking at me. I felt ill and thought I might vomit. My body trembled and I wanted to run outside into the fresh air and perceived freedom.

Communion time came and I had to move from my not so secure pew and address the altar in order to receive communion. I envisioned myself collapsing on the way to the altar or passing out as communion was being dispensed. My mind raced and my body responded. Sweat was running down my head and splashed into my eyes. I could hardly see. I was hot and cold at the same time. I couldn't feel my feet or my hands. I was floating. It was as though I was having an out-of-body experience and I was watching this event from above.

As the usher came closer to my pew, I bolted and ran from church. Once outside, I was only momentarily relieved and took a huge breath of cold air. I staggered to the car. I had trouble getting my car key into the ignition and couldn't feel my hands on the steering wheel. How could I drive home if I didn't even feel my hands? I finally started the car and drove slowly home.

One would expect once I was home, the panic attack would stop. It didn't. The nausea became worse and I felt I had only one option, knock myself out. I took two different tranquillizers and passed out. The cycle was in full swing. Fear-adrenalin-fear, my mind created a living hell.

All of the things I used to do and loved doing, I couldn't do any more. In panic, I left football games, grocery shopping, shopping at the mall, dating, basketball games, dinner at friends' houses, and movies. I couldn't understand how all of my previously routine, "normal" activities could be so difficult.

Living with "IT", as I called panic attacks, was horrific

141

and the multitude of medications I was taking distorted reality. I felt safer and normal in the world of sleep. If I had had a choice, I would have resided in that world.

My waking hours were full of overly stimulated thoughts which resulted in physiological reactions. My body was in a sensitized state and all thoughts seemed to create adrenalin-fear-adrenalin cycles, a panic attack.

If my future were going to be like this, I really didn't want to be a participant. Again, I contemplated suicide, but never carried it out. I didn't want to die; I just wanted to be like everyone else. I just wanted to be the way I used to be, without "it".

In 1973, I purchased a "self-help" book and slowly worked my way out of the panic attacks. The descriptions of panic attacks and their effect on the body were quite understandable and it all made sense, but it was easier said than done. I had to try.

I started taking baby steps towards my recovery by going for short walks or going to the store for one specific item. It took time and I had many failures. Eventually, I focused on the successes and abandoned self-punishment of each failure. Unless you have experienced these feelings, you have no idea the mental hell one lives through.

It took me more than 20 years to conquer what is today, very commonplace in millions of Americans. Oh, if I had only known I was not alone and that someday one little pill would relieve all of the symptoms in my tormented mind and body. I conquered the panic attacks the hard way, and in some ways, I'm glad I did.

~

Message:

My sexual orientation and my jolting knee injury were my sensitizing triggers. These events set me up for a number of escapades with panic.

At the time, I had no idea how the attacks were triggered and never assumed my knee injury affected me in any way other than physically.

If you have experienced panic attacks and are still dealing with them, I hope this chapter will assist you in coping. It is easy to take a pill and feel better, but knowing the causes, the symptoms and the triggers, gives one power to prevent the panic attack or calmly live through it if one does occur.

Through acceptance of thought and recognizing "triggers", one defeats the anxiety, keeps the mind from being overly-stimulated, reduces adrenalin and eliminates the panic attack.

Is it easy to conquer panic attacks? No, but being paralyzed by one's own thoughts is worse than facing your fears. Your enemy is self.

Knowledge is power and I grew emotionally and intellectualy as I analyzed each personal bout with my thoughts. "IT" existed only in my mind but that didn't lessen the power it had over me.

My tapestry got thicker.

~

Sometimes when we fight, things get worse. It's difficult, but if we go with it, things become better. The key is our reaction to what happens to us. Go with it. Your mind is fooling your body.

CHAPTER SEVEN

The Opposite Sex

Fitting In:

As a school-aged child, I had not been attracted to the opposite sex but thought girls were fun to have as friends. Unisex bodies permeate adolescence and other than prettier faces, girls resemble boys. Nasty Ninny breasts aren't visible and I was never threatened by the thought of them when in the presence of young, female friends.

My first experience in "going with" a girl, was in sixth grade. My young female friend and I never saw one another socially off the school grounds, but that's what "going together" meant in those days. She was a cute, blond haired, blue-eyed gal who grew up to be a life-long friend.

In junior high I had three different girlfriends. Again, the social aspect was magnetizing and I learned that with a girl, I had more opportunities to be invited to special parties, school events and couple's activities. For two years ten of us learned to square dance and had fun dancing to the commands of the "caller". The times were innocent and square dancing was in vogue with all age groups.

Being "exclusive" with a girl usually meant you traded "dog tags", a faux silver or gold chain with a round circle on it. On the circle was your name engraved. "Going with" a girl meant trading dog tags, (names), and when you broke up, back went the tag.

"Slam Books" were popular and everyone wanted to read the gossip written in them. A "Slam Book" was a small book with white lined paper on which one "signed in" and proceeded to answer a series of questions on each page. The questions were usually very, very serious such as, "What is your favorite singer?", "What is your favorite song?", "Who is the cutest boy?", "What is your favorite color?", etc. Heavy!

American Bandstand set the dress standards and introduced all of the new dance moves. Rock 'n Roll was here to stay.

Every evening I would run home from junior high and turn on Bandstand. I learned to dance and began to dress and wear my hair as the trend setting boys did.

In those days it was called a "Flat-top", but today it's referred to as a "Spike".

Poodle skirts were "in" and poofy "hair-dos" were a must for girls. Guys wore clean Levis, white bucks, saddles or blue suede shoes. Dressed to kill, my junior high girlfriends and I danced on television at our local version of American Bandstand and at Lakeview High School every Saturday night. We were too cool for ourselves.

Rock 'n Roll music soon replaced square dancing and I had to learn how to "Stroll", do the "Mashed Potatoes", and "Cha-Cha". My first 45 speed vinyl record was Little Richard's " Good Golly Miss Molly". I loved the Motown sound and saved my weekly allowance to by hit songs. I was never a big Elvis fan, (Sorry!). What a time to be a kid.

Computers, the Internet and technology in general were not discovered yet and kids of all ages had to use their imaginations and creativity to survive. Most television sets were black and white only, as color hadn't been invented. Inappropriate language was never heard on television and violence was limited. Bullet holes were never seen and seldom was fake blood shown. When a cowboy was shot on one channel, he lived to ride again on another channel.

The scariest television movies at the time were "Dracula", "Frankenstein", and "The Werewolf". Now that was true horror.

Lon Chaney, Boris Karloff, and John Carradine were the masters of horror movies. Computer graphics didn't exist and most of the horror occurred on a sound stage with fake backdrops. I believed it all.

I never kissed one of my junior high school girlfriends, but did attend a number of parties where kissing games were played. The worst thing I ever did was play Spin The Bottle. Wow!

I remember sitting in a circle with an empty glass milk bottle in the middle. In turn, each member of the circle would spin the bottle until it pointed to someone of the opposite sex. When it did, a kiss on the lips was given. Such passion. As a young gentleman, no sexual stimulation was felt during these times. A kiss was more like a reward or treat for winning the game.

The really sinful game was called "Seven Minutes In Heaven" and consisted of nothing more than playing "smash mouth" with a girl for seven minutes. By today's standards, this game is like watching the Muppets.

In high school, I dated two girls but secretly had a crush on a third. As a Christian boy, I always seemed to be attracted to truly Christian girls to date. No girl ever "wanted my body", which would have scared me to death, but we did enjoy one another's company as dating couples.

High school dating usually consisted of attending sporting events, going out for pizza, going to Homecoming and Proms and crusin' the "strip". In Decatur, Eldorado St. was the strip and it was totally cool to be seen crusin' down Eldo and giving the two-fingered "hello" gesture.

Steak 'n Shake, Perry's and the Tepee were hot spots for burgers, fries and milkshakes. McDonald's dominated nothing at the time and privately owned "burger joints" were the norm. Life was simple and it didn't take much to entertain teenage minds. All you needed was a car.

In high school I never had a personal car, but I had the use of my dad's work car. That car was a hot, white 1955 Ford. I lined the back window with "fuzzy" stuff and put decals on the inside. Tire rims were blackened as the hub-caps were taken off, unless you had "half moons" or "full moons". "Mag" wheels were not known t the time.

During these times, sexual intercourse was to be an act which consummated marriage, not a recreational activity. Kids were much more innocent than they are today. Remember the preacher's son mentioned in a previous chapter, he seemed to consummate something on a nightly basis, but it wasn't marriage.

My sophomore year, I had my first female rejection, as I had a crush on a beautiful young lady who was more impressed with the football quarterback than she was the track man, me. It hurt, but taught me a lesson early in the dating game. One didn't always win with women.

Dating in college was much like that in high school. Movies, dances, pizza, long walks, etc., constituted the agendas for date night. Sometimes, just "hanging out" in the dorm lounge or going to the "stacks" at the library, were good enough.

The new James Bond movies were ahead of their time and Sean Connery was a movie hunk. Most of the guys went to Bond movies to see the hot chicks; I went to see Connery without his shirt on. I was never disappointed.

In college during my freshman year I met the right girl at the wrong time. With this young woman, I did feel sexual stimulation. On date nights, I couldn't wait until time to return to the dorms and the nightly "passion pit" escapades.

To explain, in the 60's, college girls had hours and right before curfew, couples hung around the doors in a rite of passion. As the lights flashed their final warning, lips were locked, bodies were smashed and no one wanted to break it up. That's why they were called "passion pits". What an experience.

Unfortunately, she had eyes for a swimmer and we broke up. Ironically, she never married. Sadly, She passed away June 28, 2010, while I was writing this book. We had just reunited May 24th at a mutual friend's house during a small, informal reunion. I was glad I got to tell her good-bye. Our lives had touched and it was meant to be.

During sophomore and junior years I dated little. I was more interested in intramural sports and my studies. I did date one girl but only for a short period of time. We made a great pair; I was gay and she was a lesbian. So much for romance.

While a senior, I met the wrong girl at the right time. She was three years older than I, was homecoming queen and very sexually experienced. She was a beautiful blue-eyed brunette. I often thought she just wanted to be seen in my hot '57 Chevy and that's why she dated me. It quickly ended when she became pregnant. The baby was not mine as we had never had sex.

~

Learning Experiences:

As I look back, I had experienced a combination of hetero and homosexual experiences in college. Perhaps, other students had the same experiences, but for me, I felt I was the only person who was torn between two sexual worlds. I liked girls, and they aroused me, but no matter what I felt, I always remembered my Sunday School teachers saying, "Girls are bad". Plus, I couldn't deny what had happened with Jim and Wayne and those hairy chested older men always aroused me.

As the end of senior year approached, everyone seemed to be getting engaged or "promised". I literally pulled away from all of my friends, male and female, because I was student teaching during second semester and being absent from campus was easier than facing my emotions and the final good-byes. I moved off campus and lived in a trailer with another guy who was engaged. I seldom went to campus.

I loved college and my friends and couldn't cope with the thought of parting. Harboring my fear of loss, I made a conscious decision to void myself of friendship and lessen the pain. This decision was one of the biggest mistakes of my life.

"God has given you one face, and you make yourself another." Shakespeare 8

Junior High School   College

CHAPTER EIGHT

The Missing Link

Genetics:

In the 1940's and 1950's, no one spoke of homosexuality, especially in the Midwest. The word used to describe homosexuality was "queer" or "homo" and it was a taboo subject. Throughout my childhood my only memory of someone talking about being gay, was my mother.

My Grandmother, Dad's mom, had four children. Robert was the first son born but was killed at age 16. He was practicing baseball at Fairview Park and after practice hitched a ride on the running board of another kid's Ford. He was side-swiped, knocked off the running board and died instantly.

George was the second son and he worked as a

railroad car maintenance man. He married, but he and his wife never had children. After breathing in diesel fumes for 30 years in the car shops, he died of lung cancer in 1972.

Dad was the third child and spawned Bare-Butt and Michael, the first and only two grandchildren. It was most unusual to have four children and only two grandchildren, but that's how the family history revealed itself.

My aunt, Dad's sister, was the baby of the family and the most studious. She was a college student at ISNU, (Illinois State Normal University), when I was a teenager. She had served three years in the Women's Army Corps, WACS, and was attending ISNU on the GI Bill. Liz, (name changed), was studying to be an elementary education teacher.

In the summer of 1957, my brother and I were invited to stay with our aunt and her roommate, Ginger, (name changed), in their off-campus apartment. We were alone while the girls had classes and played whiffle ball outside. Miller Park Zoo was only two blocks away so we walked to the park/zoo and we had a blast. It was like a first taste of decision-making freedom. My brother and I saw nothing was wrong in the girls' living arrangement.

Later that summer, Liz and Ginger had come home to the lake cottage and we were all swimming together.

I got out to get dried off and my mother commented, "Look at them out there. That's awful".

I said, "What's awful?"

"It's just disgusting.", my mother retorted. I didn't understand what she meant. Everyone was having fun.

After that incident, I realized Mom was commenting about sexuality, lesbians. I'm not sure how my mother knew the girls were lesbians but possibly, it was her opinion and nothing more. Never did she have a kind word for my aunt or her partner. She constantly referred to the evils of same sex love. I thought, "What if I am gay?". I could be disgusting, couldn't I?

My missing link was genetics. No one ever mentioned gay tendencies in our family. No one ever told me my aunt was a lesbian.

It wasn't until I was 46 years old I asked my mom if anyone else in our family were gay. She didn't know because in those times, no one discussed it or admitted it. I suspected others were also or at best, latent. In that era, homosexuality was a stigma for families and was a familial ill. "Homos" were like religiously demented things, not people. Being gay was worse than having tuberculosis. Queers were mentally ill.

My aunt and Ginger enjoyed 53 years of life together. Their lives were full of accomplishments. Both women were educators and both excelled in their professions. Ginger was a sports icon at a small, private, mid-western college where she pioneered women's athletics and started the first women's basketball program/team.

I spoke at her funeral and eulogized her life and accomplishments. When she passed away, part of my aunt died too.

They had had a wonderful life together and never hurt anyone via their sexuality.

My aunt ended her teaching career as a special education teacher at a local high school. She taught the physically impaired and worked exceptionally hard to make special needs children have as normal a life as possible. Both women contributed to society.

At 38 years old, I finally understood my heritage. The missing link was genetics. Genetically, I had the genes needed for a gay life, and my environment had definitely influenced, guided and directed me to become a gay man.

Science has never proven being gay is genetic, but unless you have lived the life, struggled with your feelings and tried to overcome what society says is wrong, you can never know the impact of fighting a birthright such as being gay.

As for bi-sexuality, I am not sure if one's genetics dictate this choice or if experimentation sets the stage for a final decision. I believe I was bisexual at one time, but made the final decision after feeling emotionally complete and fulfilled with a man.

No one could make a straight person be gay anymore than one could make a gay person be straight. It can't happen. Neither of these circumstances could or would be a choice. Yet, the general public does not understand, nor do they want to understand, that being gay is not a choice.

Circumstances and events can also set into motion subliminal inclinations that have been suppressed for years. Right place, right time and suppression is over-ruled by genetics, events and resulting emotions. (ie: Prison life for example)

Nothing is cut in stone. Being gay is not etched in granite. Being gay is probably not found in degrees, but as in the heterosexual world, how one behaves in either world, is always a choice.

Trust me, in our judgmental society, no one would choose this life.

As in the words of Shakespeare, "To be or not to be" (gay), isn't a choice.

CHAPTER NINE

Mid-Twenties and Early Thirties

Beginning A Career:

After graduation from Illinois State University, I obtained my first teaching position at Illinois School for the Deaf in Jacksonville, Illinois, (ISD). I had my own apartment, a new car and debts on both.

My first teaching contract was for $5,800.00 and I netted $180 every two weeks. I think I was considered poor.

I was not adept at sign language because ISU didn't believe in using sign. I had to learn to sign on my own while teaching. The hearing impaired students were patient and eager to teach me all of the (dirty) signs.

I loved the day-time teaching hours, but the nights

were full of frustration. I found myself masturbating nightly, sometimes three or four times. Each time I felt guilty and loathed my actions. However, the urge was more powerful than the guilt. Masturbation soothed my need for sex, but created an endless guilt cycle.

I was sick on and off during the school year and went home nearly every weekend. I hated living alone and being alone. Maybe I hated my inability to refrain from giving-in to sexual urges and felt a change of environment would arrest the sensations, or at best, I would be monitored which would diminish the opportunities for me to act out my sexual urges.

In addition, the city of Jacksonville and Illinois School For The Deaf, held memories of my student teaching encounter on campus. Those memories still haunt me today.

At ISD, I taught in the high school unit. I.S.D.'s campus was institutional, and most of the buildings were quite old. The high school was the oldest building on campus and had an asylum look.

The windows of my room had bars on them and neither administrators nor teachers ever told me why. Working at the school was a challenge. Nothing was new. Teachers had to "hand-crank" the mimeograph machine, materials were sparse and the atmosphere was dark and dreary. I had been warned about signing a contract in Jacksonville, but I didn't listen. None of my professors at I.S.U. wanted me to teach at ISD, but no one told me why. I found out on my own.

The Principal:

The principal of the high school was an icon. His parents were deaf and he was truly a member of the deaf world. He could sign and fingerspell as well as the deaf students and he held status in the deaf community. He was a hearing icon in a world of silence. His voice was heard through his hands.

As the year progressed, I realized I could do nothing to please the man. In truth, he hated me and was jealous of my relationships with the students. He had been "King Pin" for years and resented a new male face. He was the hearing impaired's self-appointed savior.

The kids dressed like me, wore their hair like mine and became interested in personal appearance. It was a pleasant change compared to the slovenly look most accepted of themselves before I arrived.

As a part of our teacher contract language, we were required to eat lunch with the students. I often ate with one 21 year old female student who was the same age as I was. I enjoyed her company because she was more mature than the other students.

One Friday, after school, I was called to the principal's office and told I could not to eat with the young woman anymore. Why? It looked as though I was seducing her.

Little did the guy know my sexual orientation and I wasn't about to tell him. I felt like "Big Brother" was watching my every move. He intimidated me and I allowed it.

At the end of the year, I was anxious about my final evaluation. I met with the principal in private for my final conference. The principal told me if I stayed to teach a second year, he would give me an average evaluation, but if I left, my evaluation and written reference would be excellent. Everything was subjective. He had nothing in writing to prove or disprove his evaluation of my work.

I hated my experience in the institutional setting, but more than that, I hated the little world the principal had created for himself. I was new, young, enthusiastic and actually thought I could help kids. He stripped me of many ideals associated with teaching, but I did learn a valuable lesson. The educational world is full of politics.

I left Jacksonville after only one year and returned home to start the first middle school hearing impaired program in Decatur's history. My evaluation was glowing.

Postscript:

Irony, fate or divine intervention continued to permeate my life's journey. I had interviewed for the hearing impaired position at Thomas Jefferson Middle School in Decatur on a Monday. On Tuesday, the Director of Special Education, Leonard Dobson, submitted my name for the position. It was approved by the board that evening. Mr.

Dobson died of a massive heart attack on Friday, two days later. Fate? Divine intervention? You call it!

~

Thomas Jefferson Middle School:

I arrived at the newly finished Thomas Jefferson Middle School in the fall of 1967, to begin the new, innovative, middle school program for the hearing impaired. Jefferson was located on the far east side of Decatur near the airport. The building had been built in 1966. A solid brick structure, it was state-of-the-art during those times. T.J., as it was commonly known, held approximately 700 students. It was a second year teacher's dream and a far cry from the asylum atmosphere at ISD.

I was widely accepted by the students who were fantastic. I loved my job and appeared happy. My ability to sign and fingerspell helped me tremendously and hearing students were infatuated with the skills.

Sign was a novelty and I was the conduit to a new skill. Hearing students wanted to learn sign in order to communicate with my hearing impaired students. What a welcome change to find interest in special needs children. Soon, my nine students were some of the most popular on campus.

I met a number of available females and began to date a couple of them. One rose to the surface and we became exclusive. She and I were co-sponsors of the student council and we were able to meet quality students who wanted to be involved in their education.

Many of our dates were social events sponsored by the student council, but we did go to movies, eat out and just "hang out". We enjoyed the students and found our jobs professionally fulfilling.

History Repeats Its self:

Shortly after my first year, a new, married man, (Tim, name changed), arrived to teach history. Tim was a wiry 150lb, 5' 10" man who had a certain male sex appeal. His voice was very deep and he had very male mannerisms, although no hair on his chest. We became friends and he, his wife, my girlfriend and I, became inseparable.

History repeated itself. I soon found I had feelings for Tim. As with Sean, he, too, became frustrated with me and asked me what I wanted from him. I didn't know.

I ached inside when he greeted my girlfriend with a hug. I wished it were me. I just needed a hug, a touch.

I think I drove the man crazy and after three years, he and his family moved to another city.

Again, I was unable to distinguish between friendship love and emotional, physical love. To me, they were one in the same. I wanted to express physical love to a man and have it reciprocated. I needed to know what it felt like to touch a man. I didn't understand why I couldn't be hugged as a show of caring and friendship.

Full-blown panic attacks returned. I missed many days of school and eventually ran out of sick days.

I had been living in an apartment complex with a male roommate and as the panic attacks continued, I went home to my parent's house on 22nd Place. Emotionally, I couldn't live in the apartment any more. I didn't officially move out, nor did I ever take my belongings with me. I slept on the couch at my parent's house and never returned to the apartment. My life was in chaos.

Search For The Cure:

As I continued to strive for normalcy in my life, I found myself becoming serious about the young female I had been dating.

Celeste, (name changed), was of German/Irish descent. She was an attractive, blue-eyed new teacher who hailed from Decatur. She had attended Catholic schools and was an only child of much older parents. Her mother was 45 when she was born. Actually, Celeste's birth was a phenomenon called a "dry birth". Her mother didn't "show" and no fluid existed. She was a miracle child and was destined to be the only child.

Both parents were Catholic and Celeste had a strict, structured church background. Being an only child, Celeste had the full attention of her parents. Most of

Celeste's social life was church related. Her parents were friends with specific nuns and priests within the church and at a local Catholic hospital. Celeste worked at the hospital in high school and college.

Their household was strictly matriarchal, as Celeste's mother dominated. Her father labored in factories and smoked heavily. His lungs were full of iron filings and he contracted emphysema. After a time, cancer developed and he passed away of lung cancer at age 68. I met the man one time.

I met Celeste at Thomas Jefferson and we dated for about four years. Within the relationship, I would often "back away" if we became too close. I was defensive and not sure of myself or my feelings. We called my absences "vacations".

At Christmas time in 1970, I met my parents' expectations and popped the question. Celeste accepted my proposal and my parents were thrilled. However, for the next seven months, my panic attacks were at their worst. I lived in a surreal world and often felt as if I were floating or observing from afar. It was as though I was watching someone else go through the motions of life.

Every time I participated in some activity relevant to the planning of the wedding, I grew worse. Truly I thought I was losing my mind.

We were married on June 26, 1971. I was 26, and she was 27. On our wedding day, my panic attack was so great I wasn't dressed 10 minutes before the wedding started.

My brother asked me, "Are you going?"

I replied, "Don't rush me." We made it on time.

I wasn't thinking about the wedding, marital vows or even my bride. I was thinking I would pass out, collapse or have a panic attack and have to leave during the ceremony. "IT" was paramount on my mind. I have no recollection of my vows or what happened during the ceremony. I remember nothing of the church events. A new chapter of my life was unfolding and I wasn't participating.

Heavily medicated, I made it through the wedding and actually did remember the reception. We were not able to go on a honeymoon as we were both teaching summer school and had to return to work on the following Monday.

We had purchased a house together and planned to spend our honeymoon evening at home. Surprisingly, a repair man had left the heat on instead of the air conditioning and the house registered 98 degrees. Our honeymoon night was warm to say the least.

A question you are asking is, why did I marry if I knew I were gay? I didn't know. Even though I had all of the weird encounters, I still refused to believe or feel I was gay. I was in full-blown denial and was concentrating on surviving panic attacks more than sexuality.

During our dating years, I wanted to have intercourse but abided by her wishes and her religious beliefs. She experienced the same church teachings as I had and to Celeste, sex was to be consummated after marriage. I loved her and abided by her wishes.

As with most men who doubt their sexuality or orientation, I thought homosexual feelings would disappear after I got married. Marriage was to be a cure-all. I honestly believed it would be.

In addition, in our society, marriage is somewhat of an expectation for a heterosexual man. I fulfilled that expectation and certainly did please my parents. One step closer to Dad's acceptance. I was still trying to win his approval after 26 years.

The greatest impact on Celeste and her life was her mother. Celeste's mother lived in a deteriorating neighborhood and she was being robbed regularly. As it was, she had no less than four deadbolts on each of the two doors to her home. Celeste spent most of her after school hours with her mother and often didn't come home until 7:00 p.m. after doing laundry, etc. It seemed ridiculous to be married and have her spend all of her time with her mother.

Less than a year after our marriage, as a safety precaution, we moved her mother in to live with us. To me, Celeste's mother always came first. I firmly believe the person I married was a daughter first and wife second. Mother ruled the roost and Celeste did what she said. Her mom had a much greater impact on Celeste than I did as her married partner. After the children were born, I was displaced to third and then, fourth, or at least that's how I felt.

It is important to note the differences in our backgrounds to understand how and why our marriage failed. I was Lutheran, she was Catholic. I was from a patriarchal family and hers was matriarchal. Both of my parents worked; only her father worked. My parents had a large social circle of friends outside the church; almost all of Celeste's parents' friends were within the church. My parents were much younger and had a different set of social mores, (folkways established truth/law), and expectations. As much as two chronological generations separated our parents and their beliefs and their parenting skills were quite different.

At times I would attend the Catholic church with Celeste, but she never went with me to the Lutheran church. For years, I sat in church as I had always done, alone in the back pew.

In marriage, I was looking for a mate to help me overcome my confused sexual orientation and Celeste was looking for someone to take care of her. I wanted someone to love me and show it. I wanted a woman to sit by me in the car, hold my hand when we walked and hang on to me physically. I needed to know I was a man and was making someone happy sexually. I wanted and needed emotional security as well as physical approval. I never felt either in my marriage.

In my opinion, Celeste's religious background and personality didn't allow her to be able to demonstrate love as I expected it to be shown. Little did we know our marriage goals were so different. Prior to marriage when we met with a (gay) priest, we never discussed sex as the glue for marriage. We did discuss my signing children over to be members of the Catholic church, but I refused.

Ironically, other than religion, the one area we did agree on was the subject of children and how to raise them. We did an excellent job in raising our children despite our religious and personal differences.

I have no regrets regarding the years I was married, and being a parent was one of the greatest blessings in my life.

Both children were baptized Lutheran but raised in the Catholic Church. Both were forced into Catholic instruction in second grade and this created a major source of conflict. Celeste's mother was the center of the storm and created serious emotional splits between us.

As within many homes, when structured religion is pounded down children's throats, strange reactions often occur. As it would be, neither of my children attend church as adults. Sadly, in this respect, Celeste and I failed. We have good kids, but they entertain no formal religion.

We did have other issues and sex was one of them. However, the worst mistake I ever made was moving my wife's mother into our home after one year of marriage. My mother-in-law lived to be 100. No further comments.

I have been plagued with two emotional questions for years. I have always wondered where I would be today had I married a woman who needed sex as badly as I did. Plus, what might my marriage have been had Celeste's mother never come to live with us...I wonder?

My search for the cure in the heterosexual world ended in failure.

Postscript:

In 2004, my wife and I were divorced after 33 years of marriage. At no time in this book do I want any of my behaviors to reflect on my former wife. I assume full responsibility for my actions and don't blame her for my behaviors. She must assume responsibility for her own actions and behaviors. Sadly, the priest who married us died of AIDS.

Because of our children and our grandchildren, Celeste and I get along better today than we did when we were married. I hope our positive relationship continues for everyone's sake.

Challenging Times:

As I look back, my twenties and thirties were the most challenging times in my life. Chronologically, I was mature, but what I knew of life and myself, was minimal and didn't take a college degree to understand.

I spent most of early adulthood trying to figure out what I was going to do with myself physically and emotionally, not my life as per direction or occupation. I hated what I thought I had become and worked diligently and deliberately to punish myself for being a let-down to everyone, most affectionately, myself.

I married, not out of obligation, but out of love, parental expectation and sexual curiosity. I thought marriage would be my sexual salvation. I wanted to please my parents in order to gain some expression of my father's love. I thought once I had a woman, all would be well. I was a 26 year old virgin.

Unlike my genetics, my heart and my soul were like clay. Up to this point, the hands that crafted my body and mind, never fired the clay into anything permanent. I wasn't even a work in progress, I was constantly being remolded sexually even though genetics directed my plight.

My tapestry was tattered.

CHAPTER TEN

Life Changing Events

The Accident:

A catastrophic event occurred in 1982 that changed the course of my life forever. I was jogging up the stairs at home at 11:11 a.m. on 11-11-82. Schools were closed and teachers/students were off for Veteran's Day. I accidentally crammed my side into the stair railing. That evening my abdomen looked like an "tie-dye" event. I had multiple colors of green, yellow, blue and black which formed an art canvas. I noticed that my urine was discolored, but after three days, it returned to normal. I seemed to be gaining weight, but I was eating less. Frankly, I just didn't feel good.

I felt ill for one month and collapsed at home on December 10th. I was rushed to the hospital at 10:00

p.m. and taken to the emergency room. No one seemed to know what was wrong with me and I was admitted to the hospital for further observation.

After a two week search for a diagnosis, it was decided I had knocked off half my left kidney and had a 12" hematoma, (blood clot), in my abdomen. After a 13 hour surgery to remove the hematoma and the top half of my kidney, the doctors told my wife I would be a healthy old man with one and a half kidney.

After three hours of observation, the doctor returned to my wife and told her the portion of the kidney that had been left was not setting up well and he was going to remove it to keep me from any additional surgeries. Hence, I have one kidney.

Diagnosis:

Five days later, when the pathology report came back, I was told I had renal cancer. At 38, I was the youngest kidney cancer patient in Decatur medical history. The doctors literally flipped a coin to see who would tell me the news. It came, straight and to the point. I was dying or probably would die very soon. I was hysterical.

Family Reactions:

I called my dad and his response was, "Now, Barry Allan, everything will be alright."

I thought, "Damn you, Dad, everything will be alright!

I've got cancer, get it? Cancer!!!" As usual, no help from Mom or Dad. The whole event soon became an "out of body" experience.

With the birth of a daughter in 1977, and a son in 1980, my wife appeared to be headed for single parenthood. Her reaction to my cancer was, "What am I supposed to do? I will have two children to raise alone." I couldn't believe my ears.

I felt my parents' and my wife's reactions expressed little concern or love for me. I was hurt and let-down by both responses.

To be honest, my parents were more concerned with my wife and children. I wanted to scream, "People, I'm the one who is potentially dying. Is no one thinking of me?" I was in a very familiar place, alone, frustrated and isolated only this time the potential end was fatal.

Comment:

I spent Christmas, 1982 in the hospital. I was alone almost all day and had time for introspection and deep thought. I realized that holidays are for the healthy and the living. For those of us in the hospital, Christmas was just another day.

Truly, for those in ill health and those who are dying, holidays are just calendar event and quickly pass. I altered the importance of most holidays and realize everyday is a holiday as long as one is healthy. For those who are dying and in severe pain, the day of passing is a holiday.

We dare not take one healthy day for granted.

Thanksgiving has become my favorite holiday because it represents family, friends and food. That's all one needs for a holiday if he/she is healthy.

Prognosis:

After eight weeks of healing, I met with doctors to determine prognosis and treatment. I was told the type of renal cancer I had put patients into two categories, a 99% time-line group, in which one had so many days, weeks, months or years to live, and a 1% cure group.

If the first category were projected for me, then I had so many months or years to live. However, I was told I was in the 1% group and we were going for a cure. I literally collapsed on the floor.

I had 33 maximum radiation treatments which permeated my stomach and colon. I took oral and rectal medication, but nothing prevented the nausea and vomiting. Treatment schedules were five straight days of radiation, be off on weekends, and start again on Mondays. Treatment days were hell.

During the treatments, I felt as though I was driving a car in fifth gear, but the car only had four. I couldn't read, watch television, talk on the phone or pay attention to anything. I was in fast motion all of the time.

Food was not inviting and smells made me ill. I was in a complete survival mode. Life was as basic as it could be. Mentally and physically, I was exhausted. I vomited constantly.

The radiation treatments caused long-term side effects. My diet had to be changed and such internal disorders as IBS, (Irritable Bowel Syndrome), and intestinal diarrhea were prevalent. I could not eat fruit, drink milk or eat any dairy products for 30 years.

When shopping or traveling on vacation, I was always filled with anxiety and constantly had to know where to find a restroom. One soon becomes obsessed with restroom locations.

I saw doctors every three months for one year; then, every six months for the next four years. Test after test, follow-up after follow-up, I anticipated the results and agonized over the potential message. The anticipation and waiting were worse than the tests. Could this be the time the cancer had returned? I lived in constant fear.

Intellectually, I knew my chances of beating renal cancer were small. I thought I would surely die within the next two years, if not sooner. If I died, at least I wouldn't have to deal with the gay issue any more.

I did have one doctor who made me feel special. During check ups, he used to look at my incision, run his hands through the hair on my chest and then pat me on the head. On my last visit, he looked me in the eye and commented, "I hope all goes well. You're worth it."

I never forgot his words. An intelligent, professional man complimented me and thought I was of value. Never before had I heard those words from anyone, let alone a man. I was worthy of life. I'll never forget his compassion for me as a person. Now, all I had to do was believe I was worth it.

~

The Premonition:

Oddly, one day two months into my recovery, I was walking around the sidewalk on our court for exercise. I had been reading a book about the Alpha state of the mind. I trained myself to go to an Alpha state of deep peace and could release of all conscious thought and go to sleep.

I had strange feelings of inner peace and often sensed forthcoming events.

As I was walking, I had this strange premonition. I was going to meet a special man, someone well-known in the community. Someone with a large family. The premonition appeared again and again. I found comfort in the thought. Fact or fantasy, I cherished it.

~

Divine Intervention:

The years flew by and I continued to have follow-up test after test. Three years into recovery, I had no reoccurrence of the cancer. At the end of my five year recovery cycle, the doctors told me I had been cured of that particular cancer. I was informed they knew I was going to make it after the first year, but couldn't tell me. How did they know? The kind of cancer I had was so virulent had it reoccurred, I would have been dead within six months. How reassuring!

Miracle:

Do you believe in God? Each of the doctors asked me if I had a faith. I responded, I did. They commented to me if I had not had the accident and knocked off half my kidney, I would have been dead within six months.

I would have had no visible warning signs of the cancer and by the time signs appeared, it would have been too late. The accident was like an arrow saying , "Look here, find it here. Save this man." Divine intervention?

In addition, one of the old German nuns, Sister Alaquoque, brought me a picture of a baby in God's large hand. She told me it had been blessed and she knew I was going to be alright. God had told her. I believed her. She was right. To this day, I have that picture beside my bed. Indeed, I lived a miracle. God bless Sister Alaquoque, (now departed), my angel on earth.

My tapestry was blessed with an angel.

Comment:

Sister Alaquoque was a German born woman who had devoted her entire life to the sisterhood. I truly felt she communicated with God and she instilled that belief and faith in me. She was so confident I would be alright. Her faith inspired me to have faith. Sister Alaquoque gave of herself so that others might feel God's warmth and love. I will never forget Sister Alaquoque and all others who prayed for me and gave me hope.

A special thanks to Reverend Archie Grigg, (friend and now deceased), and the members of Calvary Baptist Church who prayed for me and didn't even know who I was. A true example of Christian Spirit.

Vertrauen, Brendow-Veriag, Rheinkamp-Baerl
Plastik D. Steigerwald

CHAPTER ELEVEN

An Introduction To Gay Life

The Deception:

In December of 1982, late one afternoon during my hospital recuperation, the special education director, (my boss), came by to visit me. He was kind, considerate and interested in me as a person. The boss was 6'2" tall, gray haired and hairy. He was married and had three children. I only knew him casually and was surprised by his visit. He sat beside me on the bed and asked to see my scar. I showed it to him. Something about this man made me shiver inside. He smelled so good. I hoped he would come back to visit again, and he did, daily.

I went home two weeks later and one afternoon, someone knocked at the door, the boss. We visited for about 20 minutes and he asked to see how my scar was healing. I wore only a robe and jockey shorts. It was weird, but I enjoyed showing my body to another man. When he left, he gave me a hug. I was amazed. An emotional sensation swept through my whole body. I loved the embrace of another man.

The boss was sensual, caring and empathetic. He had a heavy beard, hairy arms and chest and was totally self-assured. I enjoyed his company and he made me feel important.

He returned four more times and each time asked to see my scar. I pulled my robe up and showed him my bare abdomen. As before, I wore only my jockey shorts underneath. He smiled. I think we were both aroused.

I admit I looked forward to his visits and the hug each time he left the house. In April, I returned to work and didn't see or hear from the boss again.

In August of 1983, he called and asked to take me to lunch. I met him at his office and as soon as I entered, he closed the door behind me. He reached out as to give me a hug, but instead, he pressed his lips to mine. My first kiss by a man. I was startled, but immediately went back for a second. The passion was incredible. We were both breathing very heavily and finally, I stopped and suggested we get composed and go to lunch. After-all, we were in his office. I really didn't want to stop.

We both seemed to go through the motions at lunch and soon after we had eaten, he suggested we leave. He said he needed to stop by his house to pick something up. I still didn't get it at this point. He was looking for a place to take me. Nothing happened that afternoon in his house because his daughter was home. He asked me to drive us to Fairview Park and guided me to a desolate area in the rear of the park. We stopped and he grabbed the zipper of my pants. I didn't know what to do.

He was my boss, and I enjoyed the male attention. I was scared, vulnerable and ripe for the picking. I was sensually aroused and had no idea what to expect. I looked up and a car was coming down the road. The boss was excited too, but stopped and decided to wait for a better place and time. I was like a child who questions nothing. I couldn't wait to see him again.

One evening after work, I looked out the classroom window and saw the boss approaching. Immediately upon entering my room, he told me he loved me and introduced me to the gay life. He was slow, deliberate and loving. He said he wanted to show me how men love one another and show me off to the gay world. He was proud to have me. I fell for it all.

The emotion and the passion were over-whelming. I heard it said on the Oprah Winfrey Show once, passion is greatest between two men as lovers. I was hooked. That evening our family had dinner with my brother and his wife. I could hardly look anyone in the eye. I made little eye contact.

I had committed the worst sin, done the worst act a husband, father and Christian could have done. My attempt at perfectionism was destroyed. I had committed and unforgivable act.

Emotional lows outweighed the highs, but natural urges and genetics are powerful forces once unleashed, and mine had been unleashed. I have not forgiven myself.

Wasn't this what I was looking for? Wasn't he the man in my premonition? He was well known and had three children. Wasn't he the man to fill my voids, to make me feel important, to make me feel wanted and needed? A dad? I was being ripped apart emotionally.

He pursued me constantly and I loved the pursuit. We met often at his friend's house and I was slowly facing major dilemmas. Do I continue this life and feel fulfilled as a sexual being or do I stop and deny myself my birthright and the reduce the mountains of guilt I was accruing?

I wasn't sure where I was heading and was most fearful of the decisions I was making. In truth, I was in over my head. The gay world may have been mine by birthright, but I knew nothing about it. I was more than a novice.

I didn't know anything about gay relationships. I had little knowledge as to what gay sex was like or supposed to be. I wasn't sure about monogamous relationships, but I knew I demanded one. I was drowning in an informational void.

About six months into the relationship, the pursuit slackened tremendously. I questioned him rigorously and received some really poor excuses. As stated, I could and would only accept a monogamous relationship. I felt he was "hunting".

One afternoon during the summer, he was working and I wasn't. I followed him to Nelson Park at lunch time. I parked my car in another parking area and walked through the rock garden to be able to view his little red truck. I was not surprised when I saw him meeting other men. He was a regular at the park and often was seen in the restrooms. At this point in time, I said nothing to him, but I was now aware of his motives and the reduction of interest in me.

He went to the Y.M.C.A. nightly and I would sit down the street and wait for him to come out. He was always alone, but what I learned was he was not alone in the "Y" steam room. I began following him wherever he went and the end result was always the same, another man.

The final blow came in the summer of 1984. Again, I wasn't working but he was. I found his truck at Nelson Park and blocked it in with my truck. I knew he was in the restroom taking tricks as they came in. Many men of all ages came and went. I watched my life unfold as each man appeared from the depths of the lower stairs and restroom. How could I have believed I was the only man? I sat quietly in the truck and waited. I was sick to my stomach.

After two hours, he came out and asked me to move my truck. I didn't. He had been caught red-handed and didn't know what to say. I climbed in his truck and unleashed a torrent of something other than "Hail Marys". He wasn't remorseful nor did he care. He appeared to be angry at me for his indiscretions.

I felt betrayed, disillusioned and dirty. I had given up my secure life for one that wasn't genuine. I had put myself through emotional hell for someone who wasn't worth it and who had no intention of loving me monogamously. I had suffered physically, emotionally and intellectually. I lost 33lbs and was emotionally drained each day. I ached all over. Gay life, as I knew it, wasn't worth it.

He called me one day and said, "I do love you, but not the way you want me to. I can't. I just can't.".

As time passed, I discovered he had introduced hundreds of men to the gay life in much the same manner as he had done to me. He was a predator and developed a huge network of men on his circuit.

In a major police "sting operation", the boss was picked up for soliciting in another park. To me, this was the epitome of hitting "rock bottom". No class, no dignity and no kind of life; not to mention the danger of contracting Aids.

As for me, he intended to use and abuse me on his sexual circuit by having a different man each night of the week. Sex, sex, and more sex. No love and no commitment. As is known on the streets, he was a "Numbers Queen" and I was a number. How pathetic of me to think I was special.

I was shocked at how many professional men in our community were closeted gay men. I learned a special gay men's club existed and met above a local business down town. What a child I was in this world. Numbers were more than I had ever imagined. Now, I was one of them.

After 11 months, and many additional infidelities, I gave up on our relationship. I had ruined everything. I disgusted myself, but it was too late. Not being an unintelligent man, I was appalled at how my emotions ruled my intellect.

My introduction to the gay life was pure deception. It was not filled with love nor fulfillment. If gay life were like this, I wanted no part of it.

Post Script:

Twenty-Two years later, the boss was found shot to death at the county fairgrounds during a burglary attempt. I did not attend the funeral. I had too many mixed emotions and he represented a part of my life I was not proud of. At one point I had truly loved him. Sadly, he had never loved me as I loved him.

I hated what he had done to me, but intellectually, I hated what I had done to myself. I was responsible for my behaviors.

Chapter Twelve

Administrative Life/ A New Purpose

Professional Change:

In the summer of 1984, I was working as an intake supervisor with J.T.P.A., (Job Training Partnership Act), finding and supervising employment for disadvantaged young people. It was a fulfilling job and I met many new faces who weren't educators.

I learned how socio-economic social classes vary and how work ethic varies per individual. Some of the youngsters worked until they received their first paycheck, then they quit. Others, worked hard and sought to work longer hours than were required. I had many openings to fill during the course of the summer.

One morning a group of JTPA workers had gathered in the office to share stories and provide feedback for the bosses. During general conversation, a co-worker mentioned that an principal's position was available at a local elementary school and I should apply. I had applied for school principal positions twice before but didn't get the positions.

I really didn't want to apply, but the group built up my ego to the point that I decided to put in an application for Washington School, a large inner-city elementary school. The school had a miserable reputation in town but I wanted to work with disadvantaged kids as I had been doing all summer.

I had been teaching at Thomas Jefferson for 18 years and wanted a new challenge. At Jefferson, I was a special education teacher, athletic director, track coach, girl's basketball coach, yearbook advisor, student council advisor, hallway display person, recreation director and liaison with the administration. I was a tired man and had little time to spend with my two children. In addition, an administrator's salary would certainly help the family and our chances to send both kids to college.

One afternoon, I was seated at my desk at JTPA and the phone rang. I answered and was told to be at the Keil Building, central office, for an interview the next morning.

I arrived early, was seated in an outer office area and had no idea what to expect. I had reviewed my notes from the previous interviews and was as prepared as I was going to be. The door to the assistant superintendent's office opened slowly and a man appeared and motioned for me to come in.

I found myself seated before two very powerful men in the school district, but I was relatively calm.

After a few pleasantries, and a series of basic questions, one of the men said to me, "If you could have the principal's position at French Academy, Thomas Jefferson or Washington, which one would you choose?"

I responded, "I have applied for Washington and that is the choice I would make, but I have been in this district for 18 years, and I think you know my skills and abilities. I guess I would go wherever you thought you could best use my talents and I could do the most good for the district and children."

The two men looked at one another, smiled and dismissed me. The interview was over as quickly as it began. I thought, well, so much for that effort. It appeared to be another interview and another failure.

Five days later, I was told I would be named principal at Washington. The Board of Education had not yet approved the recommendation, so I was bound to secrecy. I knew the district was taking a chance on me because I was only in year two of my cancer remission. I had three more years to go before I would be considered "cured" from my kidney cancer. However, I was excited to start a new career within the educational field.

On the night of my job confirmation, it was reported my salary would be $30,000. I was making $28,500 as a teacher and coach. Well, so much for rags to riches. It didn't matter, I was ready for the change and looked forward to the challenges.

My school housed 756 students, 61 staff members and was predominantly African-American. A 1925 vintage building, it was solid brick, three stories tall and was located next to a city park and a junior high school. Our socio-economic status was the lowest in the city and our children had more than materialistic needs.

I have never been so fulfilled as I was working in the inner-city with socio-economically disadvantaged kids. I loved the kids and they loved me back. I adored my staff but it took some timed before I was able to unite them.

Decatur had closed my old elementary school, Roach, and moved the entire staff into Washington. Therefore, I had two staffs to unite who were used to different administrative styles. The rookie principal had a major challenge.

In addition, I had some staff members who believed they were too good to teach at my school.

Nine disgruntled staff members left within the first two years. In 1985, we began to function as a unit. I was glad the dissenters were gone. It's amazing what the absence of two or three negative people can do for a school's atmosphere. I assume this is true in the private sector also.

In the spring of 1985, I was named as a top clothing model through a contest in our local newspaper. I was 40 years old. A full page spread was published in the newspaper and the children were ecstatic. I modeled for Seno Formal Wear, Bachrach's, Appelbaum's, Carson Pirie Scott, Rags, and other local stores.

I appeared in newspaper advertisements and was featured in commercials on the local television station. We did photo shoots in various outdoor locations and I enjoyed the adventure. What a ride for a 40 year old man.

Not only was I receiving benefits from the experience, it was a great marketing tool for my school. Public relations began to change and Washington was no longer depicted as being the worst school in the city. I loved my kids and the staff was the best in town.

The students loved to see what I would wear to school and often bought similar outfits. We were moving in the right direction---taking pride in ourselves. Our students wanted to come to school. We were learning and having fun. My staff was tremendous.

Washington's poor reputation was unfounded. Children were children and what most of them needed was love and attention. Being Black or African-American was inconsequential, but being poor wasn't.

To this day I see former students and am always greeted with a hug or verbal recognition. Most of them tell me Washington was their favorite school and the best time of their lives. What a compliment.

I spent five of my most emotionally fulfilling professional years being principal at Washington Elementary School.

Postscript:

After I was named principal, I learned my interview was purely a courtesy given to me for 18 years of service to the district. I was not really a serious candidate for the job as I was a secondary teacher in special education at a middle school; A three time loser for an elementary school principal ship. Never had a middle school, secondary teacher been named to an elementary principal's position. I laid the ground work for others to follow. As for Washington, another young lady was the primary candidate.

Soon after my name was made public, the principal at Jefferson called to inform me he was called immediately after my interview and was asked if he could get by without me on the staff. He replied, "No", but the director who called him said he would have to get used to life without me because I had blown the field away. I was shocked but was glad to get the call.

After five years at Washington, I received The Award Of Excellence in the principal category of the State of Illinois' Those Who Excel Program. Only four principals received the award. So much for courtesy.

Parts of my tapestry became public.

Age 40, Principal and Model

CHAPTER THIRTEEN

An Answered Prayer

Destiny:

During my tenure at Washington Elementary School from 1984 to 1989, I was met with varying reactions and emotions by other principals.

Some of the "old heads", (other elementary principals), didn't like me because I dressed well, looked neat and had fresh ideas regarding education. I was to be seen and not heard at cabinet meetings. The secondary principals had little respect for elementary principals so I was irrelevant to them. However, some colleagues tried to help and offered assistance.

One principal in particular was William F. Cogan, (Bill). He called and offered assistance and said I could call him any time. He was a nice guy and made a wonderful gesture to a rookie administrator.

I took advantage of the offer and called regularly. At cabinet meetings we often sat together so we could talk and discuss school issues. We became friends as well as colleagues.

Bill was one handsome 56 year old man. He had silver hair, dark moustache and was very well built. About 10 years prior, I had seen him at a school function and thought he was strikingly good looking. I had an immediate attraction to him. However, he was married and had five children.

One night it struck me. I remembered my premonition from two years earlier. I was going to meet a handsome, well-known man with a large family. Obviously, "the boss" was not the fulfillment of my premonition but maybe Bill was.

Ironically, he was the exact image of my mythical Mr. Weathers whom I created to soothe me to sleep when I was a child. Was Bill the real thing?

After a month or two, I learned Bill had a companion of 16 years. Everyone seemed to know this fact but me. One day he stopped by my office and before he left, I told him I had never kissed a man with a moustache. He smiled and said, "Maybe we will have to change that."

In the spring of '85, I stopped by his office to see him

after work. We were talking about health and specifically knees. He was sitting beside me and I referenced my knee injury and surgeries. Without thinking, I thrust my leg onto his lap. I had on shorts. My hairy leg lie before him. He nearly died.

Shortly thereafter, the district had an administrative meeting at a large local restaurant. When I entered, an empty seat was next to Bill. He offered it to me and I sat down. I was excited and felt honored to have such a handsome man want me to sit next to him.

As the meeting progressed, I leaned back in the chair and my leg touched Bill's. Instead of pulling away, he leaned his leg harder against mine. Immediately, I developed an erection.

Bill had had a couple of drinks and made his way to the bathroom. I followed and utilized the facilities also. As we stood at the sink washing our hands, both of us knew what the other was thinking. We headed for the door and I blocked it with my foot. He leaned in to me and our lips met. I'll never forget it. I had finally kissed a man with a moustache.

The kiss in the restroom was the first of two that evening. After the meeting ,I sat in my car and waited for him. He came out and began talking with a group of female principals. He got in his car and drove away. I had not indicated to him I would be waiting for him. I was saddened to see him go without making contact.

I called him the next morning and told him I had been waiting for him and he sounded as disappointed as I was. We met for lunch the next day.

It was the beginning of a long-term relationship which would fulfill two men's longing for love and companionship. Fate was the master contractor and we built on it. Bill and I shared weekend mornings together as well as lunch sometimes during the week. He was the most senior member of our administrative team and had survived numerous school superintendents. He knew how to market himself and his school.

Bill was a master administrator and someone I could emulate and model.

On April 17, 1985, we were set to attend a PTA convention in Chicago. We couldn't wait. Before I left, I went to the "boss's" farm to tell him good-bye.

He said, "Don't forget who you love."

I thought, "Love, what do you know about love?"

I drove to Chicago and Bill sat beside me in the passenger seat. Two other elementary principals accompanied us. Our check-in at the hotel was delayed and we were most disappointed. Finally, the time came and we had our first room together.

We unpacked, talked and kissed quite a lot before we joined the others in the hotel lobby. We went out for lunch and walked around Chicago for about two hours. When it came time for bed, we both looked at one another and smiled. As we began to undress, I watched Bill unbutton his shirt. I couldn't wait to see him shirtless. I was not disappointed. He had a barrel chest covered in salt and pepper hair. My dream had come true. We crawled into bed and I curled up next to him. It felt warm and natural to be in his arms. Our conversation was brisk and heavy. We held one another for hours.

I felt at home in his arms. I was safe, secure and the child in me melted into his body. Oh God, my Daddy at last. Never had I felt like this, never!

He listened to my stories about "the boss" and I cried openly about the abuse I had taken. As a consenting adult, abuse did not mean sexual abuse. I had been abused emotionally in that I gave a sincere love to someone I thought loved me only to be used as a street object.

In addition, I was totally monogamous and "the boss" was not. Plus, he lied to me about his whereabouts in order to keep me from catching him with other men. He used and abused me to get what he wanted, another trophy. Truly, he was a pathological liar and a sexual predator.

As for Bill, he made me feel whole and complete. He was gentle, kind, understanding and gracious. What a God-send. No one had ever treated me as Bill had that night.

As Bill had another partner, he could have been out for a weekend of fun and games, but he wasn't. After hours of conversation, he made love to me and I knew he was the man I had searched for since childhood. I had been born for Bill and was already in love with him.

During the waking hours we talked. Bill and I discovered something most interesting. It seems my "boss" was the same man who introduced Bill to the gay life. He utilized the same tactics. The only difference was, Bill wasn't looking for someone to love. I laughed.

How many other men had the "boss" brought into this life? Point of interest, "the boss" and the priest who married me were regulars together. What a protected world I lived in.

During the weekend we spent time enjoying Chicago and one another's company. I didn't want the weekend to end, but Sunday evening we found ourselves returning to Decatur as both of us had to work on Monday. What a weekend.

When I returned to Decatur, I again sought out the "boss" at his farm. It took only five seconds to end the relationship.

simply said, "Good-bye. I have found what I have been looking for.", and walked away.

He yelled, "I thought I told you not to forget who you love?" I never looked back.

The termination of a miserable introduction to gay life had ended. Yet, the beginning of a new life was just developing. Something inside me was at peace for the first time in 40 years. I had what I wanted and wanted what I had.

~

Building A Relationship:

As Bill and I grew closer, I was aware of his other romantic interest. Late one afternoon, after hours, he stopped by my school. I smelled alcohol on his breath. I asked where he had been, knowing the answer. I told him he had to choose, as I was only interested in a monogamous relationship. I had just gotten rid of one hunter and didn't need another. I had hit him hard and he looked puzzled and left the building.

I didn't hear from Bill for a week and then, on a Saturday afternoon, I went to his office and asked him if he had made a decision. He said he had and made a call to his lover of 16 years. Bill told him he couldn't continue to see both of us and had decided to end their relationship.

He hung up and looked at me. We made it to the stairwell and I literally "carried" him down the stairs. It was one of the most difficult decisions of his life, but he had made it for me. No one had ever made a greater commitment on my behalf. We were now operating as a unit. We were one.

As with all couples, Bill and I had some difficult moments. Those moments were a direct result of my formative years and the lack of trust I placed in my parents as well as males in general. Certainly, "the boss" did nothing to endear me to gay males.

Bill was everything I had searched for, but I did my best to push him away. I made life miserable for him at times just to see if he would abandon me the way my father abandoned me.

I think I wanted him to fail so my inner-self could say, "See, I told you so. He is no different than any other man you have ever known." He didn't always understand me, but he exhibited tolerance and patience.

In essence, Bill raised what was left of the child in me.

Emotional Maturation:

My maturation process climaxed one evening shortly after Bill moved into a new ranch style home. He was putting his invalid daughter to bed and I became frustrated. I was frustrated because I had to go home to an environment filled with hatred and anger.

I had some not-so-nice words to say and stormed out of the house. I got to the end of the block and stopped.

"What am I doing?", I asked myself. "Idiot, you are

leaving the very place and the very man you want. Why are you pushing him away?", I lamented.

I turned the car around and went back into the house. Bill didn't hear me. About an hour later after he put his daughter to bed, he came into the living room where I was sitting.

"What are you doing here?", he asked.

I responded, "Growing up". We embraced and he told me how proud he was of me. I had gone over a major hurdle in my emotional track meet.

This incident ended the years of tumultuous guilt I tried to place on Bill for being someone who cared about me. I wanted him to reject me so I could prove no one was trustworthy. Better yet, no one could or would love me. In reality, I was punishing Bill for the sins of my parents. Damn the formative years.

That night I grew up and the childish games ended. My life's search had ended. I had found the man of my dreams. I am grateful someone assisted me in defeating the jaded past of my childhood. For the first time, I was seeing clearly and making meaningful choices despite my past.

"It took a man to make me a man."

Postscript:

Bill is the father of five children. Three girls and two boys. He had lived a parent's worst night- mare when he received a phone call in 1978 telling him his 16 year old daughter had been injured in a car-bus accident.

A high school fan bus had collided with a car driven by a young driver who pulled out in front of it. The passenger in the front passenger seat was killed instantly and Bill's daughter, in the back seat, was thrown forward snapping her spinal column at the neck. She incurred a severe brain injury.

The family spent years in hospitals and rehabilitation units trying to "bring her back". Nothing worked. To this day, she is quadriplegic, mute, unable to stand or walk, unable to feed herself, unable to dress, bathe or administer personal hygiene to herself.

After work each day, Bill would go home to be her care-giver. This procedure has been done for 30 years. The man never complained and never shirked his responsibilities, all of them. Three years ago, she was moved into a group home as Bill's health would not allow him to continue care. She is now 48 years old.

At 82, Bill has given his life and his health to his daughter. He is more than the consummate parent.

Character is often defined as doing what is right when no one is looking, and for Bill, the definition fits. The man had to be a saint in order to fulfill both employment and parenting responsibilities to the fullest.

~

Another Administrative Promotion:

Being an administrator in Decatur Public Schools was fulfilling and professionally satisfying. I spent five years as principal at Washington School and in 1989, a new superintendent visited our school. He was very tall, nice looking and intimidating.

He was interested in inner-city schools and visited Washington often. He loved our school and all of the changes we had made to the physical structure. Rooms were brightly painted and our hallways were lined with American flags as well as foreign flags from nations around the world. We had transposed a school into an embassy atmosphere.

Our lower level was renovated and when completed, we had some of the finest kindergarten facilities in the city. Effort, that's what it took; effort and teacher dedication. We had both.

Within the new administration, two new central administrative positions were created. One was the Director of Schools for Curriculum and the other Director of Schools for Instruction. I got the inclination the superintendent wanted me to apply for one or both of the positions.

I had been at Washington for five years and felt my "bag of tricks" was empty. I worked so hard to develop innovative programs and establish good discipline and classroom management. Emotionally and physically I was drained. I needed change and applied for both positions.

I went through the interview process and became more interested in the positions as I learned more about them. Working at the central office was quite an accomplishment in Decatur Public Schools, especially if one had come from a middle class home on the east side of Decatur. East-enders were blue collar and usually not college educated. I had no political backing and certainly didn't belong to any posh country club. All I had going for me was my work ethic and reputation as principal at Washington.

After my interview, my family and I spent the weekend in Arlington Heights, Illinois, visiting friends. I was physically out of Decatur, but my mind was racing as I thought about possibility of being named to education's elite. It would certainly be an economical and social move for me and my family.

In addition, it would be a major social coup for me as Decatur's social strata rarely found east-enders among the elite. Those accolades were left for the wealthy west-enders. Back in the day, that's how it was, a caste system by any other name.

The following Tuesday, I was called by the superintendent and told I was selected to be the Director of Schools For

Instruction. I couldn't believe it. I had made it, but I knew I had to prove myself daily, or I would be out of a job.

In June of 1989, I moved into my small room at the Keil Building, (central office). My salary was $48,000 which was about $4,000 more than I was making as a principal. The Director of Schools for Curriculum was starting at $56,000 because he was a secondary administrator and I was just an elementary principal.

Once I heard the rationale for the salary difference, it made no sense to me. After two years, the superintendent equalized our salaries. I will always be grateful to the man for his recognition of me and my skills as a professional.

Part of my job was to observe all non-tenured, first and second year teachers, four or five times during the school year so I could provide recommendations for retention or termination. I loved this aspect of my job and utilized my evaluation experiences to improve instruction. The young teaching minds were challenging and motivating. Mr. Buttz was respected. No more "Bare-Butt", at least not to my face.

I tried to never forget the reason I had been promoted and the real reason administrators have a job. Teachers! I was always loyal to the teachers and fought for them and their classroom needs. One of the greatest compliments I received was, "You never changed."

In 1991, I received my second state award in the

State of Illinois Those Who Excel program. I received the Award of Excellence in the Administrator Category. I was so proud. I was good at what I did. Being gay was irrelevant. However, I never forgot my roots.

In 1996, my director's job was eliminated. I had to reapply for another administrative position. I didn't prepare for the interview and was disgusted that I had to reapply for any position. I was named Director of Special Programs in charge of librarians, pre-school, Title I, district award programs, Title VI, spelling bees, Administrative In-service, etc. It was a monumental task. I knew I could meet the challenge.

My partner, Bill, supported me through all of the changes even though, technically, I became his boss. Believe me, it was only in a professional sense. Bill was my emotional boss.

Threats:

Our relationship met every challenge. At times, our jobs were in jeopardy and certainly our families were threatened.

Shortly after Bill and I began seeing one another, his wife started getting anonymous letters stating he was gay. She knew, but tolerated it. She, in turn, called my wife to see if she knew of our relationship and to see if she, too, was getting letters. She was.

The letters continued to be sent and would often

give details about where we were and what we were supposedly doing. Some even detailed our plans to attend out-of-town conventions and seminars.

Bill and I just wanted to be left alone. We weren't shoving our relationship into anyone's faces and were very discrete about our meetings. It was our life and yet, an attempt was being made to make it public.

Eventually, we found the letters were being sent by Bill's previous partner. His anger was so virulent one afternoon we found a note under the windshield wiper of Bill's car. In bold letters it stated, "FAGGOT".

Both our wives confronted us and all hell broke loose. In our opinions, we deduced it was public image that angered our wives as much as our relationship. Their image was at risk. At first we denied their allegations, but eventually, we just told them the truth.

No ramifications occurred because both women seemed to enjoy the luxuries our jobs afforded them as well as their status within the community. Not many women could say they were married to a principal or central administrator in Decatur Public Schools. We weathered the storm, maintained our professionalism and did our jobs.

In addition, I had promised myself I would not leave my children or get a divorce until the children were grown and on their own. It had to be this way in order for me to live with myself.

Believe it or not, some gay men do have principles. As for Bill, he was Catholic and would never get a divorce. We managed. Bill's wife passed away in 1996, and he retired the next year to care for his daughter. He had served education and children for 44 years.

In 1999, after 34 years, I retired from education. I continued to do professional development seminars for ten more years and served as an off-campus student teaching coordinator for I.S.U. for seven years. I utilized my appraisal experience and director's skills to guide and evaluate student teachers. I loved the job.

~

New Home/Big Decision:

As stated in a previous postscript, Bill's daughter was severely injured in an automobile accident when she was 16. His tri-level house, her age and his age, were making it increasingly more difficult to handle.

After Bill's wife passed away in 1996, he moved out of the tri-level house to escape memories and to provide for his invalid daughter.

In 1999, he bought a one level ranch style home north of his original home. I wanted to live with him. I got that chance in 2000. I had my right knee replaced in November in St. Louis. Upon return to Decatur, we thought I would recuperate better at his ranch style home rather than my bi-level with nearly 20 stairs.

I soon learned it was very easy to live with someone you loved. I spent three weeks at Bill's and did not want to go home.

In 2001, I had my second cancer, colon, and realized if I didn't make a choice soon, Bill and I might never get to live together. Besides, I was back on the five year recovery plan for the second time in my life.

In 2002, both of my children were on their own. We had taken our last family vacation to Gulf Shores, AL, and when we got home, the children entered their own worlds and personal destinations.

In July of 2002, I was visiting Bill because his sister had arrived from Arizona. I wanted to meet her and be involved in the part of his life I had never known. We took several small day trips and in our discussion, I had commented I wanted to have a big dog before I died but my wife said we/I couldn't have one.

In the local newspaper was an add for Golden Retriever puppies. The three of us decided to go and look at them. I was immediately committed. I knew if I bought a big dog, I couldn't go home. So, I made a choice. I wrote the check for a beautiful puppy we named Sadie, and never went home. My big dog was my key to freedom.

I moved in with Bill in July of 2002. At first I committed

to the marital separation as being enough, but as time passed, I wanted legal separation and/or divorce. I knew I would never go back to my old home and filed for divorce in 2004.

The sensation of being one with Bill was fulfilling. We did not have to live separate lives any longer. Both of us have commented our two lives seemed unrelated. One would function just as well in one life as he did in the other. We seemed to have two sets of purposes, responsibilities and destinies. Both needed tending.

I'm sure many readers will not believe we felt our lives were separate and/or we were making excuses. One has to be faced with these kinds of decisions in order to judge. Our decisions were never easy and not without some degree of guilt. Unless you've "been there", don't judge.

Today, we are living a dream neither of us thought possible. We are good men, good fathers and good citizens. Together, we both know we were not born to be damned.

In many ways, Bill finished the job my parents couldn't do. He role modeled manhood and set my sexuality. No woman ever successfully made me feel like a man. Bill was my destiny. I loved him and was in love with him.

My search for my sexuality was over. I had everything I had ever wanted all wrapped up in one person. I was born to be Bill's. It was our destiny and we both believed it.

My authentic self had surfaced and the pain of living a robotic life for others was now over. My lifelong search for a man to love me had been finalized. The emotional void in my stomach had been filled. My prayers had been answered and the premonition had come true. For the first time in my life, I felt complete.

One piece of my tapestry was complete.

Picture of Bill when we met, Age 56

Chapter Fourteen

The Priest And The Prodigal

Validation:

Bill and I are anomalies as we have nothing in common except our love for one another, our kids, our dogs and faith in God.

Bill loves opera; I hate it. I love sports; Bill hates them. I am athletic; Bill isn't. I am analytic; Bill isn't. Bill is Catholic; I am Lutheran. I like meat; he likes pasta. He has O.C.D., (Obsessive Compulsive Disorder); I don't, well, maybe.

Catholic? Yes, Bill chose to be a Catholic while attending high school. He was raised Methodist. I was born and raised Lutheran. During our 25 years together, when we were out of town attending school-related/job-related conferences, we always found a Catholic church to attend on Sundays.

After I moved in with Bill in 2002, I attended Catholic services with him on Saturday evenings and then frequented my own Lutheran church Sunday morning. I am not sure why Bill never went with me to the Lutheran Church, but I went with him because I loved him and he wanted me to go. No other reasons were necessary.

One Saturday, Father Tom, (name changed), was recounting the story of the prodigal son as the homily, (sermon). Father presented the biblical version of the story as we have known it to be.

Father Tom gave a quick synopsis of the story and stated he had heard another version which he wished to share.

It seems a father had two sons. One was straight and the other gay. Over the years, the father couldn't accept the gay son. He wasn't totally fond of the straight son, but felt he was a more Godly child than the gay son, who was unfit and destined for Hell.

As time passed, the gay son was asked to leave. He was given money and sent out of the home. The house was to be left to his straight son and his wife. The father lived with them.

As the father aged, he and his daughter-in-law did not get along. She did all she could to get the father out of the home so she and her husband could have everything for themselves.

Eventually, the father was placed in a nursing home. The straight son visited often for a while. Then, his visits were limited to once a week. In time, they ceased all together.

The father was miserable, sad and lonely. He decided to call his gay son to try to make contact. The phone rang and the gay son answered.

When the gay son heard his father's voice, he wept. His dad told him how unhappy he was. The gay son went immediately to visit his father. They quickly made amends. The prodigal father had returned.

As it would be, the gay son moved his father into his home which he shared with his partner. The father lived many enjoyable years with the two men.

Finally, age and illness consumed the father and he passed away. As a courtesy, the gay son called his brother to tell him of their father's passing and asked if he wished to be a part of the funeral planning.

The straight son responded, "No, I had him for years. Now you've got it all.", and hung up. He did not attend his father's funeral.

The gay son and his partner buried the father.

In God's name, Amen.

After the homily, the church sat in silence. The priest bowed his head and sat down. Silence, pure unadulterated silence prevailed.

What is the significance of this homily? First, it was the only time Bill or I had ever heard the word "gay" used in any church in a positive way.

Secondly, it showed God puts no labels on sexuality. He only looks into the hearts of all of his sheep. In this sermon, the father was the prodigal and returned to his true home, with the son who loved him.

Bill and I left church uplifted that Saturday. We felt proud to hear a priest relate an emotional story about real life as it is here on earth. The son's sexuality was irrelevant but his love for his father was unconditional, as was God's love for the gay son.

It felt good leaving church feeling like a human being and not a perverted "thing".

My tapestry had just been validated.

CHAPTER FIFTEEN

My Relationship With My Father

Anonymous:

t appears most gay men have significant stories about their fathers. However, I know of gay men who have had perfectly wholesome relationships with their dads. In many instances, father-son relationships are either diffused or estranged. Mine was "from a distance".

As for me, I had a father whom I adored. Little did he know I loved and admired him so much. However, with his German background and domestic issues in his boyhood home, he was never able to express himself to me. We had no father-son relationship.

Dad's saving grace was Mom. I never knew if Dad told her to tell me I couldn't kiss him good night when I was four, or if Mom had just lied. Dad may have never known of the incident. Whatever Mom's reason, it had a formidable impact on me and set the direction of my future.

Dad was a handsome, athletic, well-built, hairy-chested 5'10" tall man who started working at the Wabash Railroad in his early 20's. He started as a car man, brakeman and fireman. Eventually he became an engineer and drove such famous passenger trains as the Wabash Cannonball, The Blue Bird and The Banner Blue.

Most of Dad's career was spent engineering a freight train from Decatur to East St. Louis. At one point, I remember Dad carrying a gun to protect himself at the "end of the line", as he put it.

Dad would be gone for days and I missed him. He traveled from Decatur to East St. Louis, would lay over for a night and then return to Decatur.

While he was gone, I quickly picked up on my mother's insecurities. She was a very fearful person and it showed. To this day, I am equally fearful and am not a risk taker.

For example, I will not take risks just to have fun nor have I ever drunk, taken drugs or smoked. As for fear, founded our unfounded, I go where I am supposed to be and do what I am supposed to do as per my self-imposed expectations. I know my limits.

I hate to travel to big cities and always wonder what

will go wrong while traveling. Mom used to be a "worry wart" when we traveled as a family and I absorbed every worry. "Cause and effect" permeate my mind.

I have no recollection of my dad every holding me or touching me. I have no memories of him kissing me or tucking me in at bedtime. In fact, I tucked myself in. Mom nor Dad ever tucked me in or read me a bed-time story. My bed and my room were my personal sanctuary.

When I was four, I accidentally over-ran the bathroom sink and water ran everywhere. I remember Mom yelling for Dad to spank me. Again, it was Mom demanding I be punished. She was angry and Dad wasn't involved in the incident until she brought him into it. He hit me hard two or three times, and that is the last memory I have of him touching me. Dad shook all over when he finished spanking me. He looked harried.

I often wonder if Dad had been physically abused as a child and hitting me, rekindled traumatic memories. It was as though he had done something he had promised himself he would never do.

I saw a similar reaction once when a neighbor boy verbally ridiculed me into submission with a series of "Bare-Butt, Bare-Butt, Hairy ass and in a rut.", comments. Dad heard it and stormed out of the house. I thought he was going to physically harm the 17 year old. I was only seven and could hardly defend myself.

Dad chastised the boy and demanded to see the boy's

father. When the father came out of the house, he and Dad had harsh words.

In fact, the adult stated, "Hell, he is a damned big sissy, Bare-Butt". Dad could have had a stroke as he was bright red and shaking all over. He defended me, but paid a price. He never did it again.

Dad and I seldom shared experiences. He was a railroader and I didn't know much about trains, nor did I have interest in them. Conversation was limited. Once, we talked about my riding with him in the engine and going to East St. Louis. I never took advantage of the offer and regret it to this day.

Intellectually, Mom and Dad were never capable of helping me with my homework and I was forced to be an independent child. I functioned in an independent world. My life, my emotions and my problems were my own. I learned never to pose questions to my parents.

Dad never complimented me for my grades, induction into National Honor Society, or any athletic accomplishment. I was never praised, but never criticized either. I was nondescript. I didn't exist. Invisible!

It wasn't until I was named principal at Washington my mother told me how proud Dad was of me. He would tell his friends his son was a school principal. He never told me. He served as a volunteer in my building along with his friends from Golden Kiwanis Club for each of the five years I was principal. Truly, it was the only thing

I remember the two of us doing together. I was proud of his participation.

As an adult, I did learn one relevant aspect of my dad's behavior. Dad was never able to sit through a church service. On Christmas Eve, he would drop us off, drive around the corner and go home. I didn't know it, but Dad had panic attacks. Genetics? My aunt, my dad, my uncle, all had panic attacks; the Buttz family was certainly "blessed".

As a family, we frequently left places before events were over. I never knew why. The excuse Mom gave was, "Dad doesn't feel good." In those days no name existed for the attacks, but the physical manifestations were the same as the ones I had years later.

Dad would be filled with anxiety, sweats, nausea and a need to "get out". A complete panic. What a legacy!

After I lived through panic attacks, or the body's adrenalin hell, I prayed to God to keep me alive in case either of my children were so prone. Senior year in college, my only son developed panic attacks. I opened up, shared my past and my physical reactions. Together, we worked him through the attacks with only short-lived medication. I was able to do for my son what Dad couldn't do for me. Another answered prayer.

Dad just didn't know how to show his emotions for anyone but my mother. Mom was his angel and probably saved him from a life of despair. He worshiped her. She was all he needed to be complete as a man.

Dad's Tapestry:

Dad's parents fought tremendously as my paternal grand-father was an alcoholic. My grandparents lived across the street from my childhood home and when I would go over to Grandma's for a cookie, I had to pass the throne, Grandpa's red chair. As Grandpa never left the chair, I knew he would be in it. However, all was well as he couldn't see me and I couldn't see him. A cloud of smoke encased the chair and Grandpa always had his eyes shut. I darted by and felt safe. I had no idea how Grandma lived with him for nearly 60 years.

He eventually smoked and drank himself to death. I was scared of the man and seldom spoke to him. I didn't miss him when he died.

Dad used to tell stories about sitting in the upper stairwell at his home listening to his parents fight.

He said he thought his head would blow off, (headaches), so he walked the streets at 3:00 a.m. in the morning to ease the pain and relieve the pressure. Dad hated conflict, especially parental.

As a child, athletics meant more to dad than academics. He used to enter the front door of Stephen Decatur High School and go right out the back door. Dad saw no relevance for education. Athletics were his outlet both emotionally and physically.

Academic eligibility cost him a basketball state championship in 1936 when SDHS, Stephen Decatur High School, won the state basketball title. Dad graduated mid-year and was not on the team.

I think I would have preferred negative attention from Dad rather than no attention. Literally, he had no response to my presence at all. I was an incidental in his life, or so it seemed.

Dad never asked me how my day went or what was going on in my life. He never asked me how I felt about anything and every time I approached him about "feelings", he turned mine off.

I suppose my parents did the best they could at the time, but I certainly suffered as a result of their choices for me. I am NOT a victim, but I certainly learned how to cope at an early age, and I was not intellectually mature enough to process my parent's intentions, especially my name. Why did Barry Buttz have to be my name?

In the 1940's, Dad did what a man was supposed to do. He went to work, supported his family and that was it. In those times, men weren't supposed to be in touch with their feelings or their inner selves. In truth, I had a good dad who probably felt he fulfilled his family obligations to the fullest.

Better Make Memories:

At age 45, my parents had really made no memories with my children. They were not the typical doting grandparents and never baby-sat or treated the kids to a "sleep over". All holidays were spent at my home and Grandma and Grandpa Buttz would stop by on Sunday evening for coffee. Grandma and Grandpa were labels, not earned titles.

With both of my parents aging, Bill told me I needed to make memories with them before something happened to one or both. I had discovered the wonderful island of Gulf Shores, Alabama, in 1988 and annually, my family made the pilgrimage to paradise.

In 1993, I asked my parents to go along. They accepted the invitation and we departed Decatur in June. After the 14 hour drive, we arrived. I could tell Mom and Dad were excited. The accommodations at Summer House were like being in a swank hotel. We all loved the condo with the "wrap-around" porch on the 9th floor.

Dad loved the whole scene. He rented a chaise lounge on the white sands and would sit by the Gulf for hours. Mom was an enthusiast also, even though she could not swim. Together, Mom and Dad played golf and spent time by themselves. In the evenings we always ate out and played miniature golf or rented go-carts.

Mom and Dad went with us for four years and we made wonderful memories. My children still refer to the years that Grandma and Grandpa went on vacation with us. Thank God for Bill Cogan.

A Quiet Death:

At 11:00 p.m. on September 7, 1997, Mom called me and said Dad was not breathing and was blue. I told her to call 911. I knew what had happened.

When I arrived, the coroner was taking my dad, covered in a sheet, out of the bedroom. I walked over and kissed his head through the sheet and whispered, "Good bye, Pop". In death, I finally got to kiss my dad. He had passed away quietly in his sleep. It was God's reward for being a good man. Mom's life had just been changed forever.

The Funeral:

Hundreds of people attended his funeral. Dad was active in the community and took part in the Wabash Fellowship Club, bowling, golf, the Elks, the Moose and the Golden Kiwanis Club. I have never heard so many positive comments about anyone in my life.

Dad was very well liked and respected. For that I was proud, but it was as though mourners were describing someone I didn't know.

As I glanced into the casket for the final time, my thought was, "I never really knew you, but I loved you. God, how I loved you."

As per my dream so many years ago, Dad did die in the house on 22nd Place. Recently, I went to an Open House as the house was up for sale. The realtor asked me if I were interested in buying a "doll house". I responded the house had been my boyhood home and I just wanted to see how it had changed. I mentioned my dad had died in that room, pointing to the bedroom. The realtor turned white. I left the house consumed with my childhood.

I searched my whole life for a father substitute and believe I was sensitized to the gay life for paternal love and gratification.

My tapestry and my heart had a hole in them.

Dad, Mom and I, 1946

Ralph Buttz, Johns Hill Jr. High, 9th grade, 1932

Dedicated to Ralph Buttz Jr., 1918 - 1997

Chapter Sixteen

My Children

Damned Good Dad:

Living two lives can be perceived as deception and/or overt lying. For me, the two lives I led were unrelated.

My relationship with Bill was in no way connected with my life as a father and husband. No, I did not want my cake and be able to eat it too. I simply had two different lives. I was relevant in both. I can hear your comments now.

When a man is unsure about his sexuality and marries, what follows is a discovery process. As a 26 year old virgin, I truly believed all would be well sexually once I married. I was married 13 years before "the boss" recognized a vulnerable, scared, cancer laden man and introduced him to the gay life. Even then, I only reached out to take an empathetic hand as I met cancer head-on and needed the safety and security a man offered.

However, even after the addition of a second life, my life as a father was still paramount. Why? I had an opportunity to undo what had been done to me by my parents. I had a chance to instill in my children a foundation for their lives. A foundation filled with love, security and familial ties.

My daughter, Jennifer, was born on March 4, 1977. She was a beautiful baby who seldom put her head down while in the neonatal unit of the hospital. All of the other children slept, but my girl kept her head up and looked around. What a kid.

I was the proudest man in the world and loved having visitors at the hospital so that I could show-off my baby girl. All was well until the fifth day when the nurse handed her to us and said, "Good Luck". I had no idea what to do with a newborn baby and the shock of actually taking the baby home, was overwhelming. What did I think was going to happen? I'm not sure, but like all first-time parents, I was uneasy and wondered if I was ready to be a dad. Trust me, I was.

The hardest part of early life for Jennifer was her colic. She cried night and day for three months. As I was still working I had to sleep in the back room and even with "headsets" on, I could still hear her crying. I felt she was crying because of something I had or hadn't done.

The pediatrician said she would continue to cry for three months and then the underdeveloped digestive tract would mature and she would quit crying. To the day, three months later, it stopped.

On April 15, 1980, my son, Jason, was born. He was a blond baby with a smile that could melt butter. Our two children were lovingly planned and totally wanted.

A son was a total surprise. We had been told he was a girl and the heart rate indicated he was. Unknown to us, as we left the prepping area in the hospital and headed to the delivery room, the heart rate dropped. The nurse didn't tell us. Once inside the delivery room, and delivery occurred, the doctor said, "It's a boy." I cried openly. A healthy baby boy. Who could ask for more, one girl and one boy.

My married life was typical in the early years as Mom and Dad were young teachers who had two children. As stated previously, my mother-in-law moved in the year after our marriage and at first, it worked out well, as we had a built-in baby sitter.

However, Grandma wasn't the primary care giver. While Jennifer was in the hospital nursery, one of the nurses told us her mother loved to keep children and had just said good-bye to a child she had kept for 13 years. It was at this time, Grandma Burton was introduced to our family.

Every morning I dropped the kids off at Grandma

Burton's house. She was a 70 year old angel. The kids grew to love her and think of her as family, a real grandma. No one could have had a better woman to care for their kids. When Grandma Burton passed away, we all felt the loss. She was one of a kind. Jennifer and Jason were teenagers when she passed away. We all shed tears.

As a result of Grandma Burton and working parents, the kids grew up with all the luxuries money could provide. Toys, games, educational technology, and tons of clothes were the norm. Both children attended John Adams Elementary, the school at the top of the hill south of our home. They could walk and did not have to ride a school bus. What a blessing for working parents not to have to worry about bussing.

I made sure I was omni-present, (always there), at all extra-curricular events in and out of school. Both children took swimming at early ages and Jennifer took "baton" and dance. Parades, dance reviews, we did it all. Jennifer was tall for her age and actually played on the boys' basketball team in sixth grade. In junior high school and high school she played center on the girls' team. My life was full of sports, travel and spontaneous meals.

Jason started little league baseball at age five and played summer baseball through high school. We spent hours on the road following his teams. I looked forward to his games and the full schedule. I helped coach his little league baseball team for five years and coached his YMCA basketball team for two years.

In order to ensure motivational classes, Jennifer and Jason played musical instruments in elementary and junior high school. I sat through many an elementary and junior high band concert praying it would be over. Those junior high choir concerts weren't too fantastic either, but I was there. All band students were grouped into classes together so band and music could be easily scheduled.

Jennifer and Jason made show choir in junior high school and carried their singing and dancing talents into high school. In 1990, Eisenhower Elite Energy high school show choir was started and we were involved as ground-breaking parents. Twenty years later, EEE is one of the top Midwest show choirs.

I enjoyed every second of our involvement in little league baseball, high school baseball, high school basketball and show choir. I took off work and traveled to Virginia, Florida, Wisconsin, Indiana and all over Illinois with the teams and EEE. I filled a parental void for myself by going, but wouldn't have missed one memory with the kids.

Sur Name:

One difference I clearly noted in my children's high school education and mine, was the lack of negative emphasis on their sur name. My son never had anyone chide him for being a Buttz and my daughter seemed to have had the ultimate in compliments for her name.

She was the center on the high school basketball

team and when opening the game for the center-court jump ball, the team and cheerleaders would chant, "Leap Booty, Leap". The play on words was a tremendous acceptance for someone having the last name Buttz. I was grateful both of them never experienced what I had.

My parents never came to any of my school events and I missed that support. By not attending school events, their absence indicated to me a lack of interest in me as a person as the unwanted child. I made sure my children knew Dad would freely give of his love, time and emotional energy, to be present for their childhood memories. I was redoing history, my own.

Family Expectations:

As a family we had strict expectations for such events as evening meals, eating out and family outings. We vacationed together as a family unit, but the kids could always ask a friend to accompany us. Missing a family meal was unacceptable. Guests were welcome and our table was a source of sharing and growing as a family. Dinner time was a very special time in our home. If we ate out, we went as a family. Our kids were not allowed to skip a family meal in order to eat at McDonald's with friends. It didn't happen.

My son, now 30, who lives in Chicago, recently told me the things he misses most from his childhood are our evening meals together, family vacations and the sense of family. We must have done something right as parents.

Both of my children finished high school and graduated from college. Jennifer graduated from Eastern Illinois University in Charleston, Illinois and Jason from Illinois Wesleyan University in Bloomington/Normal, Illinois. Jennifer married and has my beautiful grand-daughter and Jason has found someone special in his life.

Jason is making plans to move to Amsterdam to join his young lady. I hope the arrangement becomes permanent and he is happy. I am thrilled my children are straight and don't have to live in turmoil as Dad did.

Family tradition and language provided the impetus, (driving force), for attending college. We always said, "When you graduate from college.", not "If you graduate from college.". Each child fulfilled the expectation.

I never chose to get a divorce while my children were dependents as I did not believe in being a weekend dad, nor did I want to leave them with their mother and grandmother for their only source of sexual identity. It takes Mom and Dad to raise a family and I never shirked that duty or responsibility.

Gay Ramifications:

I often wondered if either of my children suffered because of my perceived orientation. One incident ignited this fear in me. One night a friend of my son's called and asked to speak to him. I told him to hang on a second and I called for my son.

The friend did not know I was still on the line. I heard him say, "He sounds like a fag. Yeah, I wonder where Mr. Cogan is? Ha, Ha, Fag!"

My heart sank and I was fully aware one or both of the kids could have been verbal abuse targets as a result of my relationship with Bill. If they ever were ill-willed targets, neither of them ever mentioned it to me.

I can only beg their forgiveness if my perceived orientation caused them any anxiety or grief while growing up. It was never my intention for my two lives to collide with them in the middle. I pray if they did not know the circumstances then, they understand my whole story now and love me as Dad and nothing less.

Responsibilities:

As a protective father, and carrying the burden of fear of loss, I found myself being overly-protective while the children were growing up.

When they were ill, I made the calls to the doctor and took off work to take them to their appointments. The responsibility for their well-being over-whelmed me and it still does today. I am happy when my kids are happy and healthy. When they are not, neither am I.

No matter what happened between their mother and

me, we did something correctly, as we have two lovely children who contribute to society and are not "takers" or "users". Both are extremely intelligent and never were involved in drugs, drinking or other teenage prone activities. I appreciate my children more and more each day and both are the love of my life.

Other than good health, the greatest gifts a man can have are children and unconditional love. I have both.

Labels:

Loving fatherhood and my children so much, I have asked myself, "Am I gay or bisexual?" I think the answer lies much deeper than a simple choice.

The text of this book clearly shows how many factors dictate one's sexual fate. As an example, sexually, life in prisons becomes traumatic for many men and women. However, the sexual urges may dictate a homosexual experience, even though a man or woman isn't gay. It happens all the time.

Thus, putting a label on one's sexual performances or partners, might be misleading. Conditions, situations, environment, and of course, genetics, dictate the outcome of one's choices and decisions. Unfortunately, neither bisexuality or homosexuality is acceptable in our society.

I am empathetic for any person who wants to have children and can't. I know straight and gay individuals who want children and either can't have them or can't find them to adopt. Being straight or gay is irrelevant in effective parenting. Society is quick to judge gay couples as not being "fit" parents. Intellectually and emotionally, I think it's the gay "label" that is more distressing than the ability to parent.

The loss of a child is a parent's nightmare, but never having one can be equally emotionally distressing and depressing. I had the opportunity to counsel one of my teachers regarding child birth. She had come to my office 10 times to talk about fertility and having a baby. Nothing was working and she appeared near a breakdown.

On a Friday afternoon after school, she visited my office again. The signs were clear she was struggling. Then, I offered the following:

"As a parent, I know wanting a child and not being able to have one is a terrible thing. You are putting yourself through emotional hell and a ton of financial stress with no results. We both acknowledge an inability to have children puts a terrible strain on couples who want them, but have you ever thought what it would be like to be a child and not have anyone want you? I mean, you are seven or eight years old and are consciously aware that you are not wanted? I can't imagine what that would feel like, could you?" She looked at me and said nothing.

I said, "Yes, I mean adoption. Think about it, OK."

On Monday she came in and told me she and her

husband were going to adopt. Four months later, they received a four day old bi-racial child from Peoria, Illinois. That child is now 14 years old.

My point? Why would gay couples feel any differently about not being able to have a child or being denied a child because of their orientation? All people have feelings, including gay ones.

My tapestry is full of colors.

CHAPTER SEVENTEEN

Brother Lost/Brother Found

Destiny Earned:

I devote this special chapter to my brother, whom I love dearly. His life and my life were intertwined as no other brothers' lives would be. We were of the same parents, but if one asked him about his childhood, he would have a completely different perception of our family and our lives.

My brother, Michael Robert Buttz, was born on February 6, 1948. He was a special little guy and Mom and Dad seemed thrilled with him. I was staying with my maternal grandfather the night of my brother's birth. Grandpa Galamback and I were singing, "I'm Looking Over A Four-Leaf Clover" I was sitting on Grandpa's lap and recall the time with fondest memories.

My maternal grandfather, John H. Galamback, was special because he cared about me. Grandpa was 6'1" tall, gray headed, thin and wiry. He had a tremendous sense of humor and loved life. He was of Polish-German descent and his parents actually came to America via Ellis Island. As a child, he spoke Polish, but lost the ability to speak it over the years. Grandpa was the only male who ever gave me attention and I will always remember him for that gift.

When Dad came and told me I had a baby brother, I felt threatened. I didn't need or want competition. As it was, Dad didn't love me. Thank God Grandpa was holding me.

In 1949, Mick got scarlet fever. I remember the orange quarantine sign on our front door. We couldn't go out of the house and no one could visit. Mick was isolated in my parent's bedroom and I could not see him. I had to take a little pink pill in order to keep from getting the disease. Mom was a basket case and constantly cried because Mick might die. I picked up her emotional fears and thought I might die too. No one was worried about me.

As a four year old, I perceived Mom's grief as being more love for him and no concern for me. All of the attention was being paid to Mick. I got none. To me, Mom and Dad loved Mick more than they did me. Truly, I was ignored and shoved aside during this time period.

In a child's mind, two and two equals five. I perceived

Mick as the chosen child. I had to work hard to do everything right. He didn't have to do anything and he was always right, according to my parents.

Growing up, I treated my brother badly and often teased him as others had teased me. I was a terrible brother. I used to watch my dad and my brother play catch, but was really never asked to join in. I was jealous.

I relentlessly demeaned him and ridiculed him. I made fun of him playing cowboys and teased him about his invisible friend, Rehum.

I was brutal and didn't build any relationship with him that would perpetuate close family ties in the future.

As we got older, Mick was all that I wasn't. No one made fun of his name. He had tons of friends and was a three sport athlete in high school.

His grades weren't as good as mine, but he was everything I really wanted to be. We were never close as adolescents, teenagers or young adults.

When I was away at college for four years, Mick literally lived as an only child. His relationship with our parents was much stronger than mine. I was the outsider. To Dad he seemed to be all that I wasn't and never could be. I was jealous and withdrew from emotional ties.

In 1963, Mick enrolled at Western Illinois University in Macomb, Illinois. I didn't understand why he wanted to attend Western, as it was in the middle of cornfields near the Mississippi River. As he began his college career, things really weren't going well. In truth, he was flunking out.

I was sent by my parents to give him a "Come to Jesus Meeting". He resented my presence at WIU and thought I had come on my own to degrade him. I hadn't.

What was his issue? A girl. His girlfriend was at ISU and the two of them didn't function well apart. They needed to be together. Transfer came to a head one day when they passed one another going the opposite directions on the same highway. Each was traveling to see the other at their respective universities without the other's knowledge.

He transferred to ISU and immediately became an above average student. Mick was much more dependent than I was. I had never had anyone to be dependent upon, other than myself.

Mick graduated from Illinois State University in 1970 and became a physical education teacher. His girlfriend, Pam, graduated in elementary education.

The couple got married in 1970. I was not asked to be his best man. I thought it odd, but bowed to his wishes. He stated that Pam, his wife to be, couldn't decide which of her sisters was going to be the Maid Of Honor, so they weren't picking any brothers or sisters. To me, that didn't make sense as I was his only brother. I was hurt. I tried to discuss it with Mom and Dad, but they quickly spurned all dialogue claiming, "It's his choice, now don't make trouble.". True, it was his choice

When I got married, he was my best man. No other choice. Even though I did nothing to deserve the title of "big brother", I had no idea why he resented me so much. I wouldn't find out until years later when I almost died.

As we got older, we still did not share much time or many activities together. We were distant and not connected emotionally. I truly don't think Mom and Dad did anything to make sure we were close. Mom and Dad were happy with one another, and that is all that mattered. Mick and I simply went through the motions of family, but a canopy of love never engulfed the Buttz family.

After my divorce in 2004, Mick and I were openly estranged. We never talked or communicated. I thought our estrangement was due to his perception that I had "walked out" on my wife or my sexual orientation. I was totally wrong.

Although I really never knew the reason or the cause, I created my own destiny with my brother. However, things were about to change.

Near Death Experience:

Last year, in January of 2009, I had a routine colonoscopy. During the procedure, I was perforated twice, became septic and nearly died. I spent one month in the hospital and six months in home recovery.

Mick came to see me regularly. I could tell he was concerned and truly cared. One day, my sister-in-law, Pam, visited my hospital room and we began to talk. I asked her if she knew the reason for our distance. She told me Mick thought I believed he had nothing to offer. He was ignorant and unintelligent. I think my treatment of him delivered the perceived message of " I am better than you are." That's why he resented me. Today, I totally understand how he could feel the way he did.

I thought about what Pam had said, and after recuperation, wrote him twice and explained why I treated him as I did. I told him about how Mom treated me and how I believed he was the special child. I explained how my name hurt me so badly and that, in reality, he was what I wanted to be.

I didn't think him stupid or uninspired. I was jealous. As brothers, we were both ill-equipped to understand our emotions as children and perception is truth. The child in me wishes I had my childhood to live over so I could be endeared as his big brother. I wouldn't waste a second chance.

Within the content of my two letters, I asked for his forgiveness and he gave it. Even if he didn't understand my feelings, he forgave me.

I have judged myself severely and harshly for my

behaviors directed towards my brother. I can only use the time we have left to let my love for him kindle memories we can both take to our graves. I had mentioned to him once that I did not want either of us to stand at one another's casket and ask, "Why?".

Today, we are closer than we have ever been. In the thralls of the fire, a miracle was born. I needed my brother as he is my only connection to our immediate family.

With years of resentment and conditioning, I had ruined the very thing I needed most, my brother. I pushed away the one person who might understand. I gave up my rights to be his brother.

Life was spinning out of control, and I had no idea how to stop it. I thought I would be able to control life's direction, but I couldn't. My life was destined to be what it is today.

Sadly, I had the same impact on my brother's formative years as my mother did on mine. Digest that statement and you'll understand my feelings.

Tapestry ruined; Tapestry mended.

Postscript:

On July 24, 2010, we celebrated our "first ever" Buttz family reunion. Mick's children, spouses and six grandchildren, my daughter, spouse, and grandbaby, my aunt, former wife, Bill and myself, created what we hope to be an annual event. What a relief after 50 years of separation.

A picture of innocence. Christmas, 1952

Follow-Up:

Another significant factor arose as Mick aged. As a child, he needed an inordinate amount of sleep. I often teased him about being "lazy". This factor also attributed to my making fun of him and taunting him as being unmotivated.

In 2005, Mick was diagnosed with hemachromatosis, a blood disorder in which too much iron is produced and if untreated, can cause death. One of the side-effects is the need for sleep and rest. Mick had this disease his whole life and its detection explained the need for sleep in childhood. The disease is passed from both parents who must carry the gene. I have been tested and do not have the disease.

To the reader:

Never take your status in your family for granted. One has to work at being a Mom, Dad, brother or sister. The time you have together has no guaranteed limit. It could be years or just the next few hours or minutes and a loved one could be gone.

As you part during the day, make sure to say, "I love you". Regrets come when we least expect them. I never solidified my big brother status and wasted years of cultivating friendship with my own flesh and blood. Thank God, I got a second chance.

Chapter Eighteen

Nine Lives of the Gay Man

Born To Be?

If one truly believes God wanted me dead because I am gay, then I should have died years ago. For some reason, God heals me and allows me to live. My life must have purpose. I have faced death more than once.

Here is a synopsis of my nine lives.

- At age five, I nearly drowned. It was summer, 1949, and our family was at the lake cottage. I was on the dock with my grandmother when I turned and stepped off the dock. The water was about 12ft. deep. Eyes open, I remember being under water and not being able to breathe. I had my hand over my head. Grandma Buttz heard the splash, saw my hand and pulled me out of the lake. I could not swim and was, indeed, drowning. She caught my hand as I was going under the last time. I was terrified, but remember the incident well. Life one was spared.

- At age ten, I incurred a severe head injury. I was in sixth grade at Roach Elementary School and was playing "Red Rover" on the playground at recess. I tried to plunge between two girls whose arms locked under my chin throwing me head first to the pavement. I was dazed and couldn't move. I remember the commotion and someone saying, "Call an ambulance. Someone call his parents." As I lay there, I could hear the siren in the distance. It was coming for me. I hated sirens, ambulances and even fire trucks, as their presence usually meant disaster. Mom arrived just before the ambulance and was crying. I remember being put in the ambulance, but Mom could not ride with me. I had a fear of ambulances and hated to hear the sirens. I was alone and scared. I remember the screaming siren and how cold and bumpy the ride was. Now, I was inside an ambulance and it felt like a tomb. I was admitted to the hospital and had a head x-ray. Most of the emergency room visit I do not remember. I awakened in a hospital ward, along with 33 other patients. The boy next to me had just had his appendix out and was very ill. I gained more fears about being in a hospital and being seriously ill.

I was diagnosed with a serious concussion and was hospitalized for three days. I would lapse in and out of consciousness. One fact was most significant. I begged my parents to stay with me. However, Mom and Dad would not spend the night. I was alone in a "ward" and visions of sugar plums were not dancing in my head.

- At age 16, I was nearly killed while looking for materials for a homecoming float. My buddies and I were at a construction site in a large warehouse. One of the boy's fathers owned the warehouse and we needed wood to build a set for the float.

I had found some wood but discovered they were behind some metal doors. They didn't look dangerous, just large and heavy. I moved something in front of one of them and heard a crashing sound. Ten of the thousand pound metal doors fell on me and were crushing my head.

Suddenly, I slipped under a permanent saw bolted to the ground floor. The doors crashed over me, hit the saw and I was unharmed. I should have been killed. My head did hurt and was bruised, but I escaped death. I remember driving in a daze back to the float construction site. A guardian angel had been with me.

- At age 20, I sustained a serious knee injury to my right leg. I have explained this significant event in a previous chapter, but will highlight the incident quickly. I was doing a long jump demonstration for a summer school class at ISU. I landed out of the pit and my right leg snapped. It was being held in place only by the skin. I became physically limited and was not drafted for the Viet Nam War.

- At age 38, I had my first cancer, kidney cancer. As previously described, in 1982, I had renal cancer. A left nephrectomy was performed and I have only one kidney. The surgery was 13 hours long and I lost a day during recovery. I remember waking once, seeing what appeared to be hundreds of tubes coming out of me, and I went back to sleep immediately.

- At age 54, I had a total knee replacement of that injured knee in 1965. At this ripe old age, I had my right knee totally replaced in St. Louis, MO. One of the easiest surgeries I have had and was home within 24 hours after the surgery. I recovered quickly and spent weeks in physical therapy. What a miraculous medical advancement.

- At age 63, I had my second cancer, colon cancer. I had had a series of colonoscopies over the years and nonmalignant polyps were removed. In January of 2002, I had a routine colonoscopy and the doctor found nothing. I did not feel good and in June, was changing insurance carriers and asked for an additional colonoscopy. I was listening to my body and reacting to intuition. The doctor said he never did two colonoscopies within six months. With insistence on my part, he agreed.

The doctor found he had missed a polyp that had been growing for over 10 years in the location of the juncture of the small and large intestine for over 10 years and it was malignant. I had colon cancer and a colon resection. I was hospitalized for five days and had a slow recovery. I was told by doctors in Peoria that I had a potential law suit against the doctor, but did not pursue it. I was alive and that is all that mattered. The doctor left Decatur within two weeks.

- At age 64, I had my third cancer, thyroid cancer. I visited a fabulous doctor to get a diagnosis for a lesion on my upper lip. Instead, he felt my neck and said, "There it is." What was "it"? .Thyroid cancer! I had the tumor removed. During recovery I had draining tubes and filling balls dangling from my neck. I could not shower. Recovery went well after removal of the drains. I am on a 20 year recovery plan.

- Also at age 64, I had a thyroid ablation. I swallowed a $5,000 radioactive pill to kill residual cancer cells in my throat. The worst part about the ablation was total isolation. No one could visit me and/or medical staff were only allowed so many seconds near me. Food was dropped off at the door and I had to get it for myself. All garbage had to be bagged, tagged and destroyed as a contaminated substance. If the thyroid cancer ever reoccurs, I will have to revisit the process. Thyroid cancer needs follow-up for 20 years. Sound like fun? It wasn't.

- Age 64 was a bad age. My next trial was atrial fibrillation. I not only had atrial fibrillation, I also had an atrial fibrillation ablation, all in one year, 2008. My heart would beat so fast, I would become weak and have to sit down. No one ever dies from atrial fibrillation, but strokes or blood clots are common if the fibrillation condition is not treated. Personally, I believe the radioactive pill I took for the thyroid ablation caused the artial fibrillation.

- One more incident occurred at age 64. As described in a previous chapter, I had double perforation of my colon. I was perforated twice during a routine colonoscopy which required a second colon resection. I nearly died. Words cannot describe the pain and suffering I experienced. Being septic was worse than any of the other conditions I had ever had, including the loss of a kidney. I spent a month in the hospital.

- And yet another age 64 event. I was sent home too early after the corrective surgery for the colon perforation, and the wound became infected.

My son had come home from Chicago to care for me and I truly needed his assistance.

After a week, he needed to return to work. I was not progressing well and he hated to leave. I remember watching him drive away Sunday night and laid back down in the chair to rest. I felt terrible. I awakened Monday morning and went to the restroom. I could barely navigate. As I sat down on the stool, the stitching in my stomach literally burst. I am not sure what blew out of my stomach but it splashed off the wall. I grabbed my stomach, a towel compress and fell to the floor. I managed to grab a telephone and dialed 911.

When the ambulance arrived I was in so much pain I almost didn't feel anything. The ambulance ride was fast and rough. I returned to the hospital in a septic condition. My daughter and Bill were in the ER with me and I remember her telling me, "Dad, don't look." The ER service was horrendous and the doctor didn't see me until and hour and a half later.

The veins in my arms were so collapsed from the previous week, the nurse had to put the "IV" in my foot. When the doctor did arrive, his exact words were, "Oh Shit!" Literally he began to expunge the infection with his bare hands. My daughter left the room. The wound was three inches long and about two inches deep.

I had sepsis, (poisoning of the blood by pathological micro- organisms). My coloring was pale gray and I was listless and lethargic. I spent three weeks more in the hospital barely hanging on to life. I had a wound vacuum in my stomach for three months. Every other day the wound vacuum sponge had to be changed. I can't tell you the pain I felt when the sponge was removed from the two inch deep hole in my stomach. Recovery took six months and as I write this book, I am almost back to normal.

Today, the hole in my stomach is large and has no muscle tissue below it. My abdominal muscles are not connected and my stomach pushes out. It is a permanent reminder of how quickly one's life can be changed, forever. My body is not "model perfect" any longer. 76% of the people who contract sepsis die. I was in the 24% who make it.

- And finally, one more incident at age 64, In July of 2009, I had gall bladder surgery. Shortly after the second colon resection, my blood tests still indicated infection. My gall bladder had been destroyed. Literally, it was removed in plastic bags as no form existed. It, too, was infected and was filling my body with infection. I had had three surgeries in six months.

In addition to all of the above surgeries, I have had the following procedures, surgeries or injuries: Two cataract surgeries, hernia surgery, numerous arthroscopic procedures and a broken wrist

As I read this synopsis of my personal confrontations with illness and death, it reads so easily. Needless to say, I didn't live these events easily. Pain, suffering and recuperation can be described, but unless personally experienced, a reader can only be empathetic. I am not a "complete man" and have no body parts to donate to anyone. I am the "bionic man" without the bionics.

I cannot donate blood nor can any of my organs be donated to save the lives of others. I would have gladly shared my organs so that others might live, but that will never be the case.

In reality, I have had more than nine threats to my life. As our purpose in life seems to change over time, I feel writing this book could be another purpose for my life.

God could have taken my life at any time. Therefore, I know He does not hate me as a gay man as He created me. He fills me with love and my guardian angel protects me. Believe it!

A tapestry can tell a story of pain, but feels no pain.

Comment:

Times exist when I have degrees of survivor's guilt. Cancer is so mentally, emotionally and physically debilitating, it's hard to believe one is cured, even when told so. You never stop looking over your shoulder.

The anticipation of cancer's return is almost worse than being told it has returned. I find myself rushing through life in anticipation of the next diagnosis. The beast is but a diagnosis away. Death becomes a scheduled event instead of an unknown destiny. The agony of your potential fate is always in the back of your mind. You run from what "could be" instead of "what is". Internal peace is never a companion

CHAPTER NINETEEN

The Gift

Definitions:

Webster defines "intuition" as the immediate knowing of something without the use of conscious reasoning, and "instinct" as the inborn tendency to behave in a way characteristic of a species. (Webster's New World Dictionary)

We visibly see instinct demonstrated each fall and spring as geese fly south in their "V" formation for the winter, and then, return home in the spring. Instinct is also demonstrated in animals as they care for their young. How do they know what and how to give this care? It's instinct or inborn. Instinct seems to be associated more with animals than with humans, although I believe humans do posses instincts.

Intuition, is more commonly found in the human species via strong urges, or "hunches". Sometimes these feelings or hunches are warnings. Yet, at other times, they can be very positive. Intuition could also be a "gut feeling" about someone or something. It could be a feeling of confidence and liking or one of discomfort and disliking without known foundation or fact.

We have all had these feelings and possess some degree of instinct and intuition. However, I seem to have enhanced versions of both, almost a "sixth sense".

My instinct allows me to listen to the callings of my body so that I can utilize my intelligence in a decision making capacity to protect myself or my health. Instinctively, I move to protect myself or act upon my feelings. The contents of the preceding chapter should emphasize my need to heed my body's warnings, (i.e.: cancer). Heed the signs.

My intuition has always been my best ally in knowing people, their intentions and basically, what they are thinking in regards to me or others I care about. In other words, a good judge of character in people. I am not usually wrong.

As all individuals have both, instinct and intuition, I would say mine are enhanced or sensitized due to physical and emotional conditioning as well as sexual orientation. I have always had to be my own personal advocate. Intuition is like having a "built-in" personal defense system.

Manifestations:

I am totally connected to my children and instinctively know when the phone is about to ring. I feel it before it happens. I am right most of the time. Many parents have this type of telekinetic ability with offspring or family members.

I have had many experiences I cannot explain. One mentioned in this book is the premonition about meeting a well-known man who had a large family. This vision appeared shortly after my body was sensitized due to the removal of my kidney and neural stimulation by radiation therapy. I did not solicit or dream it, it was a factual event in my mind. It happened, I saw it, and it came true.

I have had many other events that have scared me to death, but at the same time, established that my senses are unusual. One such event happened in 1970.

I was living in Timber Cove Apartments near Lake Decatur and was in an awakening state prior to going to school to teach. I envisioned an accident involving a black and yellow car. In the parking lot, I had a yellow and black Oldsmobile 442. I could literally hear the sirens and see the fire trucks and ambulances rushing to the scene.

After showering and dressing for work, I started down the Rt.. 36 and turned onto Airport Rd. Shortly after turning, I saw traffic backed up. It appeared to be an automobile accident. As I moved slowly in traffic, I could see that a car had run off the road and had lodged in a deep ditch. It was on its side and was heavily damaged.

As I peered through the passenger window, I caught a glimpse of the car. It was a black over yellow Dodge Charger. I began to perspire profusely. My hands shook and I released the steering wheel. Coincidence? You tell me.

I didn't know if the "vision" was to warn me about a possible personal accident involving my car or simply verified that one had happened. I took the whole incident very seriously.

In 1967, another incident occurred while chaperoning a Thomas Jefferson student council event at Scovill Park. Decatur was sponsoring an annual big name boat race and the sounds of hydroplanes humming on the lake were deafening.

To look at the lake and the races, I had taken 15 students onto an over-look ramp about 35 feet in the air. It was supported by only two huge wooden beams. Suddenly, I got the feeling the ramp was going to fall into the lake or something bad was about to happen on the lake.

I calmly walked the kids off the ramp and the moment the last child exited the ramp, one of the racing boats flipped and flew into the air throwing the driver from the craft. I was terrified and one of the students asked me if I was alright.

I have the uncontrolled ability to know things are going to happen before they do. I can't control or create these premonitions, nor do I know what will happen, but things do happen. I have often thought it would be a true gift if I could control my thoughts and be able to specifically see and know what was going to transpire, but I can't.

I do know these skills are heightened when I am in a sensitized state or in the waking hours. When I am most stressed, I am most sensitized and in touch with my instincts and intuitions.

Another incident happened one morning while I was waking. The phone rang at 8:30 a.m. and it was my dad. He never called me at that hour. I was afraid something was wrong. I was having a dream about him at the time he called.

He said he had just bought a new car and wanted to come by and show it to me. Jokingly, he said, "What do you think I bought?" At the time he was buying the car, I dreamed or "saw" the incident. I saw him buying a new Ford, brownish in color. I shared what I thought he had bought.

He was dumfounded. It was a Ford product, a Mercury, and the color was exact, metallic brown. I have no idea what or how I "saw" this event, but I did.

These are but a few of the weird things I have witnessed or experienced. I utilize my "gift" to steer clear of places and events that could be dangerous for me or my family.

When my kids were in college, I would often warn them about places on road trips they would take on weekends. For example, I would tell Jennifer to be careful at a certain crossing or curve in the road. The places existed but I had never been there. She would often say, "Dad, how did you know?" Sometimes, accidents had occurred at these places or a dangerous curve existed in a desolate area.

A more recent event happened here in Decatur as I was traveling home from doing an errand. I normally take a certain cross-town road to get home but something told me to turn a block sooner. I listened to my thoughts and turned. In the newspaper the following morning, was an article about a fatal accident that happened at the exact time I would have been on the original road, had I not changed my mind. It's more than coincidence.

Just today, an incident occurred that made me cringe. Wednesday is our male-bonding lunch day. Weekly, four friends go for lunch and we usually take a road trip out of town. I had this strange feeling Lynn, friend, was not going to be able to go. He called at 8:00 a.m. and we talked about transportation arrangements. He was going.

After he called, I went outside to mow the lawn. I looked up and saw Bill flagging me down. I drove near him and stopped the mower. He said Lynn had called back and stated his son had been taken to the emergency room and he would not be able to go for lunch. I can't explain it, but the call validated my original thought, Lynn would not be going.

As a finale, this incident nearly cost me my life as I did not heed my warning. As previously described, in 2008 I had a routine colonoscopy and my colon was perforated two times ending in a near death experience. However, what has not been revealed is that the night before the procedure, I had a very vivid dream warning me about the procedure.

The dreamscape was all in black and the environment was horrific. I saw a black figure pointing into a grave that was intended for me. I was told to cancel the medical procedure. In the dream, a black "X" appeared over my bed as I slept. It was a warning.

When I awakened, I was totally aware of the contents of the dream, but I didn't heed the warning. I felt uneasy as I entered the hospital because of the dream, but I didn't have the "faith" that my warning was real. I paid a severe price for not listening to "my gift".

As I lay in the hospital near death, I knew I was going to die. Without verbalizing, I mouthed the words to Bill, "I'm not going to make it." He looked at me with tears in his eyes and nodded.

That evening when my general practioner, (doctor), came in, I told him if he didn't do something differently, I would surely die. At 11:00 p.m., a tall, good-looking Indian doctor came into my room and sat beside the bed.

He said, "I have been reading your file for three hours and we are going to make some changes."

Heretofore, the sepsis in my blood was being treated with a general anti-biotic and not one specific to the type of bacteria I had. The new doctor was able to match the bacteria in my blood with an effective anti-biotic and intravenous injections were begun immediately. He saved my life. How? The general surgeon had taken me off all anti-biotics the day before and I would have died. He had given up. Had I not demanded "a change", I would not be writing this book.

Predictability:

Along with intuitive and instinctive skills, predictability skills seem to complement the two sensations. I have always been able to predict possible outcomes of situations based on knowledge, intellect and experience. I firmly believe my intuition and instinct have given me excellent abilities to predict outcomes or relate to "cause and effect" circumstances. However, I think it's much deeper than that.

Professionally, I used my gifts to hire staff who would best serve my students. I hired no one I had to fire because of a poor choice and/or who was a "bad fit" for my staff.

Also, I have been able to use both instinct and

intuition professionally with students and parents. I am a good judge of character and can usually tell what a parent wants and what a student needs. Maybe it's just experience, but I could readily predict a child's behaviors before they happened. I made it a point to know the child and anticipate his behaviors.

Is it possible I have no gift at all, but simply possess well-honed skills? In either case, I believe events in my life have caused me to be more conscious of my intuitions and instincts than are most other human beings.

I truly believe I have some "gift" that enhances my life. I stop short of calling it a true "sixth sense", but all that occurs cannot be explained.

Whatever my gift, I am grateful. It has served a gay man well.

My tapestry is blessed.

Follow-Up:

Yes, our bodies do talk to us. Maybe not in words, but they do tell us when they need attention. Be in tune with your body and listen to what it is telling you. Then, act on it. Self-awareness may save your life

Chapter Twenty

Coming Out

Confirmation:

For me, writing this book is my actual "coming out". Many friends and contemporaries have suspected my sexual inclinations, but I have never confirmed it until now. As for family awareness, I have no idea who knew or didn't know about my other life.

After "the boss" pursued me and was in my life, my wife seemed to know more about his past than I. She had a secretary at the central office confiscating mail between the two of us and would often listen-in on telephone calls from him at our home.

In addition, once she confronted me, I didn't deny our relationship. Shortly thereafter, she went to my parents as well as my brother and sister-in-law and told them. I didn't have an opportunity to explain myself. I was guilty as charged. Neither my parents nor my brother ever asked me to explain or give my version of events.

My mother cried and asked me "why", but she didn't want to listen to my responses. She just wanted me to be heterosexual. I told her my sexual orientation was in my genes but she felt I could change if I wanted to.

Her words were, "You weren't raised that way." Again, she seemed to accept some responsibility for my "condition" and viewed my sexuality as a familial embarrassment or shortcoming on her part.

As a reader, you now understand why "A Prayer For Bobby" was so inspirational and significant to me. I had lived the life.

Mom:

In 1998, a year after Dad died, my wife and I moved Mom into our home. We had a horrendous fight about her coming to live with us. I simply pointed out her mother had been living with us for 30 years and she shouldn't be complaining about my mother living with us. I couldn't understand her reluctance to allow my mother to join us other than she didn't want Mom to see how things really were between us.

Mom invested $46,000 to pay for an addition to our home. We added a living room/bedroom, walk-in closet and full bathroom for her living accommodations.

Celeste's mom lived upstairs and Mom lived beneath her. Both mothers lived with us for two years before Mom entered a nursing home. Eventually, my mother-in-law followed.

Mom and Dad had always openly supported my wife over me and didn't believe me when I told them Celeste's mother was first in all circumstances and/or that she dominated every move my wife made.

Late one afternoon, Mom called me to her downstairs room and said, "Honey, I think I better understand what you have been through living with the two of them. While I don't understand your relationship with Bill, I can understand how you felt pressured here and why you sought love elsewhere. Living here, I see it for myself."

At that moment, I loved my mother more than ever before in my life. I thanked her, gave her a hug and we both cried. Mom had finally understood why I felt so lonely and used. I never had knowledge of any of my mother-in-laws financial matters as my wife never shared them.

Wife:

My "wake-up" call regarding my wife's love for me was her reaction to my having renal cancer. She was not upset about me dying, only her living alone and supporting two children. It was all about her, not me or even us. Truly, "What about me...?", was all I heard. I was assumed dead before I actually died.

Sexually, I felt she was never interested in me. I was a conduit to a secure, stable life and "the boss" threatened that security. I functioned as an enabler and after my divorce, good friends came forward and told me they had been aware of her using me for years. I was amazed. I had no thoughts of being used until my announcement of the first cancer. With her lack of emotion, I knew I was expendable.

In other words, it wasn't a husband or a partner she was losing, it was a meal ticket. My central administrative position provided status in the community and gave her certain privileges other teachers didn't have, (ie: Department head, student teachers, instant name recognition, etc.) I share these observations as personal opinions.

Aunt:

My aunt always seemed to know I was a "member", but never mentioned my relationship with Bill or her relationship with Ginger. It was understood and accepted between us. She has always treated both Bill and me with love and respect.

Brother:

My brother probably knew, but when my wife told him, it was confirmed. Today, I feel no animosity from him regarding my sexuality. Our poor relationship was due to my pathetic treatment of him as a child. I am grateful for my brother's understanding and love, He's a great guy.

Children:

As for my children, I openly talked about my sexuality with my son when he was going through panic attacks. I had to ask him if he was experiencing anxieties due to sexuality and he assured me he wasn't. I prayed he wasn't going through what I had in regards to sexual orientation. For him, panic attacks were triggered by stress.

Sexuality orientation could have been a factor in my son's panic attacks, so I admitted my orientation in order to save my son the trials I went through. If sexuality had been an issue, I could have, and would have, been able to counsel him. My father never shared with me his life with panic attacks. Sexual orientation was not the cause.

Even though we never discussed it, I must credit my daughter's intelligence and assume she has correctly connected the dots to create an accurate picture of my relationship with Bill. She will always be Daddy's little girl and nothing will change that. Obviously, my sexuality means little to my children as my relationship with them has always been "rock solid". I am their dad and that is all that matters.

Other relatives, never mentioned my sexuality. One assumes my business is just that, mine or my orientation is irrelevant.

Friends:

Friends might have thought Bill and I are gay partners but no one has ever talked to us about the topic. Some of our acquaintances or work contemporaries stopped speaking to us after I moved in with him, but most of them operate on what they think they know without confirmation. They're guessing.

For Bill and myself, everyone who knows us realizes we live together. Rocket science is not necessary to comprehend we are more than friends. Because of our age difference, 82 and 65, many people who don't know us think we are father and son. If someone asks me where "Dad" is, I simply say "in time out at home". They laugh.

Bill's Family:

Bill had similar experiences in his married life. He worked, earned money and his wife spent it. Bill used little for himself and often did without so his wife could raise the children while he worked. He received little credit for earning the money she spent. One of his children has repeatedly said, "Well, Mom raised us", but what was left unsaid was, "....with the money Dad earned".

That said, he had more confrontation with his wife about me than he did his previous partner. I was not the reason Bill's marriage was strained, but I was a problem because his previous partner only wanted him occasionally. I wanted a permanent live-in relationship.

However, we knew circumstances had to be perfect for

us to be able to live together. By perfect, I mean, all other responsibilities had to be fulfilled and/or completed.

One significant incident occurred for Bill before we went to a convention in Las Vegas. A Cogan family meeting was called by Bill. Bill's wife called him out and accused him of infidelity. The five Cogan children were caught in the middle. Bill's wife threatened to call his sister in Arizona and tell her about her brother. She did. She had no mercy.

Two times Bill's wife approached me at work and threatened me. Once, she wanted my fingerprint to see if I was the one sending the letters to her home. I gave her my fingerprint and insisted she have it checked. I was not the one sending letters to anyone.

The second time she confronted me in the parking lot of the central office building and threatened to tell the superintendent about me. I responded, " Well, come on. I'll go with you. You see, if I lose my job, so will your husband and then, your meal ticket will be gone. You might even have to go to work. The problem with you is, you just want his name and his money, and I want him." She stomped on my foot, got in her car and drove away. Life was supposed to be so simple.

As for genetic implications, one of Bill's children is gay as well as a niece on the maternal side of the family. Genetics, one can't avoid them regarding the predisposition for disease and/or being gay.

After his wife's passing, I did not move in with Bill until six years later. When I did, his children were very cold and un-accepting. They never referenced our home as anything other than "Dad's" house. It took some time for them to realize I was not the problem. Actually, their father was as responsible for me moving in as I was. It has taken us eight years to break down many barriers in order for me to be accepted as a caring part of the extended family. They know I care deeply and unconditionally for their father.

Times have changed over the eight years Bill and I have lived together. Initially, all work efforts were 50/50. Age and Parkinson's Disease have taken a toll on Bill's ability to work within the parameters of our partnership. I am now a care giver. For me, it's my destiny. Having 17 years difference in our ages, I knew this day would come. It just came so quickly. Fortunately, I love the person I am caring for and am grateful I am still here to be able to meet his needs.

You:

If you are dealing with the issue of "coming out", my advice is to get it out earlier rather than later. I realize "coming out" depends on location, employment, age, etc., but adjustments take time and education. After initial shock, family will usually come around. Friends will continue to be friends and acquaintances will come and go. Let "acquaintances" go if they can't accept you as you are.

You can't help who you are and what you are feeling. Don't allow others to say you can change. You can't. In addition, don't take guilt trips for being you. Stand strong and live your life respectfully and without shame. As with me, what you are isn't who you are.

Twists:

My wife and I were married on June 26th. Bill's wife's birthday was June 26th. Bill's wife was a nun. My wife considered being a nun. Both women were Catholic and ecumenical ministers within their respective churches. Both women viewed sex as a duty and/or for the procreation of children only. For Bill and me, our lives were destined to cross.

My tapestry might be a copy of another.

CHAPTER TWENTY-ONE

The Church and the Myths

"Nothing in education is so astonishing as the amount of ignorance it accumulates in the form of facts."
Charlotte Bronte[9]

What Is "Fact"?

Educational facts and religious facts are both often lost in a sea of ignorance and personal opinion. In today's fast paced world of technology and the Internet, "fact one" can be disputed a thousand times with the click of a mouse. As a child, I grew up in a world of facts spread by word of mouth, pulpits and textbooks. Opinion permeated facts and from those grew myths which were viewed as truths, even though content was often antiquated and inaccurate.

Addressing the age old myth being gay is a choice, I submit a number of "facts" that relate to the final product of "being gay".

One doubts that degrees of gayness exist. However, part of the diagnosis of being gay would depend on how it is defined. Head counts are difficult because so many people won't admit to their gay tendencies. Other gays are locked in a closet somewhere. In addition, many people appear to be bi-sexual. It's hard to submit one definition for what it means to be gay or find valid numbers per definition.

Personally, I know my environment forced me to seek male attention. I know Mom's taunting and actions soured me against women's bodies, especially breasts. Plus, the church railed against gay relationships but also cautioned against pre-marital sex with girls. If the right combination of genetics, predisposition and environment occur, one could easily mature into a gay being.

For me, I can't remember any choice involved in being gay or not being gay. The only choice one has is how he/she lives the life within the life. That being said, the same holds true for heterosexuals.

I cannot condone openly gay relationships, as one would not condone open relationships in the straight world. The spread of HIV and other socially transmitted diseases is a result of irresponsible people in both worlds, gay and straight.

Soliciting tricks in public parks is revolting to me and beneath a man's dignity. Hunters and predators are not the norm in the gay world. Sadly, society believes they are the norm. It's a mythical image gay men have.

Pedophile:

The one sexual label which bothers me more than any other is the term "pedophile". Pedophile is an emotional media label quickly placed on men having sex with boys. However, older straight men having sex with younger girls is labeled "abuse", not pedophilia. Both are examples of pedophilia.

The media avoids such labels for straight men and hence, the public views that abuse differently. Hence, the misconception exists that all gay men prey on young boys.

Being gay does not mean being a pedophile. Most of America would group the two labels under one umbrella. As for myself, for example, I am drawn only to older men. Boys, younger men, and even men my own age, are not of interest to me. I am not a pedophile.

I do know of gay men who seek younger gay men, but even then, these younger men are of age, consenting and are not children.

Children are off limits to mentally competent, stable gay or straight men. Having said that, I recognize that some readers will take offense to me using adjectives as competent and stable to describe gay men. Sorry, many of us are just that, competent and stable.

Nowhere in any medical journal will one find homosexuality as a mental illness, whereas, pedophilia certainly is. Recognize the difference.

Facts and Justifications

Other individuals use THE HOLY BIBLE to substantiate and support their views about gay men and women being eternally damned.

I have heard the story of Sodom and Gomorrah utilized so many times as justification for God damning the gay world.

In truth, God did not destroy the two cities for the gays, lesbians or prostitutes therein. He destroyed the cities because Lot could not find 10 people who believed in and/or feared God. Read "the facts" in THE HOLY BIBLE and see for yourself.

No gay people respond to their gayness in the same way. The difference in gay men's choices and behaviors is found in onset or recognition of one's gayness as well as personality and character. Some of us know instinctively, others fight it for years and many individuals try to balance the two worlds as I did. Personality and character dictate how one "acts out" or lives the gay life. The same is true in the straight world, is it not?

Some of us marry in the hopes the feelings will go away, but others remain single or simply wait for the right partner to emerge. Risk takers just play Russian Roulette on the streets.

Thus, facts, myth, and reality about homosexuality are based upon perception. If one is open to education and changing one's mind as a result of education, myth can become fact. If not, myth remains truth and prejudice continues.

In these instances, individuals do not want to be educated and/or intend to change their minds, no matter what they learn. Sadly, men are more fearful of homosexuality than women. Our culture makes sure gay men are not observed as "normal", stable or competent.

In addition, religious interpretations never allow for change regarding God's Word. In a true Christian spirit, it is easier to renounce than it is to claim. It is easier to condemn than it is to accept.

It's interesting how many times fact is predicated upon opinion. Gayness is a fact, not an opinion. It's a truth that is hard to claim and/or accept, but most of all, it isn't a myth.

~

Christian Fellowship:

Life without gay people would have been most

interesting. The impact gay absence would have had on history, The Arts and the Performing Arts would be staggering. Life would surely be shortchanged without the many contributions of gay men and women.

Many conservative religious groups feel gay men and women cannot have faith or believe in God. They believe gays live a life of sin and are damned by their choices.

Of course, defining a "life of sin" would be the challenge. Too many gay people have been driven away from church by repeatedly hearing sermons which doom them to death and eternal fire.

Let me share an example of one man's Christian fellowship within the hallowed halls of the church. This incident actually happened to me.

First, I'll set the stage. Trinity Lutheran Church, Decatur, Illinois.

Six well-known church families met for 40 years to study THE HOLY BIBLE in their homes. Three of the male members were church elders. As a group, they were the pillars of the church. They were religious role models for all other church members; the holiest of the holy, if you will.

It was Sunday morning and I was seated in the last row at church. One of the bible-study elders approached me and said, "May I talk to you for a moment?"

I said, "Sure".

The elder said, "People in the church say you left your wife for a man and are living in sin with him. If this is true, you can't take communion today. If you do, it will mean eternal damnation for you."

I sat quietly for a moment completely overcome with the boldness and judgmental audacity of this man.

Quietly, I replied, "I did get a divorce and moved in with a man. He is 82 years old. I'm humbled at the members of the church are so interested in me and my life."

The elder said, "Oh, he's 82?"

I replied, "Yes".

At this point, the elder looked pleased and responded, "Oh, then go with God. Enjoy communion. God bless you."

I sat dumbfounded. I had just been given permission to attend communion in my own church, by a "non" judgmental Christian.

What had this man thought? Was I a pedophile? Did I break up someone's marriage and steal a man? When he found out my charge was 82, all was well. Was age an acceptance factor? So goes the judgment of the church.

I was astounded at the extra-curricular discussion that occurred during Bible study. Maybe I wasn't the only one who needed forgiveness.

As I sat there, I wasn't sure what to do. I pondered for a moment and said to myself, "This is my church. I have been a member here for 62 years. I am not going to storm out as though I am guilty of anything." I bowed my head and said a prayer for the well-intentioned gossipers in the pews.

Without a religious foundation, I would have never been able to cope with the trials of my life, especially the illnesses. I needed hope, forgiveness and love. In God, I found them all.

I refuse to allow church nay-sayers or even preachers in the pulpit to dampen my faith or my spirit. I will not leave the church because of ignorance therein.

The radical Christian Right is better at judging than it is at being judged.

Postscript:

Very few words in the English language make my skin crawl, but one always gets to me. That word is "fellowship". What does fellowship mean? Webster defines fellowship as "a group of people with similar interests."

Is it something only Christians do? Is fellowship simply socialization? If it is, then why don't people say, "Come and socialize with us."? I hate the word and how emphasis is placed on fellowship as opposed to friendship. To me, the word is religious rhetoric.

~

CHAPTER TWENTY-TWO

Is It Still Open Season On Gays?

Things Are Better, But--

I am not sure why I feel education could change personal religious beliefs or individual perspectives about gay men and women. It appears once cultivated, some perceptions never change, especially those which seem to threaten masculinity in men. As it is, our country is bursting with sexual predators, domestic violence, child abuse and cruelty to animals.

I just put down the newspaper after reading an article about cruelty to dairy cows. Stabbing them with pitchforks, beating them with crowbars and hitting them in the face really seems to full-fill the "macho" image. In our local paper, the following headlines have been found:

"Kitten--Killing Cop Wants Job Back"

"Mom Kills Herself In Front Of Girl Nine"
"Parents Charged with Killing Boy"
"Cat Nailed To Pole"
"Puppy Beaten To Death"
"Boys beat baby llama to death"
"Woman Gets Probation For Abusing Puppy", (a
baby Pit Bull with an electrical cord around its
neck found in a trash can.)
"Man shoots puppy"
"Man Throws Child In Front Of Car" STOP!

I had to put the paper down. What kind of mind can
hurt or kill defenseless children, helpless animals or
other human beings?

A few years ago here in Decatur, we had an incident
where beautiful flamingos were killed at the local zoo and
their heads placed in mailboxes around the city. The act
was senseless and the perpetrators were one 19 year old
and two male juveniles. Malicious children! The reason
for the killings was, "because they were there".

Yet, by comparison, being gay rates below a level of
indignation one would feel for the flamingo murders.
Who cares if a gay is injured or killed? Don't they have
it coming to them? Didn't they get what they deserved?
Faggots don't have rights or feelings.

The "macho" image is cultivated in movies, video
games and extreme fighting games. Street crimes are
higher than they have ever been and people seem to react

violently to things they don't understand. In particular, children have become "numb" to violence.

Recently, here in Decatur, a man was riding his bicycle home from work. He was attacked and beaten by seven youths. One youth jumped up and down on his head until he was unrecognizable. The saddest fact is, over 100 people witnessed this senseless act and did nothing to assist the man. No one came forward to give any details or identify the perpetrators. The seven were caught and are awaiting trial.

We have become a nation which accepts violence. In some instances of violence the public is outraged, in others, no one seems to care. I'm appalled that life means so little, especially gay life.

As a nation, have we lost sight of the value of life? Any life? Cruelty to animals is out of control. Certain dog breeds are being utilized to fight and/or die and even though its illegal, it's justified as being cultural.

Working with the Decatur Human Society I have learned some individuals seek free kittens or puppies in the newspaper adds and claim them as pets, only to use them as "bait" or "training" animals to be killed by their fighting dogs. What has America become?

Personally, I believe if one has the capacity to hurt an animal, he has the capacity to harm a human.

Other than misdirected aggression, or a jaded sense

of control and power, I'm not sure what a man gets psychologically from hurting a defenseless animal.

Bill and I are the proud owners of seven rescued dogs from the Humane Society. They are wonderful animals who have been abused, beaten, not groomed or fed, abandoned or simply discarded on the streets. Our priceless babies are as follows: Sadie, (Golden Retriever), Sophie, (Labrador Retriever), Muffin, (Snudel), Bentley, (Poodle), Shelby, (Jack Russell/Pointer Mix), Simone, (Poodle), and Pepe', (Rat Terrier/Chihuahua Mix). The hours of love we receive from their presence has no money limit which can be put on it. We simply don't understand our society.

Hence, with violence escalating in our culture, gay men and women are still in a state of "Open Season" in some areas of our nation.

To some individuals, gays are less than human. All gays are bundled under one "collapsed" umbrella without allowing for individual differences and/or behaviors. What's more, the lay public continues to believe being gay is a choice.

Political correctness and awareness to gay issues resonate in political arenas, but "red neck" hate crimes still exist. In most instances, the new laws carry rhetoric but have little impact on prevention. I appreciate the initiation of Hate Crime Laws, The Matthew Shepard and James Byrd Jr. Crime Prevention Acts, but feel their impact is of little consequence to the offender. They are not a deterrent.

The victims suffer immensely, while the offenders are slapped on the hands, or spend a short time behind bars. In my opinion, to the offenders, it's worth it. The victims got what they deserved!

To me, legislation is for politicians. Living with the torment often associated with being gay has nothing to do with laws. Explain the law to your hecklers while they are shouting obscenities at you. Talk kindly to your attacker while he is beating you. Explain your rights as a gay man while the crowd hurls insults at you. Yes, our laws are really working well.

In 2008, 1,617 cases of hate crime abuse were reported in the United States. The following is a break down of those figures:

- 58.6% was anti-male homosexual bias
- 25.7% was homosexual bias
- 12.0% was anti-female bias
- 2.0% was heterosexual bias
- 1.7% was anti-bisexual bias
  James R. Byrd 10

Abuse and/or violence was levied at more than 800 gay men.

The real gay issues aren't about religion, going to hell or even equality. They are about money. Gay marriage, domestic partnerships, etc. are about money, not equality of men and women. Again, politics plays the greatest role in limiting gay unions or marriages.

I have witnessed similar attitudes in our public schools regarding rules and/or laws. Nothing a teacher or principal can do is serious enough to make a child change behaviors or conform to school rules and regulations. Nothing! School rules don't scare students because our laws don't scare them. In fact, having spent time in jail is almost a "badge" of achievement. No shame exists.

Calling people gay names, bullying, beating people up are considered "growing up activities". Remorse, understanding and changed behaviors are not the result of laws or rules. I'm not sure how one changes minds or behaviors that are so firmly rooted in our society and structured religion. Gay men and women seem to threaten the very soul of those who claim to be Christian. I am Christian and I threaten no one.

Discipline in many of today's schools is out of control and it's the same lack of control we have on the streets and in the community. Suspension and expulsion from school only puts the kids where they want to be, on the streets.

Why is it so difficult to tabulate statistics related to hate crimes and/or gay hate crimes? Many people are attacked due to perception only. How one dresses, looks, walks, etc., are cause for attack. Value judgments are made daily towards that which is out of the ordinary.

Most gay bashings are under-documented and/or not reported. Many people fear losing their jobs and simply don't report abuse.

In addition, for women, and the rape of lesbian women, many of these cases are viewed as sexual assaults and not hate crimes. Hence, statistics are often misleading and are on the low side. In 2001, the FBI reported that 13% of all crimes against women were due to bias incidents. (Internet, GLBTQ Encyclopedia, 2001)

In 2008, hate crimes were up 2% and numbered 7,783 cases. Seven resulted in murder. Most hate crimes occur as follows:

-
- 1/3 vandalism or destruction of property
- 1/3 threats and intimidation
- 1/3 physical violence
  Harry Kimball 11

Expecting humane treatment for gays seems to be too much to ask. In some regions of our country, our image is one of a subversive subculture which needs eradicating. "Death to faggots!"

It's still "Open Season".

Postscript:

While principal of an elementary school, I had two first grade, twin, girls who thought Daddy was for oral sex. These were not animals, they were children.

We had a child in kindergarten who was plunged out of the shower with a toilet plunger because he didn't get out when told. He had a huge red bruise on his chest. His father said he had a right to discipline his child.

Finally, I had one sixth grade boy who told me he had seen it all and done it all. He had.

I had taken the young man home one day for a "time out" afternoon. As we approached his front door, he said, "Get ready.".

We entered the house to find a young baby alone in a basket atop a curio table. No adults were visible. When the youngster yelled, a head popped up from the couch. It was his mother. Shortly thereafter, another head sprung from the couch. Another young female appeared and was totally nude, as was the mother. The boy looked at me and said, "I told you so." Discretion was not being demonstrated.

I put my arm around him and we exited the house. I didn't know whether to laugh or cry. He was a kid living in an adult world and we were expecting him to function appropriately in school. I took him back to school and he and I walked around campus and picked up trash. He became one of my best buddies and caused me no more problems.

Punishing him was a waste of time and changed no behaviors. Interest in the young man as a person, and a hug once in a while appeared to be a miracle potion. The youngster learned to control his behaviors and recognize better ways to handle his frustrations.

I couldn't change his living situation, but I certainly could understand him and his behaviors.

I have always felt, as educators, it is our obligation to send a child home in the afternoon liking himself better than when he came to school in the morning. The most successful teachers are not always those who have the knowledge, but those who can impart the knowledge in a manner which children feel loved and successful, even amid errors.

"It's difficult to paint a picture of yourself, if you don't know the person residing in you."Unknown 12

Update:

In today's local paper, a small town 17 year old boy allegedly allowed his pit bull to attack a 75 year old man. According to witnesses, as the dog bit, chewed and tore at the man, the boy stood with his arms crossed and did nothing.. Have we lost all compassion? I expect little as a gay man.

Most Americans remember the brutal murder of Matthew Shepard in 1998. He was found beaten and tied to a fence in Wyoming. He died alone.

The most recent incident of "Open Season" on gays

occurred just two days ago as a Rutgers University student jumped off the George Washington bridge and committed suicide. Tyler Clementi was despondent after roommates posted sexual pictures him and another man on You-Tube. The agony this young man felt led him to take his own life, as it did Billy Lucas, 15, Asher Brown, 13, and Seth Walsh, 13. No one deserves to be bullied or humiliated for being who they are, and certainly no young life needs to be tormented to the point of suicide.

Tyler's story is proof that "Open Season" still exists on gay men and women. I pray for the families of the victims and cannot possibly know how they feel. Suicide is a permanent solution to a temporary problem. Sadly, understanding and acceptance of gay birthrights seems to be a permanent social ill. We must continue to endure until our nation becomes educated and realizes we are human beings with feelings, skills and abilities that contribute to society.

As for the young, gay souls reading this book, you may witness change in your life time. Never give up. Those berating you are the ones who need our prayers. Change is coming!

CHAPTER TWENTY-THREE

Homophobia

Definition:

Homophobia is defined as a culturally determined phobia manifesting itself in such antagonistic behaviors as fear, revulsion or contempt for homosexuality. (Internet,www.Wordiq.com) In short, hatred of gays.

Causes of homophobia range from religious dogma, sexist beliefs, repressed desires and/or family procreation. (Internet, Wordiq.com) In many instances, homophobics exist simply because they are not comfortable within themselves. Some studies link homophobia and deep hatred towards homosexuality to repressed homosexual feelings within oneself. (Internet, American Psychiatric Association, 1987)

Violence is often the end result of homophobics acting

out their hatred and aggression. "The vast majority of victims of anti-lesbian/gay violence, possibly more than 80%, never report the incident often due to fear of being "outed"" (Internet, New York Gay and Lesbian Anti-Violence Project Annual Report, 1996)

Homophobia And Religion:

The saddest commentary regarding homophobia is the use of religion to rationalize anti-gay prejudice.

The headline in today's paper read, "Minister reveals struggle with homosexuality". (Herald and Review, August 3, 2010, Associated Press) A Lutheran minister in Minneapolis revealed he is attracted to men. As with many professed homophobics, he has verbally opposed homosexuals leading congregations and/or being ministers. However, he has denied his brithright and stated he has done no wrong because he has not acted on his feelings. He isn't gay.

This minister was one of the most vocal against same-sex marriage and gays serving as clergy. Also, he stated one can believe in God if he fights the urges for same-sex attraction and simply says "no" to it.

In addition, he is attending a Catholic support group called "Courage" which assists people in resisting same-sex urges. It is all said and done in the "name of the Lord".

I'm astounded! This man is in total denial about his

sexuality and equates his ability to have faith in God with heterosexuality. As a gay man, I have acknowledged my birthright and live a decent life within it, but I am still a Christian.

As for attending support groups to deny yourself what you have inherited genetically, I ache inside for the participants who walk away from these groups feeling "cured" and/or are able to deny themselves natural sexual urges. The pain and suffering must be excruciating.

It's time someone stood up and said, "I am gay and I believe in Jesus Christ. I was born gay and know I will not be damned because I am who I am. Jesus died on the cross for all men and women. Sexual orientation is irrelevant." There, I've just said it.

For this writer, God is the only judge, not men who profess to know God's will or who have reconfigured God's words to fit their own beliefs. One can rant, rave and quote THE BIBLE all he/she wants, but it doesn't change the genes a gay man/woman were born with.

What's Right/Wrong with Homophobia:

What's right and what's wrong with homophobia? What's right is perceived. Why? Religious writings and instructional intent have been twisted and interpreted by man for centuries. God's true intentions will never be known by man. When arguments arise regarding sexual orientation, if one quotes THE BIBLE, discussion appears to be over.

What's right is that real men are offended by the mere thought of a gay man. Making fun of the queer takes the suspicion off the offender. If I speak loudly against the "homo", I won't be suspected as being gay.

Hatred of gays is the foundation for Homophobia. Hatred's roots are based upon opinion, perception and religious teachings.

What's wrong with homophobia is what's perceived as being right. Man thinks he knows God's intentions and interprets THE BIBLE as per need. Diverting suspicion regarding sexual orientation enhances machismo and solidifies one's standing in the straight community. Truly what's wrong with homophobia is its foundation, (hatred); learned hatred fostered through verbalized opinions passed on from generation to generation.

Hate:

Hate as we know it is defined as strong dislike or ill will for something, (Webster's NEW WORLD DICTIONARY). One would assume the dislike or ill will would be predicated upon personal experiences and/or opinions formed from education or research.

However, older readers will remember World War II and Hitler's rise to power. Hitler preached hate as he tried to establish an Aryan Race of blue-eyed, blond haired Germans. He rose to power utilizing hate to instill fear in his own people.

Who was hated? Of course, Jews were the main focal point but also included were the mentally ill, physically impaired, and gays. Anyone who wasn't "perfect" was a target.

Younger readers may not know gays were targets in WWII without reference to nationality. A German gay was just as likely to be killed as would be a Jewish gay. In this respect, the Third Reich was indiscriminate.

Hate is an evil concept usually formed from opinion and hearsay.

Within this hatred one finds opinions which have become facts as they traveled from mouth to mouth generation after generation.

Hitler utilized hate and fear to create one of the most lethal killing machines in history. Oddly, it is said Hitler had Jewish heritage.

It is easy to hate. Generalizations, opinions, outrage, and even jokes can set the stage for prejudice and hatred. In addition, hatred seems to be addressed by the proverbial "they". It is very easy to hate when hate has no face.

In reality, hatred is faceless. However, add the face of a father, son, mother, daughter, wife or husband, and hate becomes much more personal and a lot more relevant.

When hate has a face, re-evaluation of one's perceptions usually transpires.

As intelligent readers, we need to limit comments about any race, culture or sexuality to that which can be proven, as opposed to that which we have heard. How do those who are not gay know exactly how gay men and women feel and act? It's a mystery to me how so many people can be so vocal and yet be so misinformed.

Hatred of gays seems to fall under one large umbrella without discrimination of culture, race, character, individual differences, or contributions to society. Hatred is a terminal cancer for all who possess it.

Awareness:

In my formative years and most of my adolescence, I had no knowledge of gayness or any known association with it. Only when I heard my mother express her opinions about my aunt, did I become familiar with sexual orientation prejudice.

Mom's facts were full of opinions, hers. She had never researched sexual orientation nor had she ever personally experienced gay relationships. She was so filled with mythical opinion she hated boy dogs because they did "nasty things". My male dogs are the most loving animals I have. Mom was wrong. As a young gay male, I was a product of my mother's opinions and learned to loathe myself because of it.

Rationale For Inclusion Of This Chapter:

You might be asking yourself, why did I include this chapter in my book? The answer is simple and powerful. I firmly believe my mother was homophobic.

To me, my tapestry wasn't pretty.

Why Mom, why?

"In itself, homosexuality is as limiting as heterosexuality: the ideal should be to be capable of loving a woman or a man; a human being, without feeling fear, restraint, or obligation." Beauvoir 13

CHAPTER TWENTY-FOUR

Personal Homophobic Experiences

Having felt the pain of mother's "sissy" and "pantywaist" comments as a child, I have not been immune from homophobic slurs as an adult.

In this chapter, I will share some of those experiences.

International Reading Convention, Toronto, Canada:

In 1986, Bill and I had gone to Toronto, Canada, for an International Reading Convention. We had just exited the Novotel and were going out for dinner. A group of young teens were seated at an outside café across the street.

As we walked by, I heard one of the young males say, "I smell something gay."

I turned and looked at him and he visually gave me a look such as, "Do you want to do something about it?"

Being 40, I decided maturity would over-ride my emotions and decided to walk on. Inside, I was thinking, "If you smell something gay, it must be your own breath blowing back into your face." Oh, how I wanted to retort. However, now you can understand why I walked on.

This young male was bellowing gay slurs at the top of his lungs in the midst of a crowd. I had to ask myself, "Why?". As with so many males, it could have been to divert attention from himself or direct attention to himself as the "gay basher". Immaturity and poor decision making were probably the real reasons he drew attention to himself.

In any case, even from a distance, the young man seemed threatened by our presence, and we were guests in a foreign country. Who cares about the gay fags, right? Feelings? What feelings could they possible have? Married with children? I doubt it! We were judged by appearance and nothing more.

~

Deep South:

Another significant judgment occurred in Gulf Shores, Alabama. In 1988, Bill and I were returning from a convention in New Orleans and had decided to spend five days at the beach. We checked in at Summer House in Orange Beach, AL, and were really enjoying our stay.

One afternoon we were going out for lunch and had gone down the elevator to the parking lot. On the 10th floor of the condo, a group of six young high school students were lined up along the railing. It was spring break time and the beach was full of young spring breakers.

I started to open up the door to the Cadillac and I heard loud "cat-call" whistle. Then, "Wow, look at that. Hey Honey".

I glanced up and one of the boys waved effeminately. I mentioned it to Bill and we started to get in the car. He stopped and said, "I'm not taking this .....". He got out of the car and headed to the 10th floor.

When Bill excited the elevator, two of the boys were entering.

Bill said bluntly, "Do you have something to say to me?"

One of the boys said, "Um, no sir."

Bill responded, "Someone must have something to say or they wouldn't be smarting off."

The other boy said, "It wasn't us, Sir. It was one of the other guys."

Bill left them with the following comment: "If you have something to say, at least have the guts to say it to our faces and not 10 stories up."

He turned and got back on the elevator. Case closed. We had no more trouble with the boys.

Even the possibility of one being gay seems to stir emotions in young men who know nothing about the subject. Society, upbringing and certainly stereotyping, prompted these young men to make derogatory comments about men they didn't know. Two men, both good looking, neatly dressed, getting into a nice car, certainly they must be gay.

I had to wonder what language these boys had heard at home regarding homosexuality. In addition, I wondered what "facts" they had been given from their parents about sexual orientation . I think I know.

~

Gulf Shores, Alabama:

About the same time as the above incident, I was in a grocery store in Gulf Shores and two men were talking about how things had changed since the first time they visited the island.

One of them said, "Yeah, if it keeps up, we'll be getting more things like that.", and pointed at me.

He didn't think I saw or heard him, but I did. I had just been equated to a "thing". I knew he meant "gay thing".

Again, I was judged by appearance only. Interestingly, I wasn't dressed much differently than the two men.

I walked on feeling as though I had no retort or no rights. Any altercation would have been my fault, no matter who started it. Remember, we were in the Deep South and the Confederate Flag was flying.

What I did conclude was that these adult males were probably demonstrating the same behaviors that the young men were verbalizing from the balcony of the condominium.

In other words, cultural customs and traditions regarding sexual orientation were deeply ingrained in the beliefs of the white male in the South.

~

Decatur, Illinois:

Another event occurred in May of this year as Bill and I sat in a local Decatur restaurant. One of the younger men in the booth behind us made a comment about sex. Another individual commented, "Yeah, like a man who likes another man." The group laughed and it was repeated, "I mean a man who likes men." The finger pointed at me.

I felt the hairs on the back of my neck rise, but sat quietly. After looking at the group closely, one could see education was lacking and certainly for them, their way of life, values and beliefs, would never be changed by anything they read or anything I might have had to add.

Unfortunately, the comments appeared to be addressed to our booth. In these instances, these kinds of incidents confirm my belief that it is still "open season" on gays or people thought to be gay.

~

Professionalism and Prejudice:

Any gay slur hurts, but when it is combined with overt laughter when your name is presented, it leaves indelible marks on your heart.

For 20 years I served as an educational consultant and was widely known in the Midwest. As a consultant, I served as the main speaker at conventions, conferences, and teacher seminars.

Working with professional adults, one would expect a certain level of dignity to prevail in learning atmospheres. However, after experiencing inappropriate adult behaviors, one could understand why children act as they do.

Bill and I had driven to a small farm town east of Kankakee, Illinois, as I was contracted to conduct a three hour Teacher Work Day seminar to a crowd of approximately 90 teachers and teaching assistants.

This community is an all-white, farm community made up of people who moved there in the first place to escape diversity and/or multi-culturalism. It has become known as a "white-flight" community from Kankakee, IL.

Upon arrival, I could tell no one wanted to be there and I had a challenge on my hands. No school personnel offered to assist us unloading the car or setting up our materials. The men all sat on one side of the auditorium and the women on the other.

In addition, it was small school basketball state tournament time and many of the men were leaving for Peoria to attend the tournament. They were counting the minutes until departure and not interested in professional development.

As a presenter, one can usually analyze the atmosphere as friendly or hostile simply by looking at the expression on peoples' faces. This audience looked hostile and I hadn't yet been introduced.

The principal introduced me as "Barry Buttz", instead of my professional name, B.A. Buttz, and the crowd broke into laughter. One of the men was overheard to say, "Looks like a fag." The principal did nothing.

I broke the laughter by saying, "Can you imagine what my parents were thinking when they labeled me with that handle?"

As the afternoon progressed, many of the women spoke openly and loudly during my presentation. It was as though I was an affront to their presence. Once, I stopped talking and looked in the direction of the conversation to no avail. The atmosphere of the session made me question how these professionals treated students.

Most teachers I have worked with would be highly offended and demand respect if students were communicating openly during class time. I expected more and got less. At times, those of us in the profession often ask ourselves why students act as they do. When teachers act inappropriately, how can one expect more of students?

I must admit 99% of the school districts and communities I have had the privilege of addressing, were 100% supportive and professional.

When the session was over, no one really seemed upset. In fact, no one really applauded, said "Thank You" or shared any kind parting gesture. Wow! What a professional contribution I had made to this group.

Bill and I broke down the set and reloaded the car. We couldn't wait to leave. I was scheduled to do a follow-up session a month later, but no one called to remind me. I never went back to that community.

I felt the sting of both name and orientation slurs within one afternoon. As I have written, environment does impact one's self-esteem and orientation. To me, these men were no better than the males we encountered in the Deep South. Uneducated and prejudiced.

~

Laugh At Myself:

As I continued to do seminars, I learned to "get it over with" and began the workshops with some sort of self-degradation and/or joke about my name. Thus, owning my name, "broke the ice" and usually pulled in some of the "nay-sayers". I think younger audiences liked me poking fun at myself more than adults, even though the adults were supposed to be professionals and role models.

The gay or name comments still hurt because I expect adults to be more professional, compassionate and intelligent. I let my work speak for itself and my evaluations were always excellent.

~

Decatur Public Schools:

In 1992, a number of school "directors" were sitting in a conference room at the central school office. We were commenting on our perception in the community as well as within the school district itself.

Our discussion was light and we all laughed as we perceived ourselves as being misunderstood in the general public's eyes. After general comments were shared, one director interjected a personal comment directed at me. The African-American director looked at me and said, "Well the Black community thinks you're gay". He wasn't laughing and his tone of voice was accusatory. I was so taken aback I hardly knew how to respond.

Finally, I said, "And how did you respond?" I received no answer. He had a wonderful opportunity to defend a co-worker and call attention to discrimination which is other than racial. Obviously, he did not take the opportunity. I was disappointed. If anyone should understand the pain of prejudice, it should be an African-American male.

The Teaching Assistant:

A final example of homophobic behaviors occurred while I was a central administrator in the public school district. A library worker came to my office to request a day off. She commented about needing to be with a friend who found out her boyfriend was gay.

She said, "I told my girlfriend not to worry. I work for a guy and he's gay. He's married, got children and is a nice guy."

I gasped for air. I couldn't believe she had no more sensitivity than to blurt out what she believed to be true. No one had ever told her I was gay, but she certainly felt free to express it.

I expressed my displeasure with her comment and asked her to reverse roles with me to see how she would feel. Eventually, she apologized. Ignorance takes many shapes and forms.

~

Do We Ever Know Why?

I share these examples of gay slurs to illustrate no matter what professional level a gay man or woman achieves, he/she is still "fair game" for sexual orientation antagonism.

Respect is learned and earned, but gayness seems to be a fragile topic not worthy of respect. Most people who ridicule loudly, seem to fear gayness in themselves.

Macho men can't be gay, can they? It's like being in a verbal argument on the playground. He/she who yells the loudest, wins. I am always suspect of individuals who protest and preach loudly.

Paraphrasing Harry Truman, "When the guy in the 'Amen corner' begins to shout too loudly, you'd better go home and count the chickens.". Mirrors reflect only what they see.

I think the reasons are too many to count as to why individuals make derogatory comments about the topic of homosexuality.

I retired from consulting after 20 successful years. The money I earned allowed my family to have all of the extras. Vacations, cars for my kids, clothes, etc., were a direct result of my efforts and work ethic.

I never regretted my consulting ventures and

enjoyed working with teachers, teaching assistants, administrators, students and parents.

Fortunately, B.A. Buttz became synonymous with educational excellence. I was recognized as one of the top four presenters in the state. I enjoyed traveling, meeting new people and the positive impact I seemed to have on teaching.

One highlight of my consulting career was in 1998 presenting at a national convention of Title VI directors in Washington, D.C.. The small town kid with the funny name, and unacceptable sexual orientation, had made it.

~

Empathy:

I have felt the pain of verbal abuse and physically been assaulted via the spittle in my face, but my empathetic heart bleeds openly for the individuals/families who have lived through hate-crimes, physical abuse or even death. The hatred and violence is all so needless as gay men and women only want to live their lives in peace.

I am most empathetic with any other minority group regarding prejudice, but feel being gay rates at the top as one of the most hated and misunderstood groups world-wide.

My tapestry is filled with empathy.

People will always remember how you make them feel.

CHAPTER TWENTY-FIVE

The Arizona Experience

What's In A Name:

Bill has one sister who lives in Tucson, Arizona. She is six years younger than Bill and her health is not good. We decided to visit in July of this year, 2010, and made the appropriate travel arrangements.

We drove from Decatur to Bloomington/Normal, IL where the Central Illinois Airport is located. Our travel itinerary was to fly from Bloomington to Dallas and then, Dallas to Tucson. All went well. We arrived in Tucson at 6:30 p.m., which is the same time we left Dallas. Time change!

Mary, Bill's sister, is assisting in raising her two great-grandchildren, ages eight and three, who live with her and

Mary's daughter, Sherry. Mary and Sherry's new home is north of Tucson proper.

The children were a total joy and helped make our visit very special. They had been turned over to their grandmother to raise after their mother found a new friend on the Internet. Say no more!

As we established relationships, both children were very eager for attention and love. At first, we were nameless, but one evening after Bill and I had gone to bed, Mary said the eight year old, a girl, said,

"What is his name?" referring to me.

Mary replied, "Barry".

"What is his last name?", replied the child.

"Buttz", Mary stated.

At this point, the child laughed and laughed and said, "No, I mean, what is his last name for real?"

Mary said, "That is his last name". The child looked perplexed.

She giggled in her hands and said, "No, it can't be that."

You see, as I write this book, my name is still an issue, a very plaguing issue. With a name like mine, I think it's hard for people to take me seriously. The name is a joke. Hence, so is the person and that is why I constantly feel I have to earn respect as well as friendship.

I am happy to say that learning my name didn't seem to impair our friendship nor the relationship we developed. I melted like butter when the youngster cuddled up next to me.

Sadly, I have made my point.

~

The Book And Its Cover:

While in Tucson, we decided to see the sites even though it registered nearly 105 degrees daily. One attraction is Old Tucson, a western movie set and a western movie buff's dream.

The old cow-town is located in the mountains about 30 minutes outside Tucson and is an exact replica of a western town. Many stars such as John Wayne, Gregory Peck, and others, made movies in this setting. I recognized some of the buildings from certain old movies I had seen.

As I spent the morning reliving my childhood, I had the occasion to be standing on the porch of the railroad station waiting for Bill. I noticed two Mexican looking men approaching and thought, I wonder if these two guys work here or if they are they just visiting.

One guy had long hair sticking out of the back of his cowboy hat and was very moderately dressed. I judged this man by his cover.

He noticed my Fighting Illini cap and in perfectly articulated English said, "What part of Illinois are you from"?

I responded, "About three hours south of Chicago.", knowing no one would know Decatur but everyone would know Chicago.

He said, "Oh, where?"

I said, "Decatur".

He replied, "I know where that is. My partner and I have bought a house in Griggsville and are redoing it. I know where Decatur is and I know the "Block I" on your hat is for the Fighting Illini."

I was amazed at the man's diction, speech patterns and vocabulary.

I said, "I know where Griggsville is, it's near Quincy and Jacksonville. I started my teaching career at Illinois School For The Deaf in Jacksonville".

He looked at me and began to use sign language,

He signed and spoke, "Really, I am a registered

interpreter for the deaf and need to visit the school there sometime. How long did you teach there?"

I stated, "One year and then I went back home to start a new program."

He culminated the conversation, "Small world. Enjoy Old Tucson."

"Hey!", I said, "Thanks for commenting on my hat and Illinois."

I was in total shock. I had judged the appearance of this man quite incorrectly as he was one of the most intelligent, educated men I met while in Tucson.

I include these two vignettes to show how I was judged and yet, how I judged others.

With my history, one would think I would know better. I judged another human being to be something he was not. I can only guess how many times judgment was made on me.

Lesson learned!

My tapestry was ashamed.

CHAPTER TWENTY-SIX

If I Could Live My Life Over

Decisions:

In approaching the subject of living my life over, I would have to put several circumstances into perspective and qualify my "what ifs" to fit the situations.

Would I marry heterosexually if I knew for sure I was gay? No. That decision would be easy as I would not be attracted to women. I would not wish to put myself or a potential spouse in a situation of possible emotional despair or divorce.

Even at this point, I would have to qualify my response in terms of awareness to/of my gayness. If my sexuality had been established during adolescence or my teenage years, I would not marry.

However, I would seek to marry within my gay life. Commitment to one person is important to me and living monogamously is essential. I would not want to live a solitary existence as a gay human being.

In this situation, I would not have had the opportunity to have children, nor would I have known the joys of having children, but I would hope my partner and I would agree to pursue parenthood. Gay men and women have so much love to share with children who are parentless or unwanted, it would seem almost irresponsible not to adopt or attempt to assist adoptable children.

Many men live in sexual orientation confusion but do marry. I am an example. However, I have known many gay men who married and never acted on their orientation. For most of us, life is a long road of detours and roadblocks as we seek to know who we are as gay men and women. I was one who lived in denial and did not I accept myself for who I was. That I regret.

Would I repeat my current life if I had known no other? Yes, I would not want to miss the joys of being "Dad" or missing the concept of a traditional family unit. Remember, I said if I had known no other life. I was not exposed to the interactive gay life until 14 years into my marriage.

My children are a source of joy, warmth and purpose for me and I would never give them up. Accordingly, I did not get divorced until they were grown and on their own. For me, they are a source of strength and pride. The

"Empty Nest Syndrome" was more than a reality for me. I had no purpose without my children.

As for my wife, if I truly believed she loved me for myself, I would regret the divorce. In reality, I do not believe I was ever a source of sexual pleasure or romanticism for her. As we slept in separate bedrooms for over 20 years, I could have predicted the outcome of our marriage long before my homosexual encounter.

My divorce should have come as no surprise or shock to my wife as we had not been intimate for over 20 years. Her reaction to our divorce led individuals to believe I just "walked out", but that was the farthest thing from the truth. My departure should have been predictable after 20 years of no more than cohabitation.

Anyone's ego is damaged if he/she feels they are only an enabler who provides physical and financial security for their partner. I have learned at one point my wife and her mother had "stuffed away" $88,000 into a separate banking account of which I had no knowledge.

I was never a partner, lover, companion, confidant or even a friend. I have all of these in Bill. I can't imagine life without him.

Obviously, none of us has a choice regarding sexual orientation, but hypothetically speaking, if I had a choice to be born straight or gay, I would choose to be straight. Why? Society is too rigid, uncompromising and afraid of the gay world. Being gay may never be accepted as a genetic birthright.

I believe today's society is more tolerant than it was 25 years ago, but "accepting", NO! Life would appear to be easier being straight. Maybe one day, gay men and women will not be scourged for something they cannot help and sexual orientation will be irrelevant. Until that time, it isn't easy being gay.

That said, if I could take a magic pill today which would make me straight, I would NOT take it. I have history with gay life and have earned my place in this world.

What would I have changed in my life? My sur name, Buttz, has never been the issue, but had I been able to pick my first name, it would not have been Barry. Remember, a name is one of the choices we do not make for ourselves.

In addition, I would have adjusted my parent's parenting skills, altered gender identity problems, and avoided adopting my mother's fears. In combination, these issues were critical to my sexual identity and the creation of my tapestry.

Most certainly I would change my treatment of my brother. I wanted the title of "big brother", but did nothing to earn it. I can see so much potential in how our childhood could have been. If only I had not felt the stigmas associated with being a big baby or a big sissy, then, maybe I would have believed I was a big brother and could have acted accordingly. I'm sorry, I have to stop for a minute to compose myself.

Panic attacks would be removed from my life completely as well as the anxiety associated with them. Intellectually, I have gained nothing from experiencing panic attacks. I wasted so many youthful years trying to diagnose my mind and body ills when I should have been enjoying youth and the joys associated with it.

However, I did receive some degree of self-discipline and training that helped me cope when I was diagnosed with my first cancer. In retrospect, the cancer made my panic attacks seem trivial.

I would have loved to have had parents who doted over me and thought I was the only child in the world. I would like to have been the proverbial "apple of their eye" and have been loved beyond compare.

Being adored would have manifested itself in being read to before bedtime, holding hands, walking with arms around one another and sharing feelings openly. Any emotional gesture that they cared for or loved me would have sufficed.

Changing my relationship with my parents would have included warm greetings, good-night and good-bye kisses, and I would have wanted to feel they enjoyed spending time with me. They didn't.

In addition, I can only dream how it might have been had they taken interest in me as a person. For example, asking me how my day went or what I did at school or even how I felt about something. They never asked me what made me happy or sad. Most of all, I would have loved to have been friends with my parents.

Finally, the ultimate gift my parents could have given me would have been respect. Never was I asked to comment or provide feedback on family matters. I never served as a consultant for my own parents. Yes, these are some of the things I would have changed if I had my life to live over. Most children are granted these things in a natural progression of parent-child relationships. I was an island unto myself.

I can only share my experiences within a heterosexual marriage and would not recommend one marry or not marry the opposite sex. It's a choice predicated upon so many variables one cannot speak for others and their circumstances. "Cookie cutter" marriages don't exist in the straight world and it takes maturity from both partners to make any marriage work, even gay ones, (which don't legally exist).

Each of us is an individual who has a story which could rival or surpass mine. We must live with the choices we make and absorb any guilt associated with the consequences of poor choices or decisions. I certainly absorbed more than my share of guilt and self-hatred.

My sincere belief and recommendation would be to live one's life with decency and respect in either world. That said, it would be difficult to define both decency and respect for other individuals, as we all have differing meanings for the two words.

I have respect for men and women who identify their sexuality early in life and set goals and directions accordingly. Fighting one's orientation, as I did, can create difficult legal situations and greater alienations within family and employment relationships.

I fought gayness for years because my tapestry was full of religious expectations, environmental roadblocks and genetic predispositions. These events took a toll on me and detoured my sexual identity until later in life. I would have rather known early in life so I could have begun to adjust, establish goals and set a clear path for my gay future. As it was, I lived in a world of "what ifs" and sexual denial.

The point is, I can't relive my life, and I have adjusted and accepted my gay birthright. I am "OK" with it now and can't change my history anyway. I am proud of the man, person and father I have become.

If readers find themselves in my story, maybe they can direct and guide themselves to avoid the pitfalls I addressed along the way. In the end, what matters most is the quality of person we become, not our sexual orientation.

With age should come wisdom. Life presents many opportunities for regrets. It is best to focus on tomorrows and leave regrets in the past.

My tapestry is woven tightly.

In life, we are entitled to nothing.

Chapter Twenty-Seven

Love, Marriage and Divorce

History:

With the divorce rate somewhere between 50% and 60%, it is hard for me to imagine heterosexuals standing before God verbalizing vows which they probably will not keep.

I have to examine the institution of marriage and its over-all history to intellectually understand the impact of marriage in our society today.

In Biblical times, multiple wives were not uncommon. THE HOLY BIBLE at no time admonishes the practice of multiple wives. Hence, as time and history progressed, man or the Church, must have decided marriage, in its purest form, was monogamous. In those times, a woman's role was one of complete subservience to the man. At times, women were sold or traded.

Over the ages and after many religious revolutions, men changed church doctrine and established the concept of monogamy. As religious freedoms grew, so did Biblical interpretations.

As time passed and monogamy became the norm, the institution of marriage was illustrated a working man and his wife, the home-maker.

In rural areas in the 1800's, not only did families utilize subsistence farming, most marriages were subsistence in nature. Procreation was critical to the longevity of the farm. Multiple children were the norm as they worked on the farm, earned their keep and often married and built homes on family farm land. The whole process was self-perpetuating. During these times, women were no longer traded or sold.

Within urban areas in the 1900's, women seldom worked outside the home and men were known as "bread winners". The woman's job was to have children, provide meals, clean house and sexually gratify her husband. Notice, I did not mention being subservient to her husband.

Through time, marriage vows have not changed. If one actually listens to marriage vows, one can still hear the implications of women being subservient to men. My question is, have wedding vows become antiquated and/ or should they be changed?

Through the 1930's - 1960's, divorce was not easy to obtain and was only granted as a last resort. Judges usually did not rule on divorce immediately and gave couples a six months reconciliation period. If reconciliation failed, in most cases, the divorce was granted.

Within religious doctrine, adultery, which led to divorce, was viewed as an ultimate sin. Divorce in itself was a sign of religious and social failure. Divorced men and women were looked upon as being remiss in some aspect of the marriage process. Obviously, they must have done something wrong or been difficult to live with. These individuals were often perceived as "damaged goods" and not marrying material.

Unwed, teenage pregnancies brought familial scorn and girls often disappeared for nine months only to reappear as though nothing had happened. Seldom did pregnant female teenagers marry. Abortion was never discussed and was viewed as controversially as it is today.

The institution of marriage has changed over the centuries, but the vows and expectations have not. Are we asking too much of human beings to be able to keep their vows? Maybe it is much simpler.

Is it possible that the casualness which permeates sex in our society has pierced the institution of marriage?

Could it be that immediate gratification which consumes our society is another culprit? Or, is it simply that man has become so corrupt vows don't matter? As a generalization, whatever the reasons, marriage does not mean what it used to mean. It's more like a social union rather than a union of souls.

~

Vows:

It appears most mortals don't have the capacity to adhere to marital vows as they stand before God on their wedding day. The vows state, "'til death do us part".

So many variables exist in regards to marriage it appears impossible to make " 'til death do us part" statements before God knowing that one can't keep them. I guess we should give credit for "intent" or state, "at this moment in time, I do".

Variables such as age, maturity, education, religious commitment, common interests, emotional stability, children, money, etc., impact the longevity of marriage.

Divorce:

The person one marries is never the person one divorces. People change, times change and love changes. Couples who change together, might make it to a Golden Anniversary.

Divorce doesn't have to be a horrendous event, but

most of the time it is. Betrayal, broken trust, revenge, money, and child custody are usually the seeds for a bitter divorce.

Divorce can often be predicted if marital goals were never discussed or agreed upon between partners. If both partners needed and wanted something different in the marriage and one, or both, of the partners sought satisfaction elsewhere, divorce usually followed. Figuratively speaking, sex is the glue that holds most marriages together, but at the same time, is one aspect which can destroy them too.

Change and maturation are also components of divorce. If one partner changes and grows, but the other doesn't, trouble usually abounds. Couples who grow and mature together have a greater chance of longevity than do individuals who grow personally and professionally outside the marriage unit.

Education can also be a point of marital contention. If both the man and woman have college degrees and are professionals, things are programmed for success. Success may not always happen, but the foundation exists. Achieving and celebrating goals together feed the foundation. Growing together is the key.

Even though society is moving in this direction, marriage is most difficult if the wife is a degreed professional and the husband is a laborer. Male ego and immaturity seem to "get in the way". Jealousy, regret and envy can permeate the marriage. The key components for success here are maturation and character.

Society seems to most readily accept the educated, professional male whose wife is a homemaker. Why? I don't know. If I were a woman in this situation, I would want a degree and a profession of my own. Today, a woman doesn't need a man to be financially successful.

However, in today's society, it's not uncommon for both partners to have degrees and separate professions.

Money issues are another cause of bitter, emotional divorces. One or both partners seem to want to make the other person pay. If emotional satisfaction isn't provided in the divorce process, then the partner "must pay" somehow, and in this case, I mean financially.

Obviously money does little to repair emotional damage, but one or both partners seem to get some satisfaction if their partner loses money or has to pay for their freedom. Sad, isn't it.

My personal beliefs about divorce have little to do with the legal system. To me, one is really divorced the day he/she is emotionally estranged from his/her spouse. The legal process is productive for lawyers, but often both spouses lose via a process man has created to end marriage.

Unlike divorcing in the past, today it is relatively easy to receive a divorce. Reconciliation is rare and most people are just ready to move on, regardless of the consequences. Who wins? The lawyers.

Today, marriage is experienced, but the rules and expectations are different than they used to be. In fact, the reasons people marry today are totally different than they were years ago. Why? People don't seem to commit to one another for the right reasons. Immediate gratification supercedes any marital vows and "working it out" or "making it last" are foreign to many relationships.

Societal Paralysis:

In regards to marriage, it is interesting how our society emotionally paralyzes young woman early in adolescence. How? The expectation to be a bride is ingrained in girls as early as the formative years. Specifically, every little girl will have her day walking down the aisle. Being a bride seems to be every mother's dream for their daughter. "Barbie for a day" becomes a mythical expectation, but it doesn't always happen.

Emotionally, we paralyze young women and ingrain a sense of wonderment about the mythical wedding. Not all men and women want or need to be married. Yet, young girls are made to feel it is their destiny. In fact, I firmly believe society sets marriage as a goal for all women and thus, if it doesn't happen, can make them feel like failures.

In so many instances, the marriage day is about the mother, and not about the daughter. I understand many mothers feel left out emotionally and feel as though they are losing their baby, but it's time to stop the jaded expectations and face reality. Not everyone will marry.

Sadly, not all brides are beautiful and not all weddings go well, but life goes on. The wedding day is just that, a day. It's what occurs after the wedding day that is most important for longevity. It appears easy to get married but difficult to stay that way.

I have known of situations where the wedding was literally over as soon as the bride and groom said, "I do."...and I don't mean the wedding ceremony.

Being Single In A Couple's World:

If marital expectations are placed on children at an early age, I often wonder what men and women feel about themselves if they never marry. Sitting in church, I often try to analyze how single people feel when the sermon is addressed only to married couples, or on Mother's Day, sweetness and charms are thickly spread amid a mixed congregation of married, divorced or single women/men.

Are the individuals who never marry failures? Have they contributed nothing in life? Why is marriage an expectation for all people? Is marriage the only reason we are here on Earth? Does one have no purpose in life if he/she is not married? What are the reasons individuals don't marry? If you don't find a person to marry, does that mean you are unacceptable in society or that something is wrong with you? Are we to pity the person who never marries?

Think about the answers to these questions. If you aren't married, have you ever felt as though you lived in a society that is totally geared for couples? If you are married, how would you feel if the above questions applied to you if you hadn't married? Better yet, what if you are gay?

Imagine yourself as a gay person trying to find your niche in and among a world so filled with heterosexual "hysteria" regarding marriage and divorce. Gays don't have the legal right to be a marriage or divorce statistic. I'm laughing to myself. I guess we are statistics unto ourselves.

As a father, I never thought I would tell my children to live with a partner to see if the two of them were compatible before marrying. As things are in our society today, I wouldn't recommend anything else. The legal and financial ramifications of marrying and divorcing are too serious to take vows most humans can't keep.

Times have changed so much a woman doesn't need a man for subsistence living or need to stay at home as a home-maker. In fact, most married women can't stay at home as two incomes are required for basic life.

Twenty-First Century Marriage:

Marriage has a new meaning and a new dimension in the 21st Century, yet the same vows seem to apply to all people in all circumstances.

I have witnessed how members of some churches feel if they are forced to divorce. Communion is denied and congregation members often shun the individuals. They are expected not to marry again. Often, men/women who are no longer "in love" with their partners stay with their spouses because of religious expectations. To me, divorce has already occurred, just not legally. Everyone seems to lose.

The difference in loving someone and being "in love" dictates longevity. Mutual or reciprocated love is an emotion which inspires feelings between two people, but being "in love" perpetuates the marital and sexual union of the couple. Once the feeling of being "in love" is gone, the marriage has become companionship.

Historically, marriage as we know it is between a man and a woman. Thus far, statistics indicate the heterosexual institution of marriage isn't faring too well and repercussions abound.

What is the impact of divorce in our society today? As a retired educator, I have witnessed the impact of broken marriages. Single parents, inactive fathers, "link" cards, confused children, emotionally deprived children, and openly defiant children are the norm.

It is difficult to teach a child who has no idea where he/she belongs. For these children, accountability and responsibility are lost and the broken marriage syndrome is perpetuated. Children raising children never seems to work.

What is my point and why did I include this chapter in my book? Most criticism and resistance to gay marriage is resonated from members of the heterosexual groups just described, those who can't fulfill their marital obligations or keep their wedding vows.

In addition, the radical far right, which seems to have all the answers, is most vocal regarding marriage as the union of a man and a woman. They would deny gay men and women the right to be married, adopt children and have a chance at the same vows as heterosexuals.

Over the years, historians, religious authors and the church have defined and redefined the institution of marriage to meet their own values and needs. What appears to be failing in the heterosexual world is flatly denied to the gay world.

Values, beliefs, and moral decency flood religious and political plains with a hierarchy of admonishments for gay marriage. Politicians utilize anti-gay marriage platforms to ensure re-election amid rhetoric they don't understand or really believe. Yet, many politicians are having affairs on the side.

Gay marriage in no way infringes on the right of men and women to be married. In addition, gay marriage is no threat to the sanctity of marriage between a man and a woman. After all, gay men and women came from heterosexual unions. We didn't create ourselves.

At this point, I close my ears to the arguments that THE HOLY BIBLE states emphatically that marriage is between a man and a woman...or should it be "women", as it was in Biblical times? Religious wars have been fought for years regarding man's interpretation of THE HOLY BIBLE. Man has created God's church to be what he, (man), wants it to be.

Why do some states allow Civil Unions for gays but not gay marriage? In truth, the real issues against gay marriage aren't religion or gender, they're politics and money. Corporate greed and political control will continue to defeat legalized gay marriage as no business wants to recognize a gay partner in insurance policies, benefits and/or as beneficiaries. We're talking money, not political correctness.

Postscript:

After all marriage issues are debated, is our society better or worse regarding the break-down of the historical family unit and immediate issuance of divorce?

Sadly, in reference to marriage in the 21st Century; "it is what it is!"

Chapter Twenty-Eight

The Perfect Couple

One World Apart:

As said, marriage in the 21st Century is what it is, but in the 1930's, as described in the previous chapter, things were different. Mom and Dad seemed destined to be united in marriage. As reported, Dad's homelife was an abomination and he needed a "way out". Mom was a conduit and provided the only emotional sanctuary Dad had ever known. She accepted Dad as he was and didn't try to change him. She only wanted to understand him and meet his needs. She loved him without conditions.

Mom, on the other hand, came from a strong Polish-German family. John Galamback and Matilda Kashefska, were both Polish/German, and devote Missouri Synod Lutherans. Mom had one older brother and an older sister. Compared to my father's life, Mom's life was like the television series, "Life With Father". Predictable and stable.

My grandfather, Mom's dad, was a strong disciplinarian and had a tremendous work ethic. He worked in the 17 Building at Staley's for nearly 40 years and cared for a staples garden at home. Grandma was the consumate house keeper and one of the best cooks I ever knew. Dad's mom seldom cooked and was not good at it. Grandma Buttz lived in a survival mode most of the time.

Both of Mom's siblings, Karl and Leona, were strong-willed individuals and dominated most of what Mom did. My Uncle Karl was just like my grandfather and had high expectations for children's behaviors. He had five children of his own and was the patriarch of the family.

My Aunt Leona had one daughter, Nancy, my cousin, whom I loved dearly. Aunt Leona was as strong willed as Uncle Karl and her spouse was a meek little man who said little. Nancy adored her father and never recovered after his death. Why? The day Nancy's father died, she gave birth to her first son. She was not able to attend the funeral and resented not only the child's birth, but the child. Nancy passed away of complications of cancer and diabetes in 1997.

As genetics would have it, both of Mom's siblings became diabetic in their teenage years and Mom eventually succumbed as an adult. On Mom's side of the family, Grandma, Uncle Karl, Aunt Leona, Nancy and Mom, were all diabetic. Each died of complications associated with Diabetes and/or Diabetes created organ malfunctions.

I only remember one time the Buttz-Galamback families shared a Christmas dinner at my Grandma Buttz's home. Thanksgivng and Christmas family rituals were mainly held at my parent's home on 22nd Place. In her younger years, Mom did make a small effort to bring the two families together. No one else did, and thus, she inherited the right to try.

Two family cultures could not have been more different than my mother and dad's families. These cultural differences provided the emotional reasons for Mom and Dad's union.

Each of the two households provided the need for marriage. One, an escape, and the other, the conduit for that escape. Destiny provided the match. It was the perfect union.

~

Tying The Knot:

Dad's desperation to get out of his parent's house was displayed on July 8, 1939, when he and Mom eloped. They drove with another couple to Festus, Missouri, and were married.

Mom didn't need the big church wedding, nor could her parents afford it, and all she really wanted was Dad. They often referenced their marriage and how they plotted and planned the event. None of the frivolities meant anything to Mom and Dad didn't care about formalities. He just wanted a life of his own with my mother.

Around our house, July 8th, their wedding anniversary, was bigger than Christmas. Mom and Dad sponsored a big party and invited friends and relatives. Toasts were made to "Helen and Ralph", as the happy couple. To me, it appeared they were remarried annually. Dad's proudest moments were on his anniversary. He functioned like a new groom each year and was totally devoted to Mom.

Mom and Dad celebrated their 50th wedding anniversary in 1991, six years before Dad died. As a family, we rented a limousine for them to be taken to the Elks Club where we had a monumental celebration. I'm not sure either one of them saw any other person that evening even though we had approximately 100 guests.

I think my parents were sexually active until they died. They didn't know it, but I knew all of their routines before they made "Whoopie". Whenever I heard Dad getting the ice cube tray out of the refrigerator after I had gone to bed, I knew what would follow. They always had a drink before the big event. For them, sex was the glue that held the marriage together.

Not only did Mom and Dad love one another, they remained in love throughout their marriage. I firmly believe they were never just partners or companions.

No matter what my feelings were/are about how my parents raised or treated me, one has to give them credit for loving one another and personifying the true definition of marriage. They lived it.

The stage was set and my life was in the making. I was born five years later and was a planned child. One time Mom told me I was the "planned" child and my brother was the "accident", as it used to be referred to. If so, Mick was the best accident they ever had. I often wondered if guilt spawned Mom's treatment differences for her two boys. She was a very guilt laden person.

I think my mother's comments regarding planned and unplanned children were totally inappropriate. I have no idea why she mentioned it to me. I don't think my brother was ever told he was an accident.

~

My Mother:

I have developed my mother's character throughout this book, but I did want to mention some additional things I vividly remember. I'll do my best not to repeat anything I have already mentioned.

First, it is easy to see why Mom and Dad were totally devoted to one another. Dad lived only for her and only to make her happy. She was his savior and he knew it.

Mom wanted and needed Dad's attention and I was probably a threat for his time and his love. She worried needlessly, as he really never saw me as one who needed love and attention. I was a child and he didn't know how to meet a child's needs. Meet Mom's needs, yes, but mine, no.

Mom's insecurities always surfaced when Dad was gone. I watched her scramble to solve problems, panic if something went wrong with the house or household appliances, and cry instantly if she couldn't resolve issues without him.

My brother and I learned to "disappear" when Mom got in one of those moods or when we saw her becoming angry. I think she resented Dad's being gone, but his work absence was how he made our living, and she wasn't about to go to work. Being fair, most women didn't work outside the home in the 1940's.

What did Mom do all day? I remember so many visits by the Omar Man, the Avon Lady, Fuller Brush Man and the milk man. All of these services came to the home and Mom eagerly greeted all of them. She sponsored coffee "klatches", (gatherings), regularly and spent hours on the telephone. Little Barry personally knew all of the neighbor ladies.

She had special days for special events. Monday and Tuesday were wash days, Wednesday was baking day, Thursday was clean house day and Friday was "eat out" night. The schedule became a ritual.

Mom wasn't the best cook in the world, but we survived. We had a set menu and seldom broke it. Hamburgers, pork chops, (with fried apples), spaghetti, (prepared in the pressure cooker), bacon and eggs, (breakfast for dinner), and pizza culminated our menu. We never had chicken or pot roast during the week. Those items were "Sunday Only" dinner items. I looked forward to our Sunday meals.

As far as our personal care, bath night was on Saturdays. Yes, we took a bath once a week and shared the water. My brother and I were first, Mom was second and Dad lathered up last. To be honest, most homes in the '40's performed bathing rituals this way. Today, I think it would be a form of child abuse.

Parent-child interaction was always lacking in our home. I was never read to not even at bedtime. As a family, we never played board games, but I do remember some card games being played. Mom and Dad had four sets of friends who played poker on Friday nights. They rotated locations and kids were allowed only if their parents hosted the event. I was not allowed to watch.

During the times that Mom entertained, I was to be as any other child in those days, seen but not heard. Thank God for an imagination and my own personal creativity. However, most of the time I was just waiting for Dad to come home and make everything alright.

I will go to my grave never understanding my mother. I

think I understood her motivations, but only in regards to my father. It is hard for me to realize how one person can totally devote themselves to another and cast all others aside. I made sure I did not repeat this treatment in the raising of my own children.

I hear so many women talk about their children and how they could do without their husband, but not their kids. That statement was not true for my mother. She could NOT do without her husband but the kids could fend for themselves. That's how I was raised, fending for myself. I still do to this day.

I know the best marriages balance love for spouses and children, and each love is of a different kind. To me, these marriages work. Balance seems to be the correct word for everything in life, including sex.

I needed to include this chapter in my book because I had to analyze content before I wrote it. I understand why both my parents needed and wanted one another, but I'll never come to grips with the fact that I was disposable. Truly, Mom and Dad were never candidates for divorce.

It was 2:00 a.m., February 28, 2004, when I received a phone call from Fair Havens Nursing Home telling me that Mom had passed. I was asked if I wanted them to wait to call the coroner so I could drive out and see her. I told them no. I had already said my good-byes.

Six months prior to Mom's passing, Bill and I had gone to the nursing home to see Mom one Friday afternoon.

She was seated in the dining hall at a table with five other women. When we approached, all of the other women spoke and said hello. Mom did not.

After a moment or two, I said, "Hi Mom".

She looked at me and said, "Who are you?".

Bill stepped in and said, "Helen, this is your oldest son, Barry.".

She gave me a blank stare and looked right through me. Mom had no idea who I was. At that moment, Mom, as I had known her, was dead to me.

I made it through Mom's lunch and headed for the car. I ran. I sat in the car and sobbed for twenty minutes. I was crying, hyper-ventilating, and angry all at the same time. When Bill got to the car, he just put his arms around me and held me tightly. He knew and felt my pain. Mom died and didn't even know who I was. For me, it was the culmination of a life long struggle to be recognized. I lost the struggle.

When Mom passed away, we had a private, grave-side service with no visitation. She was cremated, by choice, and that relieved me of making the decision. I could not put myself through the emotional events of a traditional funeral. I just didn't feel the emotion I should have felt.

As Grandparents:

If I had to grade my parents in regards to their parenting skills, they earned a grade of "C-" or below. In regards to being grandparents, they most certainly earned an "F".

The perfect couple socialized well and were known as festive, fun-loving people. Four sets of friends played golf, ate together, traveled together and played cards together. Nothing stood in the way of their social interactions, neither their children nor their grandchildren.

My children were never invited to stay the night at Grandma and Grandpa's, nor were they ever taken on daily outings. Mom and Dad never bought them "happy gifts" or something special "just because".

For birthdays and Christmas, the ultimate sum of $25.00 was given and nothing more. As one of two sons, I got $50.00.

Once, I do remember my niece, Jill, and my daughter, Jennifer, spending the night at Mom and Dad's. My son never spent the night, nor was he asked. Point: As adolescent children, my brother and I were not allowed to sit on the furniture.

Most parents invite their children and grandchildren for dinner on a regular basis. That didn't happen! If dinner was provided, my wife and I provided it. Mom rarely had dinner for "family" and resented having to have Thanksgiving or Christmas dinners. Most of the time we had holiday dinners or my brother and sister-in-law provided special meals for them.

Mom and Dad never stopped by "just to see" the kids or take them for ice cream. They did visit every Sunday night for coffee. If the kids were present, fine; if not, it didn't seem to matter.

I am not sure why I expected them to be different with their grandchildren than they were with their own boys, but I did. Doting grandparents they were not, but doting parents were never revealed either.

I would often tell Mom and Dad their friends were fickle. If one of them, meaning Mom or Dad, died, the friends would socially drop them in a minute. That happened.

After Dad died, Mom was dropped and rarely invited to any social gathering. In fact, only one woman, out of the three, ever visited her in the nursing home. None of the men ever came.

I was angry because in my childhood, Mom always preached, "family, family, family". Yet, I never saw any evidence of it or remember being included when I had a family of my own. I hated their friends and thought they were pathetic excuses for anything other than social event "chums". They proved me right.

As I look back, I truly don't think my parents knew what to do with my brother or myself, and little grandkids presented an even greater challenge to them. They had no idea what to do with them and Mom certainly didn't want to relive her life as a young mother.

As my children grew older and participated in show choir and sporting events, Mom and Dad did attend. They enjoyed the events and shared memories with the kids. I was grateful for their interest and participation.

When Dad died, my son, Jason, took it personally and reacted quite emotionally at the "wake". His mother tried to console him and he broke away from her and lashed out verbally and physically. He loved his grandfather and it hurt to lose him. I was very moved to see the emotion.

Personally, I didn't cry until one year later when I was alone in a motel room the night before a professional seminar. I was watching the movie, "Davey Crockett", and realized how life had changed so much from those times, especially political life. Then, it hit me, I didn't have a dad any more. As a 54 year old man, I cried myself to sleep. The innocent world of Davey Crockett was gone, and so was my dad.

The perfect couple loved and adored one another. I credit them for that, but no room was left for anyone else in their hearts. I guess that's how it's supposed to be between married couples, right?

Destiny:

I often wonder if I could have done anything to avoid my destiny as a gay man. Would a name change have made a difference? Would doting, caring parents have made me a different person? Could I have been able to over-come my genetics? Answer? I doubt it!

My tapestry was predestined. I only added shape and color.

1946, I represented no competition for my dad's attention.

Chapter Twenty-Nine

My Final Thoughts

Being Gay Isn't Easy:

My intentions have been to show how circumstances evolve in the making of a gay man. For me, a tapestry, which at times, unraveled to the point of destruction.

According to the ultra-religious conservative right, I was born to be damned. According to their beliefs, most assuredly, I will be. However, one can see from my story, a choice was made for me at the moment of conception. A choice I didn't make.

Gay genetics were present in me at birth and my environment only enhanced the chances of the consummation of a gay life style. I despise the term "life style" as it implies that all gays live the same way.

Genetically, I was born gay. However, it is often events and environment which set a gay tapestry into motion and dictate its outcome. As society perceives gay men, Bill and I are not typical. We don't frequent gay bars, don't wear boas, don't march in parades, don't go to the bath houses and certainly don't live an open life style. Believe it or not, typical gay men aren't characterized in movies. Finding and living with Bill ended years of frustration for me.

In fact, as an individual, I have only known and been with two men sexually. With this admission, I am a novice when it comes to gay relationships. Most of my gay interactions have been fanaticized or voyaged.

I vacillated in emotional desperation throughout my life as I tried to coordinate and complement my religious upbringing, male expectations and sexual orientation.

I have tried to forgive my parents for naming me Barry Buttz and I will never understand why they did. However, they were not the ones degrading my name thru the years. They simply set the stage.

One can clearly see from my story a combination of wrong name, sexual orientation and environment, can be a destructive combination. I wonder if my childhood would have been different had I been named Major, Rhett, Colt, Kingston, or some other name which demands respect. I would have loved to have given it a try, but I can't go back. My only choice is what I do with my name now. As a professional, I think I have done very well. Emotionally, I have failed miserably.

When I started this book, I held overt contempt for my mother and her parenting philosophies. I have released the contempt. Why? She, too, was a product of her environment and was probably parented with the same methodologies she used to parent me. Plus, I needed to forgive her for myself. Forgiveness always appears to be for self rather than the other person.

Again, I admit I have many of my mother's character traits. I am possessive with Bill as she was with Dad. However, another reason I am so possessive is that in my childhood, if a friend came to play and broke one of my toys, I didn't get another one. I soon learned to hide my toys from childhood guests. Yes, fear of loss is learned.

Childhood was to have been a time of growth and development both mentally and physically. I think I grew and persevered in spite of it all.

I hold no ill will against my father. I loved him so much and will never really know if he didn't want to kiss his four year old son good-night or if that was my mother's method of controlling who received my father's love.

At age 65, one would think I should be able recognize the incident as only one small part of my life, but it still affects me. It is difficult for me to watch or see any affection being displayed by a father and son. I wish it were I.

I loved my dad and never got to show it or tell him, until he was dead. I only wish I knew if he loved me. I know it is in my best interest to forget the "good night kiss" incident and I have learned from it. The experience helped me to be a better dad to my children. I am probably a statistical anomaly in that I did not repeat history.

Dad and I are closer in death than we were in life. I am never too far from him in my mind and dream about him almost nightly. Maybe it's his way of taking care of me now, without Mom.

Life is harder if we don't let go of the past, and letting go is a hard lesson. Holding on to the past keeps one from moving forward. Emotionally, I have been stuck in time for 60 years. I have had many detours to finding love as a result of my refusing to let go of the past. While I loved and needed men, I didn't trust them. As for women, walls always existed and I couldn't seem to find a way through them, over them or around them.

"When I let go of what I am, I become what I might be." Lao Tzu 14

~

Know Thyself:

Living the life, I know being gay is genetic, but living freely and openly within a society which discriminates against and hates that which it does not understand, can be devastating. Living freely and openly in today's world can have serious consequences.

Sadly, consequences in youth appear to be taunting, bullying and teasing, but as one grows older, physical violence is more prevalent. As older adults, the consequences seem to be less harsh and more judgmental. People gossip, but with age comes maturity and the taunting, bullying and teasing don't have the same emotional impacts.

For you, the reader, if you are struggling with your orientation, recognize you are not alone. Others have lived and are living your life.

My life should illustrate living the life can be rewarding and fulfilling. Intelligence and success are not dictated by sexual orientation.

As a gay male, I have been able to overcome my childhood in many ways. Being a teacher, principal and central administrator required I be insightful, analytic and be able to communicate. As the Director of Schools for Instruction, I was placed in charge of all new teacher orientation sessions and had to have the ability to draw people into the profession by marketing teaching and our district.

I seem to have been able to communicate well and make friends easily. For twenty years I functioned as a professional development seminar presenter and traveled around our country assisting teachers and administrators with discipline, curriculum development and classroom management, etc. Feedback from those instructional sessions gave me tangible proof I was a contributing member of the profession and society.

I have become an excellent judge of character and possess powerful intuitions regarding situations and people. My early training gave me insight into authentic people and an ability to recognize phonies.

I worked five years in a human resources capacity coordinating staffing in our school district. Staffing involves the hiring as well as the release and retention of staff; A job which directly affects people and their lives. I was empathetic in this area due to my past experiences and acquired sensitivity, understanding and empathy for people who needed a chance.

Side Story:

As a quick side-story, while I was working at the central office of our school district, one of the "hecklers" from my high school came in to see me. He was one of the "Bare-Butt" violators and was also the catcher on the state baseball team. I had known the man since elementary school and he was, indeed, a true source of anxiety for me.

I asked him what he needed and he said, "Well, Buttz, I know in the past I did some pretty cruel things to you. But, man, I'm down and need a job and I was hoping you would put in a good word for me. I really need work and thought you could help me. You've made it man. You've made it."

I listened and knew why the man was sitting before me. He was an alcoholic and couldn't hold a job. Needless to say, with a clear conscience, I could not recommend him for a job. It wasn't our past, it was his presence that created the issue. He had alcohol on his breath during our discussion.

From what I know, about our hometown, state championship baseball team, 50% have done well personally and professionally. The other 50% had their fifteen minutes of fame on the diamond in high school.

My multi-cultural background has always been an asset. Diversity is a strength and I utilized my strength to assist children who needed to be loved. I knew what it was to be a "minority".

Postscript:

The man who visited my office died two years ago. He died a penniless, pitiful alcoholic. He resided in his parents' residence and never had another home of his own. His fame had come 48 years earlier and no own would have predicted his outcome. It's funny how high school heroes disappear and the "steady-eddies" endure.

~

B.A. Buttz

Analogy:

Sometimes educators expect too much of children. As an example, for some school children, subjects and verbs might not be the most important part of their day. Survival might be. Self-worth and being valued as a human being are critical. I was one of those children who needed acceptance and love. For those students who needed it, I gave them what I never had, interest, support and validation. I recognized myself in so many children and it was a way for me to undo my personal history.

Because you are gay, never feel your life won't be productive. You can and will find peace. Remember, being gay isn't the problem; it's people's response to your being gay that is the issue. They have the problem, not you. The key to peace in your life is your response to your authentic self. Our authentic self is our birthright. Be true to that self and you will find peace. Most of all, you must love yourself, accept yourself and believe yourself worthy.

My partner of 25 years, Bill, on right

"I am the love that dare not speak its name."
Lord Alfred Douglas 15

CHAPTER THIRTY

Conclusion

"Education is the vaccine for violence."
Edward James Olmos [16]

Avoid Being A Statistic:

As my story concludes, my life as a gay man does not. I have written this book as an educational tool for all men and women seeking internal peace, and to assist young gay men and women with their birthrights in order to avoid being one of the following statistics:

Gay, lesbian or bisexual are five times more likely to miss school because of feeling unsafe and 28% are forced to drop out. (National Gay and Lesbian Task Force, 1984

Gay and lesbian youth are four times higher risk for

suicide than their straight peers. (U.S. Department of Health and Human Services, 1989

- 83% of adolescent lesbians use alcohol, 56% other drugs and
- 11% use crack cocaine. (Dreamworld.org)
- 42% of adolescent gay and lesbians have suffered physical
- attacks, (Oystergsa/gas_statistics.html)
- 97% of public high school students report hearing homophobic remarks from peers. (Dreamworld.org)
- 42% of homeless youth identify as lesbian, gay or bisexual.

(Orion Center, Street Youth Survey, 1986)

I tremble when I think of all of the potential, youthful minds who have lived lives of pure hell due to their birthrights and society's reaction to them as sub-human individuals. Tyler Clementi will never get the chance to become the accomplished violinist he was projected to become The above statistics are tapestry components of the lives they represent.

In reality, homophobia is the cause of these problems, not being homosexual.

Homophobics don't want to be educated and refrain from it. Too many of us in the gay community assume responsibility for homophobic behaviors and we shouldn't. Homophobes should be held responsible for their actions and behaviors.

During my youth, statistics such as those above weren't tabulated because the Internet, computers and other media didn't exist. No demand existed for such data and sexual orientation was not a topic for dialogue.

Today's gay youth have a distinct advantage with the Internet, web sites and statistical analysis, but statistics don't assist one in accepting gayness and/or living the life.

I have wrestled with heterosexuality, homosexuality and bisexuality and consider the experiences part of a learning curve most individuals never have.

I have learned how I live my life is more important than any label I, or anyone else, might put on it. Character, class and dignity can be displayed in any life and sadly, all three characteristics seem to have been lost, or greatly reduced, in the American culture.

As a man, I am kind, caring and unusually giving. As mentioned, my partner and I rescue dogs and at the present time, have seven wonderful four-pawed partners. At long last, I have seven "Brownies" to fill the loss of one small dog so many years ago. I will never forget.

My tapestry will never be complete.

~

Born To Be Damned! Never!:

As educators, Bill and I have both dedicated our lives to children and believe our contributions to society were meaningful and everlasting.

In truth, being gay isn't an issue for me as much as it is for others. Being gay doesn't cause problems, people's reactions to being gay create the problems.

For those who will condemn me, I am gay, get over it. I had to. Look inside my head and my heart. Then, if you don't like what you see, fine. At least you didn't judge me for what or who you think I am. What I am isn't who I am.

Writing this book has been therapeutic and at 65, I am more at peace with myself than ever before. My story has been written from a deductive perspective, as I have dissected the events and experiences I have had in order to understand who and what I have become.

I did not piece my gay life together inductively to become what I am today. I did not have the intellect nor the maturity to be able to diagnose life's progression and recognize I was putting together a puzzle which ended in a finished picture of me as a gay man.

Only when I was mature enough and had journeyed down many of life's mind-bending roads, was I able to deductively take apart the pieces of my life's puzzle to better understand how and why I am who I am. I was a gay man in the making, not a gay man making a life.

Society makes it difficult not to feel shame for being gay, but putting my story into words allowed me to see how genetics and significant events created me. I lived with shame and guilt for years and it takes a toll. I have never flaunted my sexuality nor do I intend to. I just want to live in peace and be accepted for the man/person I am.

In addition, God has stood by my side through three cancers, and a multitude of other life threatening situations.

I know I am not a castaway nor am I a lost soul, and neither are you.

I was created as God wanted me to be and know He would not destroy that which He created in His image. When I die, I will stand before God with confidence in eternal salvation.

The possibility exists gay men and women will never be accepted in our society, certainly not during my life time. If nothing else, one would pray for tolerance and an end to violence against other human beings.

Collective salvation for Christians does not exist, nor does collective damnation for gays. Regardless of what said by the religious far right, many gays are Christian and have a strong faith. Each of us will be judged on our own merits.

I have opened my life, my heart and my soul writing

this book and realize I will face consequences. I have outed myself and/or confirmed what people thought they knew. In some circles, I will be shunned and avoided. If these beliefs come to fruition, so be it.

Within the contents of my writing, I have expressed life as I have known it. I have not intended to offend anyone by sharing what I have lived.

My intent has been to educate those who think being gay is a conscious choice to participate in a "perceived" life style unacceptable to God and society. IT IS NOT.

My choice is only how I live the life I have been given. No one is born to be damned, and being gay is not a choice. Gay children are created at the moment of conception. Cherish those children.

As with Bobby, Matthew, Tyler and all the others, nothing is wrong with me. If you are gay, nothing is wrong with you. The Creator knew He was making you just as you are and God does not make mistakes. You were not born to be damned.

Accept it, believe it and walk proudly as a chosen child.

My tapestry is heavy. All stitches in the fabric must blend before one can see the beauty of the finished product. I am the product, for the tapestry is my story. I am who I am.

"Do not follow where the path may lead. Go instead where there is no path and leave a trail."
R. W. Emerson 17

I never left a trail but only looked for a secure path to find peace in my life. No maps, no guides and no guarantees; I was too ashamed to be the trailblazer.

CHAPTER THIRTY-ONE

Assisting Yourself

Never Give Up:

As a gay community we have made many strides in the 21st Century. However, most of the strides reside in politics, laws and/or perceived rights.

Work always needs to be done helping and assisting individuals with their entry and/or awareness to being gay. Unlike my plight of having to "go it alone", resources exist today to assist those who need it.

One recommendation I would make is, don't try to do it alone. Psychological and/or psychiatric assistance is available and certainly could give one guidance and direction regarding his/her sexuality.

My recommendation to seek psychiatric assistance isn't because one is gay, but rather his/her acceptance and reaction to being gay. Be selective in choosing medical personnel. If anyone tries to "cure" you, or tell you being gay is your choice, select a new doctor. You need assistance with your thoughts, not corrective measures for your soul.

The Internet offers a wide variety of sites to discuss gayness and be educated about the life, (list in back of book). I never had any of these advantages and truly had to decide for myself how I fit into a world I didn't understand.

Many gay and lesbian organizations, as well as "hot lines", exist to council gay men and women regarding problems and/or decision making.

Literally, I had no one to talk to about my feelings and always felt frustrated and isolated regarding my orientation. You no longer have to address your fears alone nor do you have to punish yourself for that which seems to go against societal norms. As we were born, we are "normal".

Help yourself, don't wait for others to step-up and assist you. Take the first steps on your own. Make contacts, read, research, and educate yourself. You must believe in yourself and know you were born to do something worthwhile. If you don't believe in YOU, why should anyone else? Stand up, take charge and become an inspiration for others of us who need it.

I am available to assist you, talk to you or answer any questions you might have that fall within my knowledge realm. My contact information is in the "Feedback" section in the back of the book.

Make peace with yourself and find internal peace, then you will be ready for others. It can be done. The hardest thing I have found in life is to forgive myself for being gay. Yes, because of my religious affiliations and background, it is still difficult to accept myself as a gay man.

Emotionally and spiritually, being gay seems to be something I have done wrong that I can't correct. Intellectually, I know I never made a conscious decision regarding my sexuality. I have had to compromise what I know to be true, with that which I have been "taught to believe" is true. It can be done. If Bare-Butt can do it, you can. What's in a name, right?

One of the greatest contributions in life is to assist others in finding internal peace.

CHAPTER THIRTY-TWO

Epilogue

The Questions and The Answers
Making Sense Of Gay Life

Insight:

Looking back, I wish I had done so many things differently. At age 65 and my personal health history, I am totally in touch with my mortality. With this knowledge, I look at things differently than I used to and every day becomes precious.

I suffered too long because of my gay plight and wasted so many days which can never be repeated. When looking back it all seems so obvious how I should have perceived and directed my life. Yet, at the time, it was all so threatening and consuming. I was ill-informed and immature.

I'm frustrated because I firmly believe if the lay public understood the relationship of genetics and gayness, acceptance would still be lacking. Laws and political correctness seldom change attitudes or fears, and certainly not religious beliefs.

Birthrights are strange bedfellows and genetics can be an asset or a detriment. Most gay people aren't predators or mentally ill "sickos".

Yes, within the gay community, predators and mentally ill individuals do exist, but isn't that true in the heterosexual community? I don't think this fact resonates within the public. Our public tends to generalize when referencing gays. Homosexuality is an emotional button that when pushed, evokes anger, hatred, prejudice and ill-fated spirituality.

I had always hoped to be 6' 4" tall, but that didn't happen. I wanted to be "buff" and "ripped", that didn't happen either. But many of the things I do have and did accomplish, others don't have and didn't achieve. As a gay man, I haven't done too badly in a society that would grant me nothing because of my sexual label.

I am going to propose a series of questions and provide experienced answers to educate and promote a better understanding of the gay world.

I live this life and my answers are from experiences, not books.

Breaking The Myths:

- Is being gay a choice?

No, scientific evidence can prove being gay is genetic; neither can they disprove it. However, the proclivity for gayness exists in the genes. Certainly the predisposition exists.

The only choice a gay person has is how he/she lives the life within the life. That is a choice.

- Does environment impact gay predisposition?

Yes, as one can see from my story, my outcome might have been completely different barring name, self-image, parenting, religion, etc. However, the genetic predisposition in the right environment will almost always impact sexual orientation.

- Can one be bi-sexual?

Depends on who you ask. Men and women often have sexual experiences with both sexes. Experimentation could be one reason to use the label bi-sexual, but being gay could be the other. Many gay men marry, have children and later, select a mate of the same sex. Obviously they were able to feel some form of sexual stimulation in order to reproduce and have children. Some people believe that bi-sexuality does not exist. Personally, I do.

- Why do some gay people marry and others do not?

Some gay people recognize and embrace their sexuality from an early age. Others may be consciously aware of it, or at least the feelings, but never act on them. Age, onset and events in life might best explain why some gay people marry. For me, I thought it was expected of me and I loved the girl.

- Should gay people be in the armed forces?

Why not? "Don't Ask, Don't Tell" hardly handles the issues. Politicians often use the following example: If an army unit is under fire, straight military men wanting someone to have their backs and not be looking at their ass. These men are grossly misinformed about how gay people function. Believe me, if under fire, a gay man is only going to be trying to stay alive as any other man would be doing. Gay people aren't thinking about sex every second of every day. Grant us dignity and intelligence.. Being gay isn't being incompetent.

- Should a gay man/woman attend church even though the church preaches damnation for gays?

Yes. The church isn't the issue, God and faith are. Men have interpreted God's word to fit their own needs and beliefs. Doctoral dissertations have been written about THE BIBLE and its literal or figurative translation. Having a faith foundation is important for everyone unless you are agnostic or atheist. I go to church because I need to, not because I have to. When I hear stories of gay damnation, I simply allow God to judge me and not the preaching. I attend church to receive communion, which I sincerely believe I need the forgiveness of sins. Men and their beliefs should not deter our having faith.

- If I have straight friends, and they find out I am gay, could I lose their friendship?

Of course. But in reality, they weren't your friends in the first place. Friendship is an over-used word. If we have no more than five true friends in our life time, we are lucky. The rest are all acquaintances and will come and go in our lives. If they are that narrow minded, let them go. It's their loss.

- Are all gay men effeminate?

No, but in fact, most of the television and movie portrayals of gay men feature effeminate men. Why? I think straight men are threatened by the fact that a rugged-looking, normal acting man, could be gay. Effeminate men are also an easy source of humor and perpetuate the gay myth. The movie "Brokeback Mountain" was one of the first movies to show ordinary men, cowboys if you will, as gay lovers. Doctors, lawyers, construction men, athletes, cowboys, politicians are all possible sources of macho gay men. Macho men want gays to be effeminate. Effeminate men pose no threat to their manhood. Stereotypes are hard to break.

- Are effeminate men born that way?

Probably. Again, one does not have a choice as to his genetics. Events and environment are also critical components in this area.

- How should I handle being gay?

How should one handle being heterosexual? It is best if one doesn't put either life "into one's face" or try to be noticed as being different. Live your life as you would. Be yourself and don't try to prove anything. Let your talents, skills and intelligence be your guide and speak for you. Educate yourself and follow your dreams. For you, you're normal.

- Is any one environment more receptive to gay life?

If that means, is one location better than another, the answer is yes. Larger metropolitan areas in certain states offer more opportunities for gay interaction. Chicago, New Jersey, San Francisco, sections of Florida, and Los Angeles are havens for gay life. Even if safe havens exist, one has to be careful where one goes. The same is true for heterosexuals. The best environment for any gay person is within the confines of his/her own home, doing what one does and minding one's own business.

- How do I tell my parents I am gay?

It is simple, tell them directly and matter-of-factly. In

most cases, they might already know or suspect. Expect a variety of reactions and give it time. Many parents think having a gay child is something weak abnormal in them, a familial ill, if you will. Reassure them that it is you living the life and you need their understanding and support. They are living the life with you, but they are not blessed with the genes you have. Love them.

- Do all men seek younger men?

No, a variety of likes and dislikes occur in the gay world just as it does in the heterosexual world. For different reasons, some men are attracted to youth. Other gay men prefer maturity. It's a matter of need fulfillment and interest. Remember, sexual attraction to young boys is Pedophilia and is not representative of gay life. A pedophile needs mental assistance, for it is an illness. Being gay is how one was born. Pedophilia is not synonymous with being gay.

- Is it true that women who love sports are lesbians?

No, interest or participation in sports does not make a woman a lesbian. She is a lesbian due to the same genetic factors as a man.

- Are priests who molest boys gay men?

No, they are pedophiles.

- Can someone who is gay, be cured?

Cured? No. A cure is not necessary because nothing is wrong with them. Individuals who claim to have been "cured", have not been changed. They may make a conscious effort not to have a gay experience, but the inclinations are still present. They are still gay. Cure is a misnomer and an inappropriate term referencing being gay.

- How can I stop being bullied?

It isn't easy. States and local school boards should have bullying policies, but most don't. We do have Hate Crime Laws, but bullying does not really fall into any of those categories. Teachers should be a student's best ally and should be directed to document all cases of bullying reported to them. From there, the reports should go to school administration for follow-up. We only wish it would work this way. Most bullies bully because they were bullied. Males bully because they lack self-confidence. Today, Cyber-bullying is rampant and usually involves girls. If you are a parent, support your child and follow up all bullying instances reported to you. Check state and local laws regarding bullying.

- Do gay men prey on straight married men?

Most gay men don't prey on anyone. To preserve their masculinity, most straight men think they have to beat up gay men who might "hit" on them, when a simple "No" or "I'm not interested" is all it takes. If a gay man does stalk a married man, the sexual orientation of the stalker is irrelevant. As would be the case with a heterosexual stalker, authorities should be called.

- Are gay men attracted to all men?

No. Gay men and women have their likes and dislikes as any other sexual being would have. Personal interests, grooming, size, shape, etc., are a part of the dating game as would be in any other dating situation. Character, intelligence, personality, etc., are equally important for attractions as would be the case in any heterosexual relationship.

- Are Gay Pride Parades necessary?

It depends on who you ask. Some individuals feel Gay Pride Parades are an awareness social event and enjoy them. Others feel they are not necessary and believe their sexual orientation is private. Not all gay people like to parade around and be noticed. In this case, to each his own.

- If someone has a gay person in their family, does that mean others in the family might be gay?

Maybe. One would have to investigate family history to see how many gay members were present over the years. Aunts, Uncles, cousins, etc...the trend is there and often follows genetic lines. That said, I know many cases where someone is the only known gay person in the family lineage.

- If I get married, have children, realize I am gay
  and get divorced, will my kids be gay?

That too is a matter of genetics. If the genes are present, that child could be gay. If not, then the answer is simply, no.

- Do gay people contribute to society?

Of course. Theater, Music, The Arts, Politics, Dance, no end exists where a gay man or woman hasn't contributed to society. In history, many of the most feared conquerors were gay. Hannibal, Alexander The Great, etc., were known gay men, yet they were warriors and leaders. Being gay does not define what you can or can't do. Genius is not sexual.

- If my son plays with dolls, does that mean he
  is gay?

No, it means he likes to play with dolls. Give it time and make little out of the situation. Use it as a learning situation and compliment him for being a good daddy or a caring big brother. In no way make fun of the child or berate him for playing with dolls. In time, he will move on to other things. Many male dolls exist today and boys need the nurturing experience.

- Are all gay men promiscuous?

No. In the gay or straight society, how one conducts

him/herself is an individual choice. Someone who "runs around" or is unfaithful in the straight society, is just as immoral as someone who does the same in the gay society. Relationships have parameters which are set by the couples themselves. For me, I wanted, needed and demanded monogamy. I got it. We have gay friends who have been together monogamously for 43 years. Monogamy is special regardless of which society one inhabits.

- Why do so many gay people live in the closet?

This answer is easy. Society as a whole, does not accept being gay or understand gayness. Those who speak loudly against gay society are usually ultra-religious conservatives who believe they have interpreted THE BIBLE in a manner which supports their personal beliefs. Sometimes, men or women who speak the loudest may fear gayness in themselves. Until society understands, accepts and/or tolerates gay society, many gay people are forced to stay or be in the closet to protect jobs, reputations and/or family.

- In dealing with prejudice, which group is most misunderstood, persecuted or hated?

The answer is......Sexual Orientation! Race is a continuing source of prejudice and hatred, but sexual orientation is a source of hatred, anger and fear. In many countries, one can be executed for being gay. Religion is another source for prejudice which is often established and spread in the name of the Lord. However, prejudice and hatred are one level of discrimination but prejudice involving violent actions or murder is another. I would list sexual orientation, race and religion as the major sources for hatred and violence.

*Internet, GoMAG, November 20, 2007, "Gay bashing is third behind race and religion."

- Do straight men fear "guilt by association" with gay men?

Every individual response to the issue of gayness varies, but for the most part, my experience is that straight men do fear guilt by association. I firmly believe straight men profile gay men by looking for certain characteristics. A well-dressed, well-groomed, attractive man is often suspect to men who feel they must look unkempt to be macho. Occupation can and does often dictate how a man dresses, but how the man carries himself is the key. I am not sure why, but men who don't know me seem to be uncomfortable around me. I think my voice tone has some impact, but other than that, I don't believe I project gayness.

Women aren't uncomfortable around me, but men are. My partner and I have two straight friends who do not judge us, nor do they doubt our intellect or character. They are not afraid to be seen with us. Yet, we know another individual who pursued our friendship and once it was established, for some unknown reason, ceased contact with us. Once you are "outed" or present your authentic self, expect friends and co-workers to change if they had not previously known your orientation. Sad!

- Why do straight athletes fear/ostracize gay athletes?

I'm not sure fear is the correct word. Again, a lack of education is one cause for anxiety or unrest, but the age old myth that the gay athlete is getting aroused in the shower, or in street terms, "getting his jollies", establishes anxiety in straight athletes. Most gay athletes aren't focused on sex any more than straight teammates are. A time and place exists for everything and the gay athlete knows it. That time and place is not on the athletic field nor is it in the team shower room.

- Why do men think pink and purple clothing is gay?

Colors don't make a man gay. If a man has to worry about what others think if he is wearing a pink or purple shirt, he must be doubting his own sexuality and is not be secure within his manhood. One doesn't have to be an unkempt man to be macho.

- Are gay men and women a threat to the concept of the traditional family?

My response would be, how? We, as gay men and women, are created within a traditional family. Certainly two gay parents didn't create us. Most gay men and women are not afforded the right to a legally recognized wedding, and probably have a gay mate who is just a partner or, at best, recognized in a civil union. I have never understood the emotion which accompanies this question when posed by certain religious groups. Maybe it's the inferred threat to the religious concept of marriage that the general public fears, but in reality, gays pose no threat to the traditional family.

- Should gays be afforded a legally recognized wedding?

Truthfully, the issue is money, not a recognized wedding. The same issue exists for civil unions. A gay wedding should threaten no one and usually it's some insightful theologian or conservative religious group expressing concerns. Moral issues create the emotion, but finance prevents the law from being passed within state's rights. The real issues are insurance benefits, taxes, (dependents), inheritance, etc. It's about money. A final issue for gays is simply equality. What is normal for them as gay men and women is being denied. It's the principle of the thing.

- What helps gays cope in this world of hatred?

Parental/family support is vital and critical. I pray you have that in your life. If not, friendship and acceptance in homosexual or heterosexual crowds is an asset. You need someplace to talk about how you feel. Another factor is education for yourself and others If you fill your mind with awareness issues and not concentrate only on the negative aspects of being gay, you will find comfort and purpose. Finally, on the Internet you will find a list of helpful organizations which provide assistance as well as hot-lines for gay people.

- Should gay people hold hands or display affection in public?

Should straight people hold hands or display affection in public? Class and dignity are not solely for straight people. I am as conservative in one world as I am in another. No one really has to broadcast their sexuality and in truth, public display probably should be limited for all people. Private feelings need to be that, private. Common sense should prevail. Yes, I am old fashioned.

- How can I meet other gay people?

Meeting gay people is difficult depending on one's physical location. However, the straight dating game is just as difficult today. I would refrain from Internet connections as one never knows to whom a screen name belongs. Anyone takes chances in clubs or bars and church might not be filled with a preponderance of gay men or women. First-hand acquaintances or personal introductions are probably safest, but in small towns, it is almost impossible. Places of employment could be a contact point or local gay/lesbian organizations, if they exist. In truth, I am open to feedback on this question.

- Do most gay people come from broken homes or divorced families?

No! Gay people show up in all nationalities, cultures, socio-economic groups and traditional families. Broken or divorced homes have no relevance in determining if a child/person is gay. It's in the genes.

- Should a parent be concerned if their child's teacher is gay or lesbian?

No! Statistics show that student sexual abuse cases resonate more in heterosexual relationships between teacher and student as opposed to homosexual. Pedophilia is "different" issue and parents should be greatly concerned. If a teacher is a pedophile, my question would be, who did the background check? How did a pedophile get the job in the first place? Some of the finest teachers I have known are/were gay or lesbian. Sexuality does not dictate teaching ability.

- If someone "comes out" to you, what should you do?

Listen! You will probably be given insight as to why the individual chose you to share such important information. Be supportive and remain nonjudgmental. You must be a special person or the individual would not feel comfortable sharing with you. Please don't stop the individual and tell them you don't want to hear it. My thanks.

Let Common Sense Prevail:

One must remember, most people are better at rationalizing than they are at being rational, especially on the subject of sexual orientation. I have proposed these questions to evoke thought. If you know of conditions or circumstances that would alter, change or add to my responses, fantastic! You are thinking about and processing what you have read and are fulfilling my intentions. If I have failed to evoke emotion or thought, then I have written in vain.

For all readers, I offer theses questions not as a "way out" of comprehending gay live, but as a "way in" to unveil the myths and irrational personal opinions. The "way in" opens your minds and enhances your intellect regarding sexual orientation. The "way in" will open doors to life and assist you with life, love and happiness.

Some day you may be faced with a gay friend, relative or even a child who will need your support and understanding. Remember what you have read and feel the power of the "way in". Don't judge, love.

Judgment lies within a higher power and is not ours to make. We are who we are for a reason. I cannot judge, nor have I ever had a professional reference for the answers to these questions. I lived them.

My tapestry will never be complete for my story has been told only to this point in my life. Hopefully, I have many chapters to go before my end comes. In any case, I stand firm as a gay man. I managed to survive in a world of personal torment and societal hatred. I never gave up because I know, "belief" gets us there. I got there. Remember, society would have man be what it thinks he should be, and not be what he is.

In my world, I try not to stand out, for I am an ordinary gay man.

2010, 65 years old

"Remember, you are not all you are,
until you cease to be."
Dyke 18

Tapestry Personified

"You were born an original. Don't die a copy."
Mason 19

Feedback For Me

As a retired educator, feedback is critical in order to learn and grow.

- After reading the book, how do you feel?

- If you are struggling with your sexual identity, was reading the book of assistance to you? How?

- Did you learn anything about being gay you did not previously know?

- If you are a straight person, did you change any pre-conceived perceptions or opinions about gayness?

- Regardless sexual orientation, did you identify with any aspect of my story?

- Any other questions or comments for me?

If I can be of assistance and/or you need to talk or have questions, you may contact me at babuttz@aol.com.

About The Author

B.A. Buttz

B.S. Education, Illinois State University, 1966

Certification:Special Education
Hearing Impaired, K-Supervisory
Elementary Education, K-9

MED Educational Administration, University of Illinois, 1976

High School Teacher, Illinois School For the Deaf, Jacksonville, IL 1966

Middle School Teacher, Thomas Jefferson Middle School, Decatur, IL 1967-1984

Elementary Principal, Washington Elementary School, Decatur, IL, 1984-1989

Director of Schools for Instruction, Decatur Public Schools Central Office, 1989-1996

Director of Special Programs. Decatur Public Schools Central Office 1996-1999

Retired: July 16, 1999

Gay Organizations To Assist You

Research them on-line: (see Bibliography)

PFLAG, Parents, Families and Friends of Lesbians and Gays Promotes health and well-being of gay, lesbian bisexual and transgendered persons

GLADD, Gay and Lesbians alliance Against Defamation Fair, accurate representation of people and events in media to eliminate homophobia and discrimination based on gender or sexual orientation.

HRC, Human Rights Campaign Advance equality based on sexual orientation, gender expression and identity.

GLSEN, Gay, Lesbian and Straight Education Network Ensures safe schools for all children.

ACLU, American Civil Liberties Union Fights discrimination against gay people and their families.

GLBT National Help Center Meets needs of gays, lesbians, bisexuals and transgender as well as sexual orientation and gender identity.

The Trevor Project, National GLBT Suicide Prevention Help-line National suicide prevention helpline for questioning youth.

Ruth Ellis Center
Support services for runaway, homeless and at-risk gay youth.

NGLTF, National Gay and Lesbian Task Force Leading voice for justice, freedom and equality.

GMHC, Gay Men's Health Crisis Dedicated to ending AIDS and support for those who live with AIDS and HIV.

Colage, For people with Gay or Lesbian Parents Support for children who have gay parents.

AI, Amnesty International World organization, deals with human rights standards.

The Rainbow Alliance Variety of programs and services for the LGBT community.

Bibliography

Decatur Herald and Review newspaper, Decatur, Illinois, p. , 1952; p. , 1940; p. , 1962

Herald and Review newspaper, August 3, 2010, Associated Press, p.

Internet: www.Wordiq.com, p. 8; p.

Song, "Ubi Caritas", Composer, Mauice Durufle', Opus Concert, Decatur, IL, Summer, 2010
2, Duruffle' p.

Internet: www.Dreamworld.org, p.

Internet, National Gay and Lesbian Task Force, 1984, p.

Internet, Orion Center, Street Youth Survey, 1986, p.

U.S. Department of Health and Human Services. 1989, p.

Internet: www.Oystergsa/gas_statistics.html, p.

Webster's New World Dictionary, p. 9, p.

Internet, www.About.com: Gay Life
10, Byrd p.

Internet:www.http://gaylife.about.com/od/
gayorganizations/Gay_Organizations.htm pp.

Internet: www.GayNEPA.com, pp

Internet, American Psychiatric Association, p.

Internet, GOMAG, November 20, 2007, pp.

Internet, New York Gay and Lesbian Anti-Violence
Project Report 1996, p.

Internet, www.CelebriFI.com 2009
11, Kimball p.

Internet: www.great-inspirtional-quotes.com, Copyright
2005-2010
1, Buscaglia p.

Internet: www.great-inspirational-quotes.com
5, Goethe p.
7, Cummings p.
8, Shakespeare p.
17, Emerson p.
19, Mason p.

Internet: www.ThinkEXIST.com, American Journals and
Strictly Personal, 1944-1986
3, Harris p.

Internet, www.ThinkExist.com, Famous Quotes
4, Wodroephe p.
9, Bronte p.
13, Beauvoir p.
12, Unknown p.

Internet: www.ThinkEXIST.com Lao Tzu, Taoism, Chinese philosopher,
14, Tao Te Ching, 600 B.C. - 531 B.C. p.

Internet, www.All GreatQuotes.com and www. ThinkExist.com
6, Kipling p.

Internet, GLBTQ Encyclopedia 2001 p

Internet, Research 106 pp.

Internet, Xtra, Canada's Gay and Lesbian News pp.

Illinois State University, Normal, Illinois, University Motto p.

Internet: Poem, Two Loves, The Chameleon, December, 1984
15, Douglas p.

Internet: www.children.foreignpolicylogs. com/2008/04/04/education
16, Olmos p.

Vertrauen, Brendow-Veriag, Rheinkamp-Barel Plastik. D. Steigerwald
p.

Dr. Donald Dyke, Professor of Psychology, Indiana State University, 1952
18 Dyke p.

For cover information about author

    B.A. Buttz is a retired educator in Decatur, Illinois, a small Midwestern town located in the heartland of central Illinois. He was a junior high school special education teacher, elementary school principal and central administrator for the Decatur Public Schools for 34 years. B.A. was a well-known educational consultant and public speaker for 20 years before retirement in 2009. He received numerous awards in the State of Illinois Those Who Excel program.

B.A. was married for 33 years and has two children and one grandchild. He resides in Decatur with his partner, Bill, of 25 years. B.A. and Bill rescue dogs and have twenty-eight paws residing in the comfort of their home.

Mr. Buttz is a three-time cancer survivor and nearly died in 2009 after becoming septic due to a double colon perforation during a routine colonoscopy.

As a result of this near death incident, he has decided to share his life in order to assist others who might have difficulty accepting their sexual orientation or who have been emotionally, verbally or physically abused in any way. B.A.'s focus is to educate society about genetic gay birthrights.

BORN TO BE DAMNED is a nostalgic trip into one man's past to examine the torment and humiliation he felt as his gay tapestry evolved into reality. Religion, environment and genetics combined to ensure he fulfilled his destiny as a gay man.

People remember how you make them feel.

LaVergne, TN USA
24 November 2010

206096LV00004B/2/P

9 781452 094670